MAYBE WE'RE ALL DIAMONDS

my JOURNEY *of losing everything*
TO FIND LOVE EVERYWHERE

a memoir
ASHLEY ROBYN

Maybe We're All Diamonds

My Journey of Losing Everything to Find Love Everywhere

ShareLoveEverywhere.com

Cover Design by Joanna Dee Studio | JoannaDee.com

Interior Design by Transcendent Publishing | TranscendentPublishing.com

Edited by Clare Fernández | ClareFernandez.com

ISBN: 979-8-9885147-0-1

Disclaimer: The book you are about to read is a memoir. All the names have been changed to protect the privacy of those I love, and some conversations have been condensed or paraphrased and certain details adjusted or eliminated. There is freedom in embracing the beautiful and ugly truth, and this is the documentation of my personal experience, of which I have the receipts. Unfortunately, some people in my story really are this shitty … and thank God, some people who came into my life really are absolute diamonds.

Printed in the United States of America.

perfect is you being exactly who you are.

CONTENTS

this book is for you.

INTRODUCTION

dearest reader,

Did you know that there is a trend in the diamond industry that categorizes the way a rough diamond is transformed into a polished diamond? Jewelers call it the "Diamond Journey," and it all begins with pressure, heat, and violent volcanic eruptions. In my research, I learned that if you carve into a rough diamond, you are actually able to get a view of the various growth events in its history that shaped the way it looks today.

One thing you should know about me is that I don't do "small talk." After spending about three minutes with me, most folks are already well aware of this. Our individual multifaceted lives are so wonderful and complicated and layered and rich and beautiful and ugly, that simply asking "What do you do?" when we first meet isn't going to give me all the depth of who you are. What I want more than anything is to get at the magical parts of you that brought you to this very moment. To know you and to see all the glittery facets of your being.

I've got a crazy idea that people are like diamonds, formed to achieve greatness through intense heat and pressure. I want to see and celebrate that sparkle. So instead of talking about the weather, I may ask you, "What is your proudest moment so far?" or, "What color do you identify most with your personality?" These questions are how I can see YOU beyond the surface-level conversation that begins with "How's work going? Staying busy?" Ninety-nine percent of the time, that dull and tired question is going to lead to a tall brick wall that will stifle any chance of a deeper connection between us.

I spent a lifetime blocked by a wall like that, surrounded by surfacers. Surfacers are people who do not have the capacity for empathy and vulnerability. I'm certain you've known at least one or two people like this in your own life. They not only lack the ability to embrace their own darkness and depth and wonder, but they also lack the ability to cultivate intimate connection, sincere community, and candor with others. Impossible to please, but always expecting perfection. You can run yourself ragged performing in the role they write for you.

I became deeply depressed trying to live the surface life and meet the standards and expectations of everyone around me. My childhood indoctrination taught me that I was here to serve the needs of others and discouraged me from chasing after or exploring the things that mattered to me. But I'm not a surfacer. I'm a miner who was told to be a surfacer.

I spent a lot of time burying my true self so that the "surfacer version" of me was pleasing to everyone else. In my efforts to make others happy, I had become remarkably miserable. I had surrendered to the thought that maybe that's how life was going to be for me. Maybe as long as everyone else is happy, that's all that matters.

The sadness that floods my heart even now to admit that I truly believed this … whew. When your spirit is broken, you don't always realize that you deserve to be whole.

The Universe loves to use quirky humor and dark comedy to teach me life lessons. I've developed an appreciation for finding amusement in the ways I relate to the world around me because laughing at the hard parts is more manageable than having a full-on mental breakdown.

It's a classic case of, "What came first?" The crazy-making characters in my life who made me feel that I was worthless without their validation and acceptance, or the anxiety that compels me daily to go, go, go and do, do, do. I know it's not all my deeds and perfect performances that give me value. I've read loads of self-help books. I've done the prayers and meditations. On paper, I know this.

But my heart is a slow learner, and after all that she's experienced, she still struggles to believe that I am loved, I am accepted, I am safe. She tells herself some wildly absurd stories in the name of protecting herself from the familiar downward spiral into negative feelings and brokenness.

This book is a radical act of love first for me and also for you. It feels bittersweet to say this, mostly because of the healing I've needed to do to think of myself as a person who is even worthy to share her story. But the one thing I have learned for sure is that we all carry within us the gift of perspective and experience, and I firmly believe that we need to be talking about these things more honestly.

The stories contained within these pages are reflections of the people and places significant to my story, but you may notice a few familiar flecks that feel like characters you know all too well woven within every chapter.

One thing I think we have in common as human beings is that we are all on a path of self-discovery—our very own "Diamond Journey." People who transform their life by turning pressure and upheaval into opportunities, committing to constantly learning through therapy, evolving with self-awareness, growing in maturity, respecting boundaries, and deep-diving spiritually are doing brave and vital work.

If you picked up this book, I already know that you are one of those souls, and I'm so glad you're here. Chances are since you began your grand life adventure, you've been through many experiences that have stretched your heart and left you broken, exhausted, and questioning everything. Welcome to being a person! We all have "stuff" that burdens us, and not one single piece of baggage you may be clinging to makes you any less worthy of living a life full of joy, connection, love, beauty, and happiness.

I was convinced that the package of "me" was too much. I told myself that my story was too heavy to unload on people. And instead of talking about all my shit, I leaned more into my perfectionistic tendencies to perform flawlessly and "present well" to others. To be fun, to be light, to be interesting, to be easygoing … to not risk giving off any awkward vibes by making confessions of my truth.

But I have learned the hard way that when you ignore your truth, it will eat you alive from the inside out. I desperately wanted to be a blooming sunflower in a field drenched in sunbeams, but my roots were dying because I was blaming God for all my problems rather than realizing I already had the answer. I was the common denominator.

So I began the work of finding my people and getting in the weeds with vulnerability. Oh God, that word we celebrate Brené Brown for, yet we all so savagely fight to avoid. I say I want a life full of depth, and if that is true, it's time to seize the opportunity. It's time to be open. It's time to get comfortable with the uncomfortable. It's time to take that savage fight and point it toward healing and truth.

And now, the last person on earth you would ever imagine to quote a professional sports player (me) is going to pull a quote from Rick Fox, an L.A. Lakers NBA Champion (ok, he is also an actor so it's not *that* sportsy for those of you who were about to close this book already!). In the HBO documentary *Shaq*, Rick Fox said of winning the NBA Finals that championships are not won by someone handing them to you. He said, "Championships have got to be taken."

You have to come out swinging and ready to fight for what you want. Life itself is much the same. Nothing will be given to you; you have to work for it. No one is coming to bail you out or rescue you. You have to do the work yourself. You have to find a way to push past the urge to isolate for protection and the compulsion to be seen as perfect, and take a few strong steps into the light where your flaws can catch healing beams of sunshine. Get so comfortable with the uncomfortable that it feels comfortable to you.

If I want a life overflowing with meaningful connection and love with others, I have to live in a way that cultivates depth. To fully encounter depth is to step into the freedom of allowing yourself to be truly known (and this cannot happen until you truly know yourself). This process requires vulnerability—YES, bring on the vulnerability!—and according to my therapist, "Vulnerability is just being emotionally honest."

But before we go there together, I've got a short story for you ...

One breezy January morning while on vacation, I was walking along the beach in Mexico and happened upon about a dozen freshly hatched baby sea turtles scattered along the shoreline. They were all making their way into the ocean, leaving tiny trails in the sand behind them.

It was an awesome sight to see, and I stopped for a moment to watch. Suddenly I noticed that one of the little babies somehow managed to flip herself over and was stuck on her back. Her tiny fins were flapping, but she couldn't manage to gain any ground on getting back to being right side up.

After a few minutes of watching her struggle, I walked a little closer to her, bent down, and picked her up. I held her for a moment, examining her adorable, petite face, and marveled at how small her nostrils were. These things can live for over 100 years and grow to be so massive, and here I was holding one in the palm of my hand.

It felt like a significant moment. I took a quick picture of her with my phone, and then I sat her right back down in the sand, exactly where I found her. Only this time, right side up and facing the ocean. I walked away so excited that I just had this super cool encounter with nature.

When I returned home, I was telling a friend about my trip over coffee, and this was one of the highlights. After I shared, she asked, "Why didn't you just take her all the way to the ocean? Why did you put her back where you found her? Why not help her out and take her to the place she was trying to go?"

The thought of putting her in the ocean did cross my mind briefly, as I stood on the beach that day. I could've picked up half a dozen baby turtles and put them in the water.

But I decided to set her back where I found her because I can't do her journey for her. That would rob her of the experience of traveling from her freshly hatched egg into the mysterious sea. This was her actual rite of passage. If I took her all the way to the water, it would remove the richness and depth from her journey. My role was simply to help her get unstuck, and then she was free and empowered to carry on with her life however she chose.

I will remember this sea turtle and the lesson she taught me for the rest of my life. In my role as a mother, in my relationships, in my artistic expression and creative pursuits ... It's never my job to manipulate things or people into being who I want or need them to be. It is a privilege to be able to see where people are stuck and help them get back to forward motion on the path they are carving toward *their* destiny.

There are so many complicated layers to our lives and our stories and how we choose to interpret them. My big questions for you are: What is it that you are digging for? What inspires you? What challenges you? Where are you stuck?

I've discovered that I am always digging for sincerity and love. It's what I believe was missing most in my life until recently, and I've been able to transform from a girl who felt so alone into someone with an abundance of genuine, kind, and loving souls in my corner.

Many times, answering these questions is work you have to do on your own, but it doesn't have to be lonely. This book is proof of that, and it is my deepest prayer that somehow in these stories you are met with a feeling of love and support, no matter the situation you're currently in. May you find the courage to pick up your shovels, roll up your sleeves, and unearth the diamond within.

Grateful for you,

Ashley

chapter one

ROSE-COLORED GLASSES

"Trust yourself. Create the kind of self that you will be happy to live with all your life. Make the most of yourself by fanning the tiny, inner sparks of possibility into flames of achievement."

— Golda Meir

I stood sobbing as the heavy April rain fell in perfect, straight lines from the gray ceiling of clouds above my head. I was standing on the runway of an old abandoned airpark in my neighborhood, leash in one hand, umbrella in the other, my dripping wet Goldendoodle by my side. I had been waking early every day for the last month before anyone else in my house began to stir—before Conner had reason to complain of my absence. I made sure to return before anything would be required of me, before our children would need any breakfast. No one would even have to know I was gone. This time was precious, and it was all mine. One brief hour each morning. That's all I had.

Crying in this downpour felt oddly appropriate. The airpark was totally deserted when it rained, which seemed to mirror the feelings in my heart. I guess no one else was quite desperate enough to literally weather a storm just to get away from their life for a few moments. The rain was a welcome friend to me. She held my hand, stroked my hair, kissed my face, and encouraged me to feel the weight of it all.

I looked forward to being completely alone on days like this. I would be free to scream, to bawl, to shout curse words at the heavens. I could walk the length of the airpark, talking out loud to myself like a crazy person. Telling God how badly I needed him to intervene. How miserable I had become. How I didn't know if I was strong enough to endure this test.

I was filled with doubt and fear. *I can't do this alone. I need help. Please help.* This was the only consistent prayer I had been offering for years. A feeble attempt to connect with my higher power—to tap into a wisdom greater than myself—was the only coping mechanism I had available for what was now an untamable beast of a situation.

"How did we get here?" I said through tears. "Can't you send me someone who can tell me what to do, or give me the magic formula to fix this nightmare?"

When I started seriously dating during college, my mom told me to pay attention to the boys I was going out with. "Write down the qualities you like about them, and write down the things about them that you hate. Use this list to create some guidelines about the type of man you want to marry someday," she suggested. This was solid gold, a piece of my mom's advice that I took right to my heart.

Before long, I had a list of 113 things I was looking for in a husband. After a few long-term relationships, I met Conner, the man who would become my husband. Suddenly that feeling of loneliness I had grown up with started to go away. He checked every item on my list except for one: he picked his nose. I was told that "all men pick their noses," and I figured if that was true, he was my best shot at a life of love and happiness. My mom remarked how my eyes had a different sort of sparkle in them when I would return from a date with Conner, something she hadn't ever noticed with other guys I dated. Had I finally found my person?

After only a few months of dating, Conner and I moved in together. It was a classically small, fourth-floor walk-up apartment in Astoria, Queens. It was my first time not living at home. My mom suggested Conner move to New York with me since he had always wanted to live there, and she didn't want me to live with a random stranger who was subletting a room through Craigslist.

When we first arrived in New York, Conner was a freelance director for music videos. His schedule was sparse, and if he didn't have anything to do, he would spend his days wandering the streets of the city, exploring and getting "inspired." Eventually, he landed a brief unpaid internship with one of his favorite directors, Michel Gondry, and he even had the opportunity to work on a Kanye West music video—very impressive, since Kanye was pretty hot in the fall of 2005. I viewed Conner as the more creative talent in our relationship and wanted to help him cultivate his career because I deeply believed in his abilities. I just knew that someday he would catch his big break, and I wanted to support him in every possible way to make sure he succeeded.

On the weekends, the two of us would ride the subway to Brooklyn or SoHo or whatever cool spot Conner had researched during the week. We would wander aimlessly into specialty restaurants that served 54 different varieties of macaroni and cheese or rice pudding, grimy vintage shops Bob Dylan once visited, trendy boutiques, sneaker shops, and the legendary music venue, CBGB (sadly, no longer in existence).

Every day was a new adventure and opportunity to become more of a true New Yorker. When the weather cooled down in October, Conner and I visited Central Park one Saturday afternoon. There were horse-drawn carriages that offered a ride around the entire park. I dropped the hint that I wanted to take a ride in a carriage to see the park and give ourselves time to rest. The setting felt so romantic—a crisp autumn day in New York's most famous park. We climbed into the carriage, I held Conner's hand, leaned in and kissed him on the cheek, and told him how he was making all my dreams come true.

By November, Conner and I had been talking about getting married. We had only been officially dating for six months, but I had come to understand what all those other married people meant when they said they "just knew" their spouse was the right one for them. Moving so far away from home together helped to solidify and accelerate our relationship. We were all we had, and we learned to lean heavily on each other while navigating our new city and becoming grown-ups who paid our bills on time.

On December 8th, 2005, Conner took me ring shopping after work. He met me at my office on Broadway, and we took the subway to Manhattan's Diamond District, where several over-the-top jewelry stores sparkled brightly, the lighting so stark it was almost clinical. I felt like a 10-year-old girl playing house. We went inside one, and I awkwardly tried on a few rings that were out of our price range.

Once we finished, Conner suggested we stop by Rockefeller Center to see the big Christmas tree. We paused to admire the holiday sights, and Conner said we should get our picture taken. He asked a nice woman nearby if she would mind snapping our photo, but when he handed her the digital camera, he secretly explained to her how to take a video. Then as soon as she hit the record button, he turned around, got on one knee, and blurted out, "Will you marry me?"

I had about 5,000 thoughts racing through my head at that moment, the first one being, *Of course I will marry him!* and the second being, *All he said was, "Will you marry me?"* I had envisioned what my marriage proposal would look like thanks to all the 90s rom-coms I watched as a teenager. I was pretty sure he was supposed to give me some sort of swoony *When-Harry-Met-Sally*-style speech about how meeting me had changed his life forever, and that he loved me so much he couldn't imagine living life without me as his wife.

I hadn't responded yet. I stood there holding my fuzzy-mittened hands over my mouth, paralyzed with the bittersweet feeling of slight disappointment in his delivery, while also being overjoyed that I was going to spend the rest of my life with this guy that I had fallen for. I looked into his wide eyes and smiling face and answered, "Yes!" He stood, and we embraced, kissing clumsily, as he slid a dazzling ring on my finger. We walked to a diner down the street, placed an order for celebratory french fries, and expectantly talked about our future together.

Looking back at this moment, I see a young woman who was so insecure and unsure of herself and her ability to do anything on her own that she was willing to attach herself to anyone who presented as remotely "normal" compared to how she grew up. I was subconsciously desperate to get out from under my mother's controlling thumb and change my last name so I didn't share it with my father anymore. I didn't even know myself—or understand that I had so many childhood wounds to heal from. I wish I could go back in time to that girl and say, "Don't rush this just because you think it's the 'right' thing to do. You can do whatever you want."

When I was 13, my Aunt Loretta (my mom's sister-in-law) took me and my cousins thrift store shopping. I flipped through the donated formal wear and imagined these dresses in their prime, being worn by beautiful women done up all pretty for a wedding or a high school prom, with hope and excitement swelling in their hearts. My aunt was walking over to me with an overloaded armful of jeans when I spotted it.

I pulled the most delicate and understated lace wedding gown from the rack of formal dresses with puffy sleeves and sequins. This gown was strapless, with boning in the bodice and a unique ruching detail that flowed down the center back of the gown like a white waterfall, and was accented at the back waist with long green, flowing fabric adorned with tiny pink petals sewn onto the bottom.

I fell in love with that dress and thought I might be able to dye it a fun color and use it for high school prom or homecoming. The price tag on the dress was $13. Aunt Loretta purchased it for me that day, and I went home and tried the dress on. It fit almost perfectly, except it was a little loose in the chest. I looked at myself in the mirror and squeezed the loose fabric where my breasts would soon be. *I'll have real boobs by the time I want to use this dress,* I thought as I hung it up in my closet.

I never got around to dyeing the dress or wearing it to any high school dances (or having the bosom to fill it as a teenager), so when Conner proposed, I knew exactly what I wanted to wear when I walked down the aisle. Besides, my mom suddenly had her hands full helping to care for Nanny, my grandmother, who had recently been diagnosed with stage four ovarian cancer. Not only that, but something bad was going on with my stepdad, Eric. Whenever I would call home from New York, Mom would tell me how sick Eric seemed and how he was mostly just lying in bed every day, unable to get up because he was so chronically dizzy. With all that going on, I figured going wedding gown shopping probably wasn't something she had a lot of extra time for.

"It's been three weeks, and Eric has only gotten out of bed to go to the restroom or occasionally to smoke a cigarette," my mom confessed to me over the phone during one of our morning calls, as I headed down the four flights of stairs and began the mile walk to the subway station on my way to work. "He's barely eating, and he keeps it completely dark in the bedroom. He told me that any time he gets up he feels dizzy. I keep trying to get him to go to the doctor, but he won't. I think he knows something is wrong, and he's afraid to get a diagnosis from the doctor. I'm really starting to worry, Ash."

I had never heard such realness in my mom's voice. She usually had a sunny, party-all-the-time, pain-avoidance disposition, so if she was actually saying out loud that she was worried, it must be bad. But I was so far away in New York and couldn't be of any help, other than a sounding board. I thought of my mom stuck in this wretched situation, managing her mom's chemo treatment schedule and emptying her colostomy bag, only to come home to another heartbreaking situation—an extremely ill husband who refused to see a doctor and instead just laid in bed, suffering and slowly dying. I couldn't imagine the stress she was under.

After another couple of weeks, she finally convinced him to see a doctor, and they discovered a large mass in his brain. Cancer. And it was an aggressive form. His prognosis did not give him much time; this was terminal.

She tried to be excited for me and our upcoming wedding, but I could hear in her voice through every phone call that she was overwhelmed. With all the sickness in my family, I didn't want a long engagement or an extravagant wedding. We set our wedding date for Memorial Day weekend, on May 27th, 2006.

My $13 thrift store wedding dress would need a cleaning and a slight altering, so I flew back to Ohio one January morning to visit my family, and my mom and I took a trip to a local seamstress who worked in the back of a dry cleaning business. She pinned the dress in a few spots and commented on how she thought the lace looked like it was from the 1940s. Several people from the dry cleaners came over to see the lacework, and everyone was shocked to learn how I had found this dress and held onto it for almost 10 years.

We paid the seamstress $80 to clean the dress and make the fitting adjustments, and I humble bragged to my mom (and anyone who asked how wedding plans were coming along) that for less than $100, I had the most beautiful and affordable wedding dress in the history of weddings.

We booked an outdoor garden space at the Columbus Park of Roses that also included an indoor shelterhouse where we could host our wedding reception. Conner pulled a favor from a photographer friend who we booked to shoot our wedding day, and we arranged for our favorite local pizza shop, Johnny's Pizza, to cater. They made us heart-shaped pizzas, and my cousin Birdie got us a chocolate fountain. I designed our wedding cake, inspired by *Alice in Wonderland*, with topsy-turvy, Mad Hatter angles. It felt like the perfect way to start our marriage.

A month before our wedding, Conner wanted to talk. "I've been thinking," he said. "You've had sex before ... with a couple of your past boyfriends ... and well, I have never had sex. I feel like you should get tested before we get married."

When we met, Conner had shared his strong faith-based

convictions about sex and where he drew the line, so we had not been with each other in that way before our wedding night.

"Like, an STD test? Is that what you are referring to?" I asked, trying to clarify where he was going with this.

"Yeah, I just think that there's obviously a chance that you have something since you've had sex before. I need to be 100% sure that you aren't going to transmit anything to me." The way he said it made me feel like he actually thought I had an STD.

"I have no symptoms of an STD and have not been with anyone in over a year," I said.

"Well, you can never be too safe, and I can't marry you without knowing for sure," he added.

All I could think was, *Oh my God, we are weeks away from our wedding, and he is asking me this now ... Why?* But what I said in response was, "I'll call my doctor and get tested."

Then I proceeded to make one of the most degrading phone calls I have ever made, from a dark and musty storage closet at my office in Manhattan. I spoke to the nurse practitioner and explained the situation. "He knows that your last Pap came back normal, right?" she asked, trying to see if there was any way to avoid me coming in for a test I didn't need.

"Yeah, but he wants an official test just for STDs, including AIDS." I knew exactly how ridiculous this request was, but I was trying to help Conner feel more comfortable about the fact that we were entering into a marriage where he was a virgin and I was not. *It's a small inconvenience for me, and it would make him feel so much better. I can suck it up and get tested,* I kept saying to my heart.

"Ok, so we want to test for *everything* then?" the nurse confirmed from the other end of the phone.

"Yes, everything. Do you have any openings on Thursday?" I asked.

No surprise, a few days later my results came back clean, so I could marry Conner and ease his bat-shit bonkers fears. This was the first time I caught a glimpse of his controlling and wild expectations of me, and yet I didn't see the red flag.

On our wedding day, I felt anxious. I assumed it was just pre-wedding jitters. I was so grateful that Eric was feeling well enough after some chemo treatments to attend, and Nanny was also rebounding. Having both of them there for my wedding meant everything to me. Eric came into my life around the same time as the wedding dress I was wearing, and he had stepped into the role of "Dad" for me when my biological father moved away to Longview, Washington.

While my dad would be attending my wedding, I did not want him to give me away or even offer up a father-of-the-bride speech at the wedding reception. He barely knew me and had let me down so much over the years; I didn't feel like he deserved to have any part in my day. I asked my mom to walk me down the aisle and give me away, and I asked Eric to say a few words at the reception.

A week before the wedding, Eric decided he wasn't feeling well enough to give a speech and told me he was sorry that he couldn't. In a moment of weakness, I called my dad and invited him to participate in the wedding reception by saying a prayer before we served the food.

The big day had arrived. The late May sun beat down in the rose garden, and I could feel sweat dripping down my legs beneath my dress. It was 94 degrees and more humid than was seasonal for this time of year. I was beginning to feel gross and stinky, not exactly how you want to feel on your wedding day.

It was six o'clock in the evening and time to walk down the aisle. I was finally getting rid of the last name that I had grown to despise. I hated the way it sounded: Ashley Hurley. Yuck. My dad always told me the story of how he and my mom nearly named me Shirley just so my name would be Shirley Hurley. While that would've been worse, having my dad's last name was a reminder to me that I was half him. I wanted to erase my connection to him, and marrying Conner would help me do that.

My bridal party and I walked the length of two football fields to get to the rose garden, where white chairs were lined in perfect rows. Both our families sat expectantly, squinting in the hot sun. We paused behind a large hawthorn tree with twisting branches that stretched above our heads in a canopy of a much needed shady hideout, and one by one, my bridesmaids marched forward in the procession. My mom grabbed my hand, and we stepped out into the sun, walking slowly toward the rose-filled trellis. I was beginning to tear up, and my mom looked at me, squeezed my hand, and whispered, "Take a deep breath, and don't ruin your makeup."

I hid my emotions and composed myself. I would not cry in front of all these people. We repeated the vows we were given, and then it was time to seal the deal with a kiss. I wanted to take a cue from Julia Sullivan, Drew Barrymore's character in the movie *The Wedding Singer*, and leaned in for a tastefully sweet peck on the lips. Conner and I had not discussed our official kissing style for the wedding ceremony, but I assumed that it was common sense that it looked awkward and gross when people went all in with a french kiss at a wedding.

Conner had a different idea of how the kiss should go, and as he leaned in, he grabbed the back of my head with both hands and pressed his slightly perspiring lips to mine. Suddenly his tongue pushed past my lips, which I was not prepared for. As I felt the sweat on his upper lip swipe across mine, I clenched my teeth and tried to gently back away without making it look like I was as grossed out as I actually was. He leaned in, and I did a half backbend to relieve the pressure, nearly losing my balance, but I quickly recovered. I stood back up in an upright position and slapped a smile on my face, as everyone applauded our new commitment.

After group and family pictures, Conner and I made our way into the shelterhouse for the reception, and he asked why I pulled away from his kiss.

"I just wasn't expecting it to be tongue, and it caught me a little off guard," I replied.

"Most awkward wedding kiss ever," he griped.

I felt bad but tried to let it go as we made our way up the stone stairs and opened the doors to the reception where the DJ announced our arrival. Everyone clapped and cheered as we found our seats. Before the heart-shaped pizzas were served, my dad took to the microphone to bless the meal. He thanked everyone for attending our special day, and then he got emotional as he tried to come up with a story about me and how much he loved his firstborn daughter.

He addressed me directly, "Ashley, I was the first one to hold you after you were born and tell you I loved you ... and now you're Conner's wife. Marriage is one of the hardest things you will ever do in your entire life." I was beginning to feel the uneasiness of his words as his voice quivered into the microphone.

"Remember that Rolling Stones song your mother used to sing to you kids when you'd cry because you weren't getting your way? You and your brother hated it and would scream and cry while she sang this song to let you know that just because you want something doesn't mean it should be yours. Marriage is like that song," he said. Then he started singing the chorus of, "You

Can't Always Get What You Want."

I sank down into my chair and felt my cheeks get hot with embarrassment. The room fell completely silent; no one understood what he was saying. This was his best memory of me because he was never around, and his attempt at being sentimental backfired. I was regretting giving him a platform to speak on the biggest day of my life. As my dad prayed, Conner leaned in and whispered, "What the hell was that?"

The time came to cut the cake. I stood next to Conner behind the round table that displayed our cake, chocolate with raspberry buttercream frosting and a layer of colorful fondant. We cut a slice, and I felt the gritty, dried sweat on my hands from standing in the heat of the sun's beams during the ceremony. I thought about the fact that neither of us had taken a moment to go wash our hands after we had been shaking hands and hugging all our guests.

Honestly, the whole cake-feeding tradition always bothered me. But everyone was yelling at us to feed each other the cake, so I was trying to maneuver this part of the night without disappointing Conner since I had already ruined his wedding kiss. *I don't really want to have cake smashed in my face by dirty hands,* I thought. So I picked up a fork and opted for a clean cake-feeding experience. Conner had picked up a handful of cake and was lurching toward me. I bounced a couple of feet back, looked him in the eye, and said, "No. I don't want to do it that way," and handed him a fork.

"Really?" he protested.

"Yeah, I don't want a mess on my dress," I said, trying to soften the blow of my hard "no" in front of all our friends and family. We took our slices of cake back to our table and quietly nibbled while everyone else was served.

I had always envisioned a giant dance party at my wedding

reception, and even created an epic Conner-approved playlist for the DJ. Conner had very particular taste in music and was adamant that we should highly curate our music for the reception. I hadn't considered the venue's no alcohol policy, which had saved us thousands of dollars by not having to supply booze to 100 people. It turns out that without alcohol, most people don't feel brave enough to shake their booties.

It had never occurred to me that alcohol was an important factor in other people's enjoyment because it was not important to me. Up to this point, I had never had a single drink in my life, so I didn't understand the concept of liquid courage. The entire night, only six people danced on the designated dance floor, and two of them were me and my new husband. I was disappointed that our families weren't integrating and having more fun.

Close to midnight, Conner and I left the reception and drove off into the proverbial sunset toward our hotel with a to-go box of pizza. We checked into the Marriott near the airport, where the next morning we would depart for our honeymoon at an all-inclusive resort in Jamaica. It felt weird to me that everyone who attended our wedding now knew exactly what we were about to do.

I felt gross from the sweat of the day, and as I set my bag on the bed, Conner said, "I want to literally rip that dress off of you."

"Can you give me a moment to freshen up?" I asked. "I just feel super disgusting and unattractive."

"I don't care if you smell bad," he said.

"Ok, but I do," I replied as I grabbed the frilly lingerie I packed and went to the bathroom for a quick shower.

I was feeling so anxious about being intimate with Conner. We had lived together and had fooled around a lot during that time, but we had never actually done the deed. Even though I'd had sex before, none of the experiences were attached to positive feelings or memories for me, and I had never really enjoyed it. Sex was more like something I viewed as a necessary element of keeping a boyfriend interested, something expected of me when our relationship reached a certain level.

This will be different from what I've experienced in the past, I told myself while I showered. *This is real love. This is my husband.*

I slipped into the lingerie and awkwardly fumbled out of the bathroom. It was dark, and the light from the bathroom beamed into the room as I made my way toward him. He kissed me and leaned me back onto the bed. As he hovered over me, I began to feel tears trickling down my face, which turned into full-on sobbing a moment later. And with the tears came a thought. A dreadful thought that I wouldn't dare say out loud: *I have made a terrible mistake. This cannot be the last person I will be intimate with for the rest of my life.*

"Are you ok? Is this hurting you?" he asked.

"I'm fine. It's not hurting ... I think I'm just emotional right now. This is a special night." I was saying this out loud to him, but I was really saying it to convince myself that the sadness I was experiencing was merely a bit of delayed wedding jitters.

Maybe I wouldn't be crying right now if Mom had let me cry during the ceremony, I thought to myself as Conner continued to press his soft, clammy body against mine. *I just need to get it together; this is my husband, and I have to give him what he wants if I'm going to be a good wife. It won't always be this way; we will eventually get used to each other and find a flow and everything will be fine,* I told myself as I boxed up my feelings of insecurity and uncertainty and did what I thought was expected of me.

The next morning, as we boarded our flight for our honeymoon in Jamaica, I made a commitment to myself to fix how I was feeling. Divorce was never going to be an option, so I was going to be with this man for the rest of my life, and I needed to make it work. I willed myself to be everything he wanted me to be. I would find the love I needed to push through.

"How could you let this happen?" I said out loud to God. The rain was even heavier now. I was still standing in the middle of the runway at the airpark. Full-on ugly crying. My dog looked up at me, her fluffy hair now drenched and flattened to her body; I think I saw actual concern in her eyes as if she was thinking, *Are you stuck here?* I *was* stuck.

For my entire life, I had been setting myself on fire, trying to light the path for the people I loved—to be who they needed me to be. And I had completely lost myself in the process. I knew my roles as a wife and a mother, but beyond that, I felt like no one at all. My perfectionistic tendencies made the list of "should-do's" that were dictated to me by others so loud that my own thoughts were buried under all the noise. I was trapped in my own body, hurting and broken. It felt like I was spinning in the eye of a monster tornado that was trying to destroy the last shred of hope I had left.

"Conner is holding you back," my therapist, Valerie, would say to me. I had been seeing her for four years. I trusted her. She had never steered me wrong, and she gave me the tools to navigate so many painful situations in my life. For the last two years, she had been gently telling me that I might need to consider a temporary separation from my husband.

"At a minimum, I would say three months. I'm not pressuring you, but I am here to help you if and when you're ready," Valerie offered. She tried to stay hopeful. "You guys just need a reset. You're not going to fix your problem by doing things the same way you always have with him. He isn't getting the message."

I was slowly waking up to the truth. Valerie was right, and I felt an unsettling foreboding that I was no longer able to ignore.

At the beginning of 2019, I had chosen my word for the year: freedom. What I didn't know was that my freedom would come at such a great cost. I wasn't speaking to my parents or my brother. I hadn't yet felt safe enough to open up to my friends about what I was going through. My husband was my last person—if he was gone, then I'd really have no one.

Why did God put so many people in my life who would break my heart and let me down? I looked for a sign from heaven. I was desperate and begging Him to send someone to swoop in and save me from having to experience so much pain.

"Whatever the life lesson is here, God, please help me to learn it quickly and move on from this," I prayed. I was about to discover that learning the lesson isn't the same as knowing the truth.

chapter two

IF NOT FOR ME

"People are like stained-glass windows. They sparkle and shine when the sun is out, but when the darkness sets in, their true beauty is revealed only if there is a light from within."
— **Elisabeth Kübler-Ross**

As a kid, I spent a lot of time in the security of my bedroom. Behind that closed door, I felt safe. I pretended to be Kristi Yamaguchi performing a powerful figure skating routine, leaping through the air, flinging my arms from side to side, twirling and gliding on my carpet—honestly, it was not so much a glide as it was a not-so-graceful shuffle—and blasting Mozart. Classical music felt so sophisticated, much fancier than I could ever be outside of my bedroom.

But there, alone in my room, I was exactly who I wanted to be: a refined and beloved Olympic figure skater in a flawless, frilly costume with supportive tights and parents who watched proudly, holding flowers and stuffed teddy bears ready to toss onto the ice after another stellar performance. Reality was a stark contrast to the perfectly calculated imaginary figure skating career I had concocted. Real life was unpredictable and too open for chaos and confusion.

I felt like God had cheated me in the dad department. I was never proud to be his daughter. Every family has that one relative who is ever-so-slightly off ... but what do you do when that family member happens to be your very own dad? I was ashamed of him. Even as a kid, I could sense that he was lazy and mostly unavailable to me and my younger brother, Oscar. I quickly learned to recognize when I was not wanted, which at least in my dad's case, seemed to be always.

While I was in elementary school, we lived on a couple of acres of land, and my dad always had lots of animals around. I loved that house because of its large front porch complete with a swing, but most of all because the neighbors behind us had horses that I would feed carrots and sugar cubes every chance I got. Ohio summers were great for exploring the property and visiting with the animals.

There was an old barn with fenced runs for Dad's hunting dogs, a small flock of sheep, a couple of goats, two turkeys, and a stray cat we named Missy Kay, who we found wandering in the parking lot of our community swimming pool one hot summer day. Dad would randomly take in other animals, like stray dogs, or the time he brought home baby skunks, which he said would make great pets once he had their stink sacks removed. I think we had them for about a week before they all died.

This wasn't the first time animals had lost their lives under my dad's care. When I was five, Dad brought home a half-dozen fuzzy yellow baby chicks. Oscar and I had been gone for most of the day running errands with Mom. As she pulled our bright red Eagle Talon sports car into the driveway, she noted, "Dad's not home. He must've gone in to work at the car dealership. I hope he remembered to open the back windows for the chicks; it's so hot out today. Ash, why don't you run in and check on them while I unload the groceries."

As I walked down the darkened hallway toward the door where sunlight was pouring in through the small windowpanes above the doorknob, I noticed how the dry, hot air slapped me in the face and nearly took my breath away. When I opened the door, I walked toward the crate and saw what I thought was the most adorable sight: sweet, sleepy chicks all piled on top of each other, beaks open as if they were in the most peaceful slumber.

I ran to my mom to tell her how cute it was that they were all asleep. I flung my head back, closed my eyes, and opened my mouth to show her what they looked like.

"Those chicks aren't asleep, Ashley; they're dead," she told me. "Your dad forgot to open the windows for them, so it got too hot in there, and they couldn't breathe. Their heads are back like that because they were gasping for air."

I was devastated. How could my dad forget something as important as another creature's life? I began to wonder if he was capable of caring for his own kids if he couldn't even remember that animals need air to live. Even to my five-year-old brain, this felt reckless. I recognized that he was not dependable and began to pull myself inward, trying to be invisible whenever he was around. If I didn't need him for anything, if I could ask my mom for help or do it myself, then he could never forget about me like he did with the chicks. I retreated to the safety of my bedroom, and no one ever talked about the chicks again.

Of all our animals, the sheep were my favorite. We started with three, a male and two females. The ewes both got pregnant and were ready to deliver in the springtime. I was there when one of the ewes gave birth. Dad was helping her, and I watched from the other side of the barn. She had two lambs, a white one and a black one. Dad said the black one was the runt and probably wouldn't make it. He wrapped the sheep in an old blanket and placed the six-pound bundle of fluff in my lap.

"We can try to bottle feed him to see how he does, but don't get your hopes up," he told me.

I named him Lucky. I enjoyed bottle-feeding this tiny sheep, and as I cared for him, he grew in strength and stature, and soon he no longer needed the bottle. Lucky was my friend.

One Saturday, while playing with my vast collection of troll dolls alone in my bedroom, I heard the loud gurgly rumble of a neglected muffler that sounded as if Mario Andretti himself were pulling into our driveway. I looked out my bedroom window, but I couldn't see anything, so I headed down the stairs and out the front door, where I found my dad talking to a short, dark-haired man loading our small flock of six sheep into his El Camino. Their legs were bound with rope, and the man was stuffing the sheep into his trunk and the back seats as if he were overstuffing a suitcase that was slightly too small for its contents. Dad stood by and watched. He always called this way of working without actually helping, "supervising."

I tugged on his hand. "Daddy, where are our sheep going?"

Dad looked down at me and said, "We can't have sheep here anymore. This fella is taking them to his farm."

I began to cry and asked him not to send my sheep away. I begged and said I would help more with the animals if we could keep them—if we could even just keep Lucky.

"He already paid me for the sheep. It's a done deal. Go on to your room and play," he said blankly.

I ran to my room, threw myself onto my bed, and sobbed. Inside my body, my heart actually felt hot, like it was exploding into 10,000 shards, collapsing on itself, and radiating beams of sadness and anger inside my chest. I wondered if I was dying. Why else would it hurt this much? Mom came upstairs to check on me after a while. She told me that she had made brownies, and I could have one if I came downstairs. "Sorry about Lucky," she added. "He's just an animal though, and you'll have lots more to love in your life. Now how about those brownies?"

As much as I wanted to believe her, I knew that Lucky was not just another animal. He was my friend, and I loved him. No one asked me how I felt about losing him. They just sent him away. One moment we were walking in the field together, and the next he was gone. I learned quickly that I should never get too attached to anything. As I tried to make peace with losing Lucky over a plate of Betty Crocker brownies, I made a silent vow to never have that excruciating heart-exploding feeling ever again. I didn't know then how impossible that promise would be to keep.

My two grandmas couldn't be more different from each other. Grandma Hurley, my dad's mom, was short and round, but what she lacked in height she more than made up for with her sass and stubbornness. We called her "Fat Grandma" because she was significantly bigger than my mom's mom, who we were given explicit instructions to always refer to respectfully as "Nanny." I always felt weird calling my Grandma Hurley "Fat Grandma." I knew it wasn't nice to say that someone was fat, but it didn't seem to phase her. "Call it like it is!" she'd brashly exclaim whenever we would see her.

Fat Grandma was known for being mean, loud, and mouthy. As rough as she seemed, she also had a side to her that was strangely whimsical. She had a curated collection of cheap little figurines from yard sales, dollar stores, and McDonald's Happy Meals that she thoughtfully displayed in her home. She would tell me stories about how she married Grandpa Hurley when she was only 12 years old. "Poor country families did that a lot back then," she would explain. My grandpa was well into his twenties when he married her. He was in the Army and made good money, so her father eagerly gave her away. "One less mouth for my daddy to feed," Fat Grandma reasoned.

I wasn't as close to her as I was to Nanny, but I enjoyed going to her small, three-bedroom house to see her many pristine QVC porcelain dolls arranged on the tops of each bed, surrounded by ruffled pillowcases. The toys she had set up on tables and shelves and dressers were a stark contrast to my grandfather's looming gun cabinets and NRA belt buckles. We were never allowed to touch or play with the dolls and toys, but I loved to look at them all—as long as I didn't stand too close to Grandpa's guns. They always made me feel uneasy.

Nanny couldn't be more different. She was a proper church lady who always talked to me about Jesus and my soul and how to get to heaven. She put the fear of God in me so that I was convinced I needed to say the sinner's prayer every night, just in case I died in my sleep and had sinned earlier in the day without knowing it.

Nanny was beautiful. She had a soft olive complexion and short dark hair that was hairsprayed to perfection so that not a single hair was out of place. She and my mom were the same size, and they shared clothes for church each week. On Saturday afternoons, I would sit on Nanny's floral bedspread watching as they rummaged through her closet for pretty dresses with shoulder pads, trying to decide which outfits they'd wear to Sunday morning service the next day.

I had come to understand that this weekly ritual was expected of their mother-daughter relationship. Any time Nanny called, my mom did exactly what she requested—which was usually pressuring us to attend yet another family gathering or church event. It seemed like our family was always at church; we practically lived in the 17th row back from the pulpit. Nanny expected us to all be there every Sunday morning, Sunday night, and Wednesday night. Our family was well-known and respected there.

I imagined that when I was older, I would take my own daughter to a Saturday afternoon church-clothes swap at my mother's house each week, just like any good adult-Christian daughter should. It seemed to me that Jesus expected his women to behave, sing pretty in the choir, and dress a certain way in order to make it through the pearly gates. I wanted to be the best person I could be, and the best people I knew were my mom and Nanny, so I did everything they expected of me in order to gain "more jewels in my heavenly crown," as Nanny put it.

Nanny wanted us to be the picture-perfect example of a Christian family who had it all together. It was an unspoken rule that image was everything. To outsiders, we looked the part of the perfect family, and for a long time, we had ourselves convinced that we were. She so desperately wanted others to compliment her on what a fantastic job she did raising her family. Deep down, she saw us as a reflection of herself. She was impossible to please, but we knew she loved us.

We were all caught up in this elaborate charade, each of us playing our roles, and it was obvious that mine was to follow in the footsteps of all the women before me: look pretty, stay quiet, and don't question authority. But my mom did things differently, and that made her influence on my life even stronger. I trusted her more than anyone.

Nanny had adopted a few dozen expectations of how our family should operate: Be helpful, be kind, love God, read your Bible, and pray every day. Volunteer at the church food pantry. Sing in the choir. Teach a Sunday School class. Use an iron on your wrinkled shirt. Show up to every family event on time, and visit well past clearing off the table to show you care. Talk to everyone you can about Jesus, and try to save their souls by inviting them to church. I often wonder if she felt the need for her family to be, look, and act perfect because of how imperfect her life was in the poverty-stricken Kentucky holler where she grew up.

In 1956, at just 16 years old, Nanny escaped that life. She moved to Ohio and took a job as a roller-skating carhop at a diner, where she eventually met my grandfather. They married shortly after. Nanny had a high school diploma. My grandfather only made it to the second grade before his father passed away, and he was forced to get a job in the fields of Georgia, working for local farmers. My grandparents had worked hard and scraped together a life that was respectable.

Both my grandmothers had similarly difficult upbringings, and yet they turned out so different. Whenever Nanny heard us kids saying the word "fart," she would tell us it was a curse word, and we were all forbidden to say it in her presence. I believed her and thought all my friends at school who said fart so freely were going straight to h-e-double-hockey-sticks. Fat Grandma was much more relaxed and easygoing (even about fart jokes), and my mom and Nanny didn't like that.

When I was seven, Fat Grandma bought me a beautiful wooden Victorian dollhouse for Christmas. I had been wanting a dollhouse ever since my cousin Alice had gotten her Barbie Dreamhouse. I was overjoyed when I received this gift from my grandma. I couldn't believe it was made of actual wood and not cheap plastic like Alice's dreamhouse. *This dollhouse will last forever,* I thought. We brought it home from Fat Grandma's on Christmas Day, and Dad leaned it against the wall in front of my bed so that I could see the picture of it on the outside of the box, all assembled and beautiful.

"When can we put the dollhouse together, Daddy?" I asked.

"Soon," he said. "There's a lot of small pieces; those shingles are gonna take forever."

A few weeks passed, and no one had even opened the box to try to put the dollhouse together. I asked Mom about it one night at bedtime. "Your dad is a busy guy," she said. "But at least you have the pretty picture to look at while you wait." I was upset, but I trusted my mom. She was always finding the silver lining.

Summer rolled around, and my mom and Aunt Loretta were planning a huge family yard sale at our house. We lived on a busy road and had a great long driveway and a big garage. Early Thursday morning, they set up eight-foot tables in the garage where we could prep and organize for the sale. We began tagging all the items with those neon circular stickers with prices on them. My job was to go through an old pile of clothes that no longer fit me, tagging shirts and shorts at fifty cents, and old winter jackets for two dollars.

What I discovered at the bottom of this clothes pile upset me. The box with my beautiful and still unopened Victorian dollhouse was on the tagging table. Was my mom planning to sell the dollhouse? I got up from my work and walked over to my mother.

"Mom, why is the dollhouse down here? It needs to be in my room so Daddy can put it together," I said, thinking it was brought down by mistake.

"Honey," Mom said, "Dad isn't going to be able to put this dollhouse together. There are too many parts, and it would take way too long. So we're selling it."

I protested for a moment, but I had come to learn that my feelings would be disregarded. I was "just a kid." I wasn't allowed to have a say in these types of decisions. Being agreeable kept me out of trouble.

My aunt saw my disappointment and came over to talk to me. "You know you can come by and play with Alice's dollhouse anytime you want," she said.

"I know. Thanks," I told her before moving on to the next set of items that needed tagging.

My mom never would have given that dollhouse away if it had been given to me by *her* mother. Everything that Fat Grandma ever got us was considered a lesser gift in my mom's eyes. Once, my parents threw away a brand-new grandfather clock that Fat Grandma had gifted to them. The next time that Fat Grandma came to our house to visit, she inquired about the clock and my mom's response was, "We accidentally threw it in the garbage."

I could tell Fat Grandma's feelings were hurt, and I still can't reconcile how two grown adults would not know that they put a giant grandfather clock in the trash can. Value was assigned to a gift based on how my mother valued the person giving the gift. Fat Grandma was her least favorite person, so it was easy to categorize her gifts as regifts, yard sale, or garbage can material.

I couldn't recognize this as a child, but I would learn over time how easy it was for my mother to discard relationships that didn't suit her.

Money was always tight in our house. My dad was constantly out of a job, so Mom often worked two jobs or sold Mary Kay makeup to ladies at our church to cover the bills. They argued all the time about everything from finances to Dad's interest in other women—and other topics my young ears couldn't comprehend. Hearing them fight made me feel anxious. It was like being held underwater, feeling the panic of not being able to inhale oxygen. My hands would get clammy, and I would pick at scabs or my nails, anything to quell my anxiety.

One afternoon, I sat on the staircase listening to them yell at each other. I picked at the old wallpaper in the dining room, at the very corner where the wall and ceiling met the stairs, and pulled a massive chunk off. I looked up and saw my mother storm out the front door without a word. I went to find Dad.

"Where did Mom go?" I asked.

"I don't know," he said quietly.

"Ok, well … When will she be back?"

"I don't know that either," he replied without looking up from his can of Budweiser.

My mom and I were very close. For her to leave without saying anything made my seven-year-old lungs feel as though they were full of dry ice. I went up to Oscar's room to find him playing with his Ninja Turtles.

"Mom's gone, and I don't know when she will be back," I told him.

"Ok," he said between breaths of imaginary battles and Michelangelo's clanking nunchucks. He didn't seem to be as worried as I was.

I went to my room. My safe place. I shut the door and sat on the side of my bed. I grabbed a pencil and a notebook and started drawing, hoping that she would return soon and not leave me here with Dad for too long. I didn't trust him to know what we needed or to be able to keep us alive for more than a week. He didn't know how to take care of us like she did. He didn't know the songs she sang or the way she rubbed my back at night. He didn't even know how to cook, so if Mom wasn't back by dinner, what were we supposed to eat?

As the sun was setting, I heard the slam of a car door—the kind of door-shutting sound that only happens when your hands are full, and you have to use your foot to shut it. *That's Mom's car*, I thought as I hurried down the stairs to find her unloading a bucket of Kentucky Fried Chicken and getting plates from the kitchen.

"Where were you, Mom? Why didn't you take me with you?"

"Just out to run errands and get this chicken," she replied. "Now take these napkins and help me set the table."

Dinner that night was painfully quiet. Mom and Dad barely said two words to each other. I tried to make jokes over my mashed potatoes and gravy to make them smile, but no one laughed. Oscar was there, but he was always off in some distant world in his own head. I felt like I had to do something, so I blurted out that I had picked off a chunk of the wallpaper earlier that day. They both looked at me blankly.

My dad told me that there would be a consequence for that bad behavior and got up from the table, taking his plate to finish his meal alone in the kitchen. After he left, Mom said, "Why on earth would you do that?" I put my head down and pushed my fork through the mashed potatoes, making lines like the wave-shaped ripples of a sand dune, gravy flowing through like a thick, brown river. I felt a small prick in my heart. I stiffened my back and tucked the pain away. *I will not let my heart hurt tonight,* I thought.

Not too long after the wallpaper incident, my dad started spending a lot of time in our basement. He would be down there for hours, and I was always told I wasn't allowed to go down with him. *Nothing exciting usually happens in a basement,* I thought. I figured he must be working on something amazing if he was spending so much time in that cold, dark, and scary place.

One day, Mom had just left for the grocery store, and Dad headed toward the basement.

"What are you doing down there, Dad? Can I come, too?" I asked.

"There's stuff down there that could hurt you if it fell on you. You might get squashed like a pancake. I'll be up later. Go watch some TV or play in your room," he told me.

But I didn't want to watch any more television. I was dying to know what his top-secret basement work was. I waited a moment at the top of the basement stairs, then as soon as Dad was out of sight, I followed him. I reasoned that if I just took a quick peek then I would know what was so special, and I could sneak out quietly without him knowing I was there.

I silently followed him through our endless, winding basement. Half of it was finished, with a bed and a desk in the room. He went through a door that led to the unfinished part, mostly used for storage. I passed a few boxes and old tools and came upon the water heater and HVAC unit. I watched Dad slip behind the water heater, and suddenly, I heard a door open and saw a glowing fluorescent light.

This part of the basement was cold and smelled musty. I was a little scared, but I really wanted to see what the light was for. I peeked through the door, which Dad had left half open. I saw him sitting at a table that was full of green plants, each about eight inches tall. He was misting them with a spray bottle and inspecting all the leaves. I watched him for a moment, and then he looked up and saw me there.

"Hi, Daddy ... I just wanted to see what you were doing down here. What are all these plants?!" I asked excitedly.

"This is Daddy's garden," he said with a smile. Then he got very serious and added, "Do not ever, ever, ever touch it. Now please go back upstairs and check on your brother."

As a young adult, I asked him about this memory. He laughed a little and said, "Your mom asked me to start growing and selling weed to make us a little extra money. I didn't really want to, but there was no arguing with your mother."

I found that statement ironic because I *only* remember him arguing with my mother.

When I was 11 years old, our family moved out of Nanny and Grandpa's house, where we had been living for nearly two years without my dad. He and my mom had an on-again-off-again relationship, and at that point, they were off. When we moved into the house next door to my Aunt Loretta and Uncle Rhett, my parents were giving it another try, so Dad moved with us.

I adored those few years living next door to my cousins, Birdie and Alice. They were my two most favorite people in the world. I often silently wished I was a Hall and not a Hurley. Visiting my cousin's house was always a blast. I loved playing with them, and my aunt and uncle seemed like kind, stable people.

There was never anyone fighting loudly, never anyone storming off angrily. My aunt always gave us choices, like pizza or mac and cheese for dinner, or bowling or a movie on a rainy Saturday. Also, my dad wasn't there telling me to be quiet or to go to my room. My aunt helped manage a daycare and knew that kids need to make noise and be silly.

I often wished my cousins were my sisters instead, and that I could go to gymnastics with them and learn how to do a back handspring. I got to do gymnastics for a little while, but it was too expensive for my parents, so they pulled me out. Besides, my mom was busy with work, church, and her softball team, so there wasn't much time left for us kids to have any extracurriculars.

I longed for the stability that my cousins had. My parents had such a rocky back-and-forth relationship—always fighting, cheating, manipulating, and leaving. A stark contrast to my dad growing weird plants and "accidentally" killing baby chicks, my Aunt Loretta and Uncle Rhett always seemed to have it all

IF NOT FOR ME

together. I wished Uncle Rhett could be my dad. He was strong and constant. He knew how to fix things. He was never late on paying a bill.

I've decided that if you know you're poor as a third-grade kid, your family must be dirt poor. As an adult now with kids of my own, we've struggled financially, but my kids have no clue and think we're rich. Though I wasn't even double digits yet, I recognized that we had no money. We lived in a small, ranch house that my grandfather had purchased, and Nanny would always slip my mom hundred dollar bills after Sunday lunch as we were heading out the door. My mom would pretend she didn't want it. The two of them would spend two minutes doing this giving/receiving dance. It would start with my mom, noticing Nanny reaching for her pocketbook.

"Oh, Mom, no. You shouldn't ..."

"No, Deb, I insist," Nanny would say with her soft Kentucky accent. "Go buy some groceries or new jackets for the kids."

I would watch Nanny gently push the money into the palm of my mom's hand, folding her fingers over the bills. My mom often told me the story about how Nanny was the youngest of 13 children, and her family was so dirt poor, she couldn't even afford underwear. In high school, she was voted Prom Queen, and she went commando under her thrift store dress.

Nanny loved to help other people, especially her family. She hid money from my grandfather in her car and her underwear drawer (now that she could afford those), and used it to help as many needy folks as she could. Grandpa didn't always approve of how much financial help Nanny offered others. When it came to helping her own daughter, Nanny's rescue came with an expectation for my mom to be a certain type of person. The kind of person who attended church, sang in the choir, and danced in the aisles for Jesus.

My mom tried to be this person, but I don't think it ever truly suited her. Mom was a self-proclaimed "black sheep of the family." She did uncivilized things like sneak out to smoke pot in the garage, bust out her most vulgar pelvic thrust moves during every living room dance party, and lift her shirt to flash her fake boobs to her teenage nieces, tween daughter, and son every time one of us landed on a "Lucky Day" space while playing *The Game of Life*. Not exactly church lady material.

When I was in the third grade, my parents were struggling so much that my aunt and uncle decided to step in and relieve the financial burden of the holidays. They wanted to surprise my mom and dad by helping out with our family's Christmas presents that year. My dad was trying to "live right" and had been working at a nearby church as their youth minister (how he landed that job is still a mystery to me). This job either didn't pay very well, or he had already been let go—a common occurrence in our household.

My cousins invited me to the mall one weekend to do some holiday shopping with them. I was with my uncle while he picked out a diamond tennis bracelet at the jewelry shop for my aunt's Christmas gift. The bright white lighting of the jewelry cases made the diamonds sparkle and shine like nothing I had ever seen before. I was in awe.

"I've never been to a jewelry store before because we aren't rich," I blurted out loud. My uncle laughed.

A few days later, Aunt Loretta enlisted my help to get her a spare key and help deliver the gifts to our house when my parents were away.

I was giddy with the knowledge of this surprise, and the fact that they trusted *me* to keep such a massive secret. I was so proud when my mom got home and saw all the gifts under the tree. I watched her open gifts with her name on them. Several of the smaller boxes held rolled-up cash. I don't know how much money it was, but to my nine-year-old heart it looked like my rich aunt and uncle gave my parents a thousand dollars.

I felt so special to have played a small role in this good deed. I felt like a hero for keeping the secret and helping my mom receive this generous gift. It's still one of my favorite Christmas memories because it reminds me of how love works: a simple act with no strings attached, only a desire to do good for someone you care about. That year, Christmas actually meant something more, and I was a part of something bigger than myself—something bigger than just getting a bunch of toys I wouldn't remember 28 years later.

I grew up attending the Seventh Avenue Church of God, a Pentecostal church with a handful of charismatic, Southern-style preachers who called all of us "Brother So-and-So" and "Sister What's-Her-Name" and yelled their sermons with sweaty, red faces into a microphone as if they were fighting the devil himself to get their words to reach the ears of the congregation.

Sometimes, on a wild Sunday night when the Holy Ghost would show up during the song and worship part of the service, the praise team would sing for three hours straight while everyone danced and ran through the aisles or fell out in the spirit. In Pentecostal churches, when the pastor "lays hands" on someone who wants prayer, sometimes they literally fall to the floor, dance, or speak in tongues. Ushers would place their suit jackets over women's legs when they had fallen to the ground in their Sunday dresses, shaking and praising Jesus into oblivion.

It wasn't until middle school that I realized not everyone's church services looked like mine. The first time I invited my friend Carly to sleep over on a Saturday night and go to church with us, the next morning was a real culture shock for her Baptist heart. I'll never forget the look of terror in her eyes when she saw Alex Carter, a short and heavy-set man who only got inspired to do cardio when Jesus showed up in the church service, screaming at the top of his lungs and sprinting the sanctuary aisles. Carly turned pale and sat down without saying a word.

On the way home, she had a lot of questions about why our pastor was so angry, and what was the strange language he prayed in when he touched people at the altar call, which is a time of prayer at the end of the service where sinners can be "saved." I had to explain that the preacher was speaking in tongues, which was God's holy language, and that the pastor wasn't mad, he was just delivering the message from the Lord. She didn't seem convinced. After that, any time I invited a friend to church with me, I would ask God to make it a calm service so I wouldn't get embarrassed. But God has a sense of humor because almost every time I brought a new person to church there was a wild Holy Ghost encounter.

When I was 20, I was invited to sing on the church praise team with my mom, my cousin Alice, the pastor's wife, and a girl I grew up with in Sunday School named Ava. The Holy Ghost was showing up to church more often now which meant that we were performing at shouting services more often. When I closed my eyes, standing on that orange carpeted stage, singing my heart out, I imagined I was on *American Idol* while we belted out our praises to the heavens.

As part of the praise team, we were always coached to lead worship by example. "If we want the people to experience God through worship, we have to set the tone of what that looks like," we were told. So whether we were feeling it or not, we had the mindset of "fake it till you make it," so we could show the people in the congregation how to properly worship the Lord. We all found our holy groove, and when "God showed up," as the pastor liked to say, he would fling the church doors open so the whole neighborhood could "hear what God was doing over on Seventh Avenue."

One Thursday evening as our worship team practice was wrapping up, Ava confided in all of us that her husband of just six months had a porn addiction, and she was struggling to navigate life as a married woman. She was devastated that she was considering filing for divorce, and shared her fears through slow, crocodile tears that she caught with a tissue right beneath the rim of her eye so that she wouldn't smear her makeup. Some of the ladies offered her feeble words of encouragement and prayed for her before we each made our way home.

I had no experience with porn or a husband and felt completely inadequate to offer any words of wisdom, so I just listened quietly. I was supposed to be praying for Ava, but I kept contemplating how weird it was that she was my same age and already had a baby on the way and all these very grown-up problems. We were 20 years old, and most days, I still felt as if people treated me like I was only 14. *I guess that's what happens to people who still live at home,* I thought. *We take longer to grow up.*

When I arrived home that evening, I poured a glass of sweet tea from the refrigerator, and my mom came into the kitchen to chat about what Ava had shared. "Let me give you some words of advice for your future," she said. "When you get married, if you don't provide your man with everything he wants, he will go looking for it elsewhere. If you're lucky, it will just be porn, but sometimes it is someone else, and you get cheated on."

I thought about this for the next few days and spent time reading my Bible, studying the following verse from the New Testament:

"Wives, submit yourselves to your own husbands as you do to the Lord. For the husband is the head of the wife as Christ is the head of the church, his body, of which he is the Savior. Now as the church submits to Christ, so also wives should submit to their husbands in everything." (Eph. 5:22-24 NIV)

I had grown up seeing the roles women played in the church, cooking for potluck fellowship and singing in the choir, while not being allowed on the board of elders or to even have much of an opinion regarding church-related decisions.

A good, submissive Christian wife must give her husband everything he wants, I deduced. *When I become a wife someday, I'll make sure my husband has no complaints.* I didn't want to end up like Ava, pregnant with a marriage falling apart because she wasn't having enough sex with her husband.

\|/

chapter three

INVISIBLE

"Understand this if you understand nothing: it is a powerful thing to be seen."
— **Akwaeke Emezi**

I have this vivid memory from when I was six years old. I'm alone in a room with a silver butter knife. I decided it was a good idea to gently stick the knife into an electrical socket to see what would happen. My mother had always told me not to stick anything in a socket, but she failed to explain why, so curiosity had finally gotten the best of me. Immediately, I felt an electric jolt in my fingers that traveled through my whole arm, and by pure luck and reflex, I dropped the knife.

I was terrified at the chaotic, stinging sensation that pulsed through my body for that one tiny moment. I thought I had killed myself, become a ghost, and that no one would be able to see me. I walked through the house, a bit shaken, trying to determine if I had, in fact, died in the other room. I could hear my mother in the kitchen, singing along to a Whitney Houston song and washing dishes.

I stood behind her without saying anything at all. She was wearing giant yellow rubber gloves, her hands submerged in the billowing bubbles of the dishwater. I wondered, *Can she see me? If I speak, will she hear me but not be able to see me, since I'm fully a dead ghost now?* I decided to test it out.

"Mom! Can you see me?" I shouted.

She turned around, looked right at me, and said, "Of course I can see you," and then went right back to her dishes.

When I was in kindergarten, I rode the school bus. The boy who sat in the seat in front of me was a bit edgy for a third grader, and he used words I had never heard before when he spoke to the other kids. Words like *shit, bitch, asshole,* and my favorite, *fuck.* I liked his use of vocabulary. It felt powerful to me. I wanted to see what it felt like to say those power words. I didn't understand why everyone around him would always react when he dropped an f-bomb, but I liked how he commanded their attention when he did.

I got off the school bus that day and went inside to discover that only my dad was home. I went to play in my room and decided that was a perfect place to try out this newly discovered power word.

"Fuck!" I said confidently. "Fuck. Fuck. Fuckkkkkkk!" *Hey, this is fun,* I thought.

Suddenly, my dad appeared in the doorway.

"Stop saying that," he ordered.

"Stop saying fuck?" I asked.

"I'll wash out your mouth with soap, young lady," he threatened.

"Because I'm saying fuck?" I asked again.

"That's it. Bathroom. NOW," he demanded.

I was confused. I didn't realize fuck was an off-limits power word for me. I only just discovered it, and I liked saying it. Why was he so mad? Why couldn't I use power words?

He reached under the sink and grabbed a bar of Dove soap.

As he opened the box, he said, "You're going to take a bite of this soap, and you're never going to say that word again."

He handed me the soap. It was ivory in color. It felt smooth and solid in my hand. I looked down at it and traced the "D" that was stamped into the top of the bar.

"Go on, take a bite," he said. "You're not leaving this bathroom until you do it."

I didn't think he was actually going to make me eat a bite of soap, but he did. I bit into the bar. The waxy consistency was stomach-churning. I pulled it back from my mouth and saw my teeth marks. *Don't let him know that you hate this,* I thought.

"Now swallow it," he said. I gulped. "How did that taste?" he asked.

Inside my heart, I was feeling hot anger and the urge to cry, but externally, I knew better than to show any emotion at all. I replied, "It needs salt," and at that, he swatted my bottom and sent me to my room for the rest of the day. This is the first vivid memory I have of my dad. I remember hating him because he made me eat soap and took away a word I loved—without even explaining to me why it was wrong.

I always wanted to be seen. I wanted to be like my mother. I wanted people to look at me the way they looked at her, this beautiful, confident, endlessly talented, brilliant, and witty woman who thrived in the spotlight. But once I got the attention, I was terrified and found only disappointment in my introverted heart for not being brave enough to actually allow myself to shine. *It's easier to point my tiny sparkle in someone else's direction so that they shine brighter,* was a lie I told myself in the name of self-protection.

I was so shy that I could not even order my own food at a

restaurant until I was 13 years old. My mom would order for me, and as she would point in my direction saying, "She will have the spaghetti kids meal," my face would flush with embarrassment. I would wish to be anywhere else, melting into my chair and trying to blend in with the restaurant decor.

My mother certainly wasn't shy. She had the kind of magnetism and charisma of a big-time Hollywood actress, and every man who knew her wanted her. I got sick of the boys in my fifth grade class calling her "hot." Kevin Tucker would knock on my door at least twice a week after school just to see my mom before he asked if I was home. She knew that's why so many boys would come over to ask if I could play after school, and she loved it. She always sought after the attention of men, and apparently enjoyed her MILF status at my school.

People always told me how much I looked like my mother. I believed that was the highest compliment I could ever get. Everyone thought my mother was beautiful; I thought so, too. And if they said I looked like her ... then that must mean I was beautiful, like her. But, as much as I idolized her and tried to emulate her and follow in her footsteps, I knew I could never be like her.

When we moved next door to my aunt and uncle when I was in elementary school, my dad had secured a job at a local composting plant, and my mom and Aunt Loretta did a weekly cleaning job at his office to make extra money. Alice, Birdie, Oscar, and I tagged along, helping to empty trash cans and dust conference rooms. Occasionally, Oscar would get bored with cleaning and go sit on a massive front loader tractor and pretend he was working there. Dad seemed to like his job, but one day he came home, particularly worked up.

"Daniel was putting wood through the chipping machine at

the plant and got his arm caught. He lost half his left arm today," he reported at the dinner table. I was in shock. A man lost an arm working at the place where my dad went every day. That sounded terrifying.

"Is he going to be ok?" my mom asked.

"Yeah, he'll be fine. He's gonna be set for life now with worker's comp and legal stuff. I bet he'll sue the company and never have to work again. What I wouldn't give to be that guy," he said as he leaned back from the dinner table.

"You'd be willing to lose your arm if you never had to work again?" my mom asked, sounding slightly annoyed.

"Yeah, of course!" he replied. "Do you know how lucky that guy is?"

I hurried to scoop a few more bites of food off my plate before this conversation could go any further. I knew where it was going, and I didn't want to be there to hear it. I announced that I had homework and found my way back to the safety and quiet of my bedroom. I could not believe that my dad would be willing to give up his arm if it meant he would not have to work ever again.

I thought about how much I needed my left arm. I loved being a lefty and thought about how awful it would be to lose the part of me that helped me to create art. Even as a kid, I knew I would never voluntarily give up an appendage so I didn't have to work, and this admission by my dad completely baffled me.

In preparing to graduate from high school, I applied to less than a handful of local colleges. I could not fathom the thought of moving out of state and living so far away from my family. I needed to stay close because I wanted to be able to see them as much as possible, and moving far away would give me severe family FOMO. Missing our weekly Sunday family gatherings was just not an option for me. I hated the feeling of being out of town and knowing everyone carried on with life as usual, eating Nanny's Sunday pork chops and fried okra without me.

I was accepted to Otterbein College in Westerville, Ohio, which was only about 30 minutes from my house, so I would be able to stay at home and commute to save money and avoid the stress of living in a dorm and sharing a community bathroom with people I didn't know. I thought there was too much opportunity for casualties in shared restrooms.

I was never good at public restrooms, ever since my mom told my cousin Birdie when we were young that snakes lived in the toilets of restaurant bathrooms. She would constantly ask to go pee right as the food would arrive. My mom thought that telling Birdie this story would make her think twice about asking to go to the potty unnecessarily. I had been told this tale enough that I learned to hold it in as long as humanly possible, and only asked to go to a public restroom in the case of an emergency. By fourth grade, I could hold my bladder for an entire school day, which in retrospect, I realize is not healthy.

The summer before fourth grade when I went away to church camp for a week, I reasoned that if the toilets at Chi-Chi's Mexican restaurant had snakes, then the toilets at the campgrounds out in the middle of nowhere rural Ohio *definitely* had snakes coiled up in the pipes waiting to strike my ass. Since the campground was surrounded by trees and wildlife, I figured the snakes were probably big ones, and that terrified me.

Every day my cabin had swim time at 3:00 p.m., so I peed in the pool freely to avoid the actual toilets as much as possible. I knew that it was wrong, but I was willing to risk the potential embarrassment of being spotted relieving myself in the chlorinated corner near a water jet over the horror of feeling a snake tongue tickle my buttcheek while I tried to tinkle. If I did have to go to the restroom, I made it fast, my hands quivering as I hurried to wipe and get out of there safely and without a snake bite.

On the third day of camp, I could not quite make it to my regular appointment of pissing in the pool at three o'clock, and my bladder of steel publicly failed me during morning devotions. I tensed and stood up, clenching my legs together, trying to make a swift and undetected move toward the bathroom when I felt it. The warmth of my own bodily fluid filling my underwear and trickling down my right leg, soaking my sock and slowly leaking into my sneaker.

Mortified, I sprinted across the field to the facilities as more pee kept flowing out. My body had become a bomb that I could not diffuse. I frantically pumped the lever and gathered a long strand of nonabsorbent paper towels from the dispenser, wiped my leg, and tried to wring out my sock. I filled my sneaker with water from the faucet, attempting to clean out the urine.

With my one squishy shoe, I sneaked back to the cabin to change clothes and wondered how many people there had noticed that I had just peed my pants at 10 years old. Later that night I conveniently got sick, and the camp nurse called my mom to come pick me up early. I had never been more relieved to leave a place before. I returned home to the safety of my room and a snake-free commode, tried to put the disaster behind me, and never showed my face at camp again.

I planned to study journalism and major in communications at Otterbein. When I was young, I had aspirations to be an artist, but journalism felt like a more secure career field, and I knew my mom would approve. She and I loved watching the local news stations and *The Today Show* every morning while we got ready for school and work. I enjoyed writing well enough and thought choosing a career path that could one day lead me to anchor a local news broadcast would make her proud of me. I would take the safe route and let my hopes of a career in the arts die the poetic death of unexplored dreams, only to rediscover my talents in drawing or painting as a hobby in my retirement.

My perfect plan was thrown a curve ball in the spring of 2001, at the tail end of my senior year of high school, when my pencil rendering of a young Dave Matthews for my independent studies art class was accepted to the Ohio State Governor's Art Show and selected as one of the "Best in Show" submissions. It was inspired by a photograph I had clipped out of a *Rolling Stone* magazine, and my interpretation earned the attention of the art school in Columbus.

They sent me an invitation to tour their college and meet with an admissions advisor. They also said they would like to discuss the possibility of giving me a scholarship to attend their school. When my mom heard this news, she was overjoyed. I could tell she was proud that my artwork had gotten so much attention, and she encouraged me to schedule an interview.

Almost everyone in my family was more of a jock, and I was the least athletic of the bunch. Not for lack of trying, though. I tried out for lots of sports but was never anyone's first pick for the kickball team. I knew I lacked ability, and it frustrated me that my athletic performance was never anything special. I wanted to be "the best" at something. My mom was an all-star, bases loaded, grand slam softball player. We lived at the ball fields every summer where my brother and I would play in the dirt and draw pictures on the ground in the dugout while she played shortstop. If we were lucky, the ice cream truck would make an appearance, and we would rush to the car to pick change out of the cup holders to buy Bomb Pops and Strawberry Shortcake Bars.

I tried to live up to her legacy, but I just didn't have the same natural abilities that she had when it came to sports. Once it became obvious that I was not going to follow in her footsteps as a home-run hitter, she did what she could to support my interests and cultivate my talents, enrolling me in art classes at the community center and buying me a drafting table with a swivel chair and tons of art supplies so that I could draw and create anything I wanted.

I worked there for hours drawing Disney characters and pretending to work as an artist on the latest animated feature. Creating art was always something that came naturally to me. I imagined that how I felt drawing and painting was how my mom felt catching a fly ball or rounding third base. Mom wasn't artistic. She would always joke, saying, "I can't even draw flies," when I would ask her to draw with me.

I knew my dad was more creative. Once I watched him paint a Bob-Ross-style landscape on an oval-shaped canvas in the sunroom where he had carelessly murdered the baby chicks. I was impressed with his artistry and assumed I got my creative talents from him. As I watched him with his fan brushes and oil paints, making his own version of "happy little trees" in an imagined mountainscape, I wondered what inspired him to paint that day. It was out of character for him, but I liked seeing him from this perspective.

I was used to him drilling wells, driving semi-trucks, restoring old cars, and composting. As far as I can remember, this was the only day he ever painted during my childhood, and I could not figure out why he didn't do it more. He seemed to be good at it, and he looked like he was enjoying the process. The paint dried and the picture got hung up in an unused corner of the house. I would visit it often and run my fingers over the bumpy ridges of the evergreen trees and the cloudy blue sky, quietly judging him and deciding that art and good teeth were the only decent things he passed down to me in the gene pool.

Choosing between these two great colleges seemed like a no-brainer. Otterbein had not offered me a scholarship, and it was an expensive school. They did not typically give out academic scholarships—only athletic ones—so once again my lack of sports skills was holding me back in life. But the art school was practically going to pay me to go there, and I imagined that studying the arts, with all the blank canvases and gouache paint, was sure to be a creative utopia. I made the appointment with the admissions officer.

My mother and I sat on used office furniture facing a tall man with dark hair and round glasses, wearing a navy blue turtleneck. His desk had a sign that read "Abraham Timothy, Dean of Admissions." It was early April. I nervously looked out his window at the tiny buds of green beginning to emerge from the tree branches, while he paged through my art portfolio.

"Well, you definitely have some talent," he finally said to break the silence. "You're not afraid to use darkness in your work. Most student portfolios I see," he added, "they're all afraid to put the shadows into their pieces. They lack a range of value ... but you're using shadow and light in visually interesting ways."

I was shocked to hear that he thought this. My whole life I had privately shamed myself for pressing so hard with my crayons that all the pigment on my coloring pages had a thick, glaring sheen on them. *Maybe my heavy hand wasn't so awful after all,* I thought quietly, as he and my mother chatted about the program a little more. He interrupted my thoughts and asked me, "What's your major going to be?"

"I want to major in illustration," I timidly replied. I thought back to the moment I knew what I wanted to be when I grew up. I was six years old and had just watched Walt Disney's *Steamboat*

Willie for the first time. I loved it and wanted to draw my own version of Mickey Mouse, so I got a pencil and a piece of old printer paper from my grandma's computer. The dot matrix paper was all on one continuous ream and had perforations where you could separate pages after running it through the printer.

I remember drawing the three circles for Mickey's head, one large circle for his face, and two smaller circles for his ears. I saw Walt Disney on television once explaining how he drew the mouse, and I tried to execute my own drawing exactly as he had demonstrated. I filled the black parts of the mouse's body with dark, heavy strokes of graphite, and when I had completed my sketch, I took it to show my mom and Nanny, who then showed it to my dad and grandpa. Everyone was so impressed with my work. I felt proud and knew I had found something that made me special, something I was good at.

"Oh wow, this is actually really great, Ashley," my mom said. "It looks just like Mickey Mouse!"

By the next weekend, I had my very own sketchbook and set of colored pencils. I drew as many Disney characters as I could. Donald and Daisy Duck, Pluto, Minnie Mouse ... the whole gang. Whenever I was asked what I wanted to be when I grew up, without hesitation I would answer, "I want to be an animator and work for Disney." By the time I was 11, I was captivated by *The Lion King* animated film that had just been released. Not only was it a Disney movie, but it also starred my favorite *Tiger Beat* magazine teen heartthrob, Jonathan Taylor Thomas. I was obsessed.

McDonald's restaurant was giving away *The Lion King* trading cards with purchases as a promotional item. My friend Theo Alexander from school knew I loved the movie and asked his mom, who worked at our local McDonald's, to get me every card in the collection. They put them in a clear plastic baseball card storage box, and he gave them to me one day before school. This was probably the kindest gift I had ever received. There were about 150 scenes from the movie depicted on these cards, and I set out to draw every single one of them in my spiral-bound sketchbook with freshly sharpened Crayola colored pencils. I sold my versions of the movie scenes to other kids for 25 cents per drawing, but I kept most of them because I loved them so much.

"Ah, yes. Everyone wants to be an illustration major," Mr. Timothy said as he slid my portfolio across his desk and back to me. "Kids come in here, choose to major in illustration, and set their sights on getting hired by Disney. But let me tell you, that's a pipe dream. The likelihood of that happening for most students is slim to none. It's a competitive field, you know." He folded his arms across his chest and leaned back into his swivel chair. "You look more like a fashion girl to me. Our fashion program has 100% job placement, so you'd be guaranteed a great job after you grad-uate," he added.

My heart sank down to the very soles of my feet when he said this. It was as if he knew that I was going to say I wanted to be a Disney animator. But he looked at me and typecast me for the fashion design department. I felt myself shutting down. My mom perked up in conversation at the thought of 100% job place-ment and a secure future in a creative field. It began to rain outside, and once we thanked Mr. Timothy for his time and the scholarship offer to cover half of my education, the rain had gone from spring drizzle to tropical monsoon.

I slipped off my sandals at the building's entrance and ga-thered the bottom of my long pink skirt to make a dash for the car without getting tripped up on the wet fabric. My mom and I sprinted as fast as we could to the car, drenched in 25 seconds flat. We quickly slammed the doors, and she started the car. She tossed a napkin in my direction so I could dry off, turned to me, and said, "Well, looks like you'll be majoring in fashion design!"

My freshman year of college was officially referred to as "foundation studies" by the professors and administrators at the art school. It didn't matter if you were majoring in painting or industrial design, everyone started out their first year at school with the same set of classes because they believed that we all needed to have a well-rounded art education. I was required to take courses on color theory, structural design, and anatomy.

For the most part, I was excited about my classes and thought that art school would be a breeze. I was wrong. It turns out that art school was like a creative boot camp where the school owned its students and all of our time. After the first week of classes, all of us freshmen had glassy-eyed looks of panic on our faces. Before class, kids who smoked cigarettes would stand outside the building and whisper about how the school was trying to get new freshmen who weren't serious about becoming great artists to give up and drop out.

"That's why the first year is so hard," one goth girl said as she took a long drag of her cigarette. "They're trying to weed us out."

Later that day, I went to the bursar's office to square up a few outstanding articles for my scholarship. The waiting room had eight chairs along the wall, facing the receptionist's desk, and every seat was occupied by a student. Some looked visibly upset. One boy was rocking back and forth with anxiety, looking like he might come completely unhinged if anyone looked at him funny. As I was signing a few papers, the boy got up and said to the receptionist with his voice shaking, "I'm not going to be able to do this. It's just too much. This schedule is impossible. I won't even have time for my job."

"Sir, if you'll please have a seat, we are working to get a counselor for you as soon as we can, but as you can see, the waiting room is full," the receptionist said with a dry and cold tone.

I felt uncomfortable, my cheeks flushed and hot. It was 2001, just a couple of years after the Columbine High School shooting, and I worried that this kid might get angry and start freaking out. Was he crazy enough to bring a gun into a school and start shooting? Was the creative pressure of a rigorous art curriculum enough to make someone snap?

The workload was more than I anticipated, but I was lucky. I didn't have to have a job outside of my classes because I lived at home with my mom and Eric and didn't have any bills of my own to pay. My mom said that keeping up my grades was work enough and that we would keep taking out student loans to cover the fees not covered by my half-tuition scholarship. Even without any additional stress, my perfectionist tendencies lived on, and I was beginning to get worn down.

Class critiques on our assignments were brutal. My industrial design teacher, Mr. Roberts, was a little bit deranged, but I assumed most creative people had to be at least slightly crazy, otherwise how would they uncover their creative genius? Andy Warhol was a total freak. And Van Gogh? Mad bonkers. I assumed that true artistry required a bit of insanity. I considered myself too simple and uncomplicated to be a "true creative." On the first day of class, Mr. Roberts explained to us how we would spend much of our time in the woodshop learning to use dangerous tools like the miter saw and bandsaw. He held up his right hand, which was missing two fingers.

"You don't want THIS to happen to you, so pay attention!" he warned. Then he cackled, his bald head glistening under the adjustable track lighting in the room. "Actually," he added, "I lost these two fingers lighting firecrackers when I was a young boy. But the point here is you can lose a finger on these machines if you're not careful."

Since we were still going through all the safety training for the woodshop, Mr. Roberts gave us an assignment to construct a sculptural art piece that conveyed movement using only popsicle sticks. He challenged us to create dynamic, expressive work that would move the viewer's eye across our piece to tell a story. I had a full load of classes and each professor assigned detailed "problems" (projects) that the students needed to solve with our artwork. I often stayed up until the sun was rising to make sure I had time to solve all my problem assignments for the week.

Mr. Roberts' assignment took the most time that week, and I had pulled an all-nighter to complete it, making sure I met every single requirement outlined on his syllabus. As the class began to trickle into the room on the day these first projects were due, Mr. Roberts sat at his desk and told each of us to place our work on the circular table in the center of the room for our first critique.

I nervously placed mine on the table and went to sit down in a corner of the room away from other students, in true introvert fashion. As the table filled with more projects, Mr. Roberts was looking more and more agitated. We sat in silence for what felt like an eternity, all of us just staring at him. Finally, he stood up, walked over to the table, and picked up someone's art at random. "Let's discuss this piece," he said.

We were silent for a moment, then someone said, "I like how the artist has used curved lines to express an upward motion."

Mr. Roberts looked disgusted. "This piece does NOT solve the problem, folks," he said in a harsh tone as he placed it back onto the table. He had similar reactions to the next three works he had selected for critique. Apparently, none of us had understood the assignment, and he was beginning to seethe at our ignorance. He grabbed another piece and flung it violently across the room, smashing it into the wall and shattering popsicle sticks into a hundred pieces on the floor.

Everyone gasped. I couldn't believe my tear-filled eyes. Mr. Roberts had demolished my project. We all fell silent as he ranted about how we missed the point and how all our work was garbage. When he finished talking, I got up and quietly excused myself to the restroom where I sobbed until class was over. I had to go back to retrieve my bags and hoped to miss seeing Mr. Roberts again that day, but he was still in the room when I returned.

"Miss Hurley, may I have a word?" he asked, sheepishly.

"Sure," I said, my eyes swollen. It was obvious that I had been crying.

"I owe you an apology for destroying your work. I had no idea whose piece I had picked up at the time," he added, to let me know he hadn't singled me out to make an example of me in front of the class.

"I stayed up all night making that," I told him softly.

"It won't happen again," he said apologetically.

And he was true to his word. During the remaining weeks of the semester, Mr. Roberts kept his wits about him, and I got an "A" on every assignment. I figured I was making the grade because he felt so guilty about ruining my project. I was certain he still thought all the work was shit.

The stress of all my classes was catching up with me, and I would often come home and share my worries with my mom about how I was going to get it all done. I was regularly on the verge of tears because I was so overwhelmed. I thought back to the boy in the student affairs office waiting room. *I get it now,* I thought. *That kid wasn't crazy; he was having a panic attack.*

If I would start to get too emotional about my problems in school, Mom would tell me, "No one ever accomplished anything by sitting around crying about their troubles all day. Give yourself 20 minutes in the bathroom to feel upset—cry, scream, or whatever you need to do to get it out of your system—then get to work and make some progress.

"People who are mentally strong can handle anything without the need for medications," she encouraged. "You're strong enough to handle this. I know it."

Through this practice, I learned to compartmentalize my emotions and keep a lid on the feelings that prevented me from being functional. I told myself that if my mom thought I could handle anything, then I had to suck it up and push through to make her proud.

After about 15 years of toughing it out and trying to make their marriage work, my mom finally admitted to herself and everyone else that she was done. I was 12 years old. The tension in the house was thick, and even though I didn't know what exactly was going on, I knew something wasn't right. My mom had started sleeping in my room with me, always making sure to bring her purse with her at night. She put a brass lock on the inside of my door so that my dad could not barge in on us. I didn't ask too many questions; I wasn't sure how to even bring it up. Finally, she asked him for an official divorce, and together they sat down with my brother and me to share the news. My dad sat in his chair sobbing, as my mom delivered the update, "Your dad and I love you both very much, but we need to tell you that we are getting a divorce. It's not your fault."

Dad continued to cry while muttering something about how much he loved us, and how he would still be seeing us regularly. But all I saw when he spoke was a sad failure of a man who had been lazy, didn't want to work, and failed his family. I tried to act accordingly to this news they had just given—like I cared or was sad or surprised. As he talked, I thought, *I should probably show some sort of emotion here. But I feel nothing.* It actually felt like a giant relief to hear that he was going to be moving out once and for all.

When he finally left the house that night, mom, Oscar, and I jumped up and down on the furniture he never even let us kids sit on, emitting cheers of joy that he was gone and had taken all the negativity and tension with him. Mom seemed to have had a weight lifted off her shoulders, and I was elated at the idea of having a new life that would provide freedom from tip-toeing around my father.

In the few months after they separated, we were with my dad the standard every other weekend and every Wednesday evening. I hated going to visit him. He never had any good snacks, and dinners were always so bizarre. He had switched jobs, yet again, and was now working as a corrections officer at a local prison. He would tell us weird stories about the inmates, and try to tell us what was cool about where he worked. One weekend, he was ranting and raving about this thing that he had seen some of the inmates making.

"It's called 'the Break'," he said. "What you do is you get yourself a giant trash bag, like this …"

He pulled a yellow box out from under his kitchen sink, unraveled a large, black garbage bag, and smoothed it out on the countertop. He reached into the cupboard above and pulled out three bags of ramen noodles, handing one to Oscar, one to me, and keeping the other for himself.

"Ok, so what we're gonna do is break up these noodles in the bag before we open it. Once they're all broken up, open the bag, and dump the noodles into this trash bag."

I was beginning to feel very skeptical. Why would I put these perfectly good ramen noodles in a garbage bag? Why not cook the ramen and be done?

"I'm not sure about this. Can't we just cook these normally?" I protested.

"Come on, I wanna show you this. It's delicious. You will love it," he said. We hesitantly dumped out the dry noodles. "Now, we get to add the fun stuff. Open the fridge and get out all the condiments."

"Wait, ALL the condiments?" Oscar asked.

"Yeah," Dad replied.

Onto the counter, we piled jars of pickles, ketchup, mayonnaise, mustard, barbeque sauce, hot sauce, applesauce, and that cheese that squirts out of a can. Then he grabbed a box of saltine crackers from the cupboard.

"Now what we're gonna do is pile on as much of these condiments as we want. Each of you gets to do two."

My stomach was starting to grumble. I was so hungry, and this guy was making a mess out of food that we could actually eat. But I was always told to respect my parents, so I kept doing what was being asked of me, trying to keep a hopeful attitude, but knowing in my heart that this was going to be a disaster. Oscar and I added globs of condiments, and dad sprinkled crushed saltines on top.

"Alright, now comes the most fun part." He smiled when he said this and began to close up the garbage bag and tie a knot in the end. "We have to shake this up for about 10 minutes. We can all take turns," he added.

We passed the garbage bag full of this food concoction around, shaking and sloshing it, massaging it, and even punching it a few times. Finally, he said, "It should be done!" and reached for three forks.

He opened the bag as he exclaimed, "We get to eat this right out of the bag; how cool is that?"

I was reluctant, but also famished, so I took the fork and scooped up what truly resembled a sixth grader's vomit. I attempted one bite and discovered that my suspicions were correct. This was hands down the nastiest meal I had ever been served. I refused to eat another bite, and Dad got upset. "This is what we're eating tonight, so if you don't like it, you can go to bed hungry," he barked. And so I did.

After telling Mom about "the Break," she didn't make me go over to his place as much. I preferred to stay home with her, where I knew I would be able to eat normal food.

Slowly, Dad's visits faded away for me and Oscar, and one day, he told us he was moving to Washington and getting married. This news was just as much of a relief as when my parents announced their divorce. I wouldn't have to spend as much time with him if he was all the way across the country. He said he would call us often and keep in touch, but eventually he was only calling quarterly and even forgot my birthday on several occasions.

I didn't mind when he forgot, because when he would remember, he would send me something in the mail, like a tiny jar of volcanic ash from Mount St. Helen's near his house, and then I would have to call him and thank him for the small vial of dirt he so generously gifted me. I thought it was better to be invisible, or at the very least forgotten by him. And I wanted him to be invisible to me so that I could forget about him. I made a vow to myself to stay in my lane. I was learning to blend in as much as possible. My comfort zone was in being invisible, but a life lived as a ghost only left me feeling like an empty haunted house.

\|//

chapter four

THE PERFECT MOM

*"There is no perfection, only beautiful versions
of brokenness."*

— Shannon Alder

When I was young, I always wanted to be with my mother, and she would often take Oscar and me along with her to the grocery store or on other errands over the weekends. We would see other families during our excursions, and Mom would make commentary on them as we walked by. She especially loved to point out to us the other mothers who looked tired, unkempt, or overweight, or who were angrily reprimanding their own kids with remarks like, "Don't touch that!" or "I said NO, Rachel ... We aren't buying Cocoa Puffs today. Stop your whining!"

Sometimes the other mothers would get physical and grab their child by the arm to yell at them next to the neatly stacked cans of SpaghettiOs. Without fail, every time my mom noticed these women, she would lean into my ear and whisper, "See that? Aren't you so lucky that *I'm* your mom and not that mean, fat lady? You could have it so much worse if you had that poor kid's life. At least when you and Oscar misbehave in public, I have the good sense to quietly pinch the back of your arm instead of causing such an embarrassing scene. You are so lucky."

I looked at the angry mothers and their sad kids, and I did

feel lucky. *Thank God I got this good mom,* I thought.

My mom was a vibrant, natural beauty, and everyone at church always remarked on my dad's dashing good looks. People went on and on about what a good-looking family we were, and my mother always seemed to take great pride in that compliment. Years later, immediately following my parents' divorce, when Mom introduced Oscar and me to her new boyfriend, I was surprised to be meeting a short, bald Jewish man named Eric.

He was missing his two front teeth from a hockey fight back when he was in high school. He once owned a set of flipper teeth—removable tooth implants—that gave him a full, normal smile, but his dog ate the tooth implants, and Eric hadn't gotten around to replacing them with the dentist just yet. Eric had a laugh that sounded like a chopped up hiss. It reminded me of a character from the late 1960s Hanna-Barbera cartoon, *Wacky Races,* which I would watch reruns of on Saturday mornings as a kid. I worked hard doing silly things at home just to hear Eric's laugh.

He and my mom were certainly an odd-looking couple. I thought she could do better from a looks perspective because I was taught as a kid to view looks in a certain way. Our whole family dynamic was about "looking perfect" to others, and Eric did not fit the expectation. Choosing to be with him was my mother's first big public rejection of meeting Nanny's standards for our family. She seemed happier than ever.

Eric was my mom's boss at the insurance agency where they worked. He was the exact opposite of my dad. He had a job, he saved money, he took interest in Oscar and me, and he didn't just send us to another room if we were being loud or having fun. He listened to TLC and Mariah Carey in his Corvette, and whenever my brother was in the car, Eric would put in his Jerky Boys CD and we would laugh at all the prank calls.

For several months before my mom and Eric decided to get married, he would stay the night at our house. Mom made him park two whole blocks away and walk to our house after dark because we were still living right next door to her brother and my Aunt Loretta—and also in case Nanny drove by. She told me she knew Nanny would be judgmental about Eric being Jewish since our family were such devout Christians. Plus, the fact that he was sleeping over when they weren't married certainly didn't meet the standards Nanny had for our family. But Mom loved Eric and wanted to be with him.

I was nearly 13 years old when she told us she was going to marry him. They eloped in Las Vegas, and we stayed with my aunt and uncle for a few days. Mom told me, "I know Eric isn't the most attractive man by stereotypical standards, but good-looking people with bad attitudes get ugly real fast. At the end of our lives, we're all old and wrinkled anyway … Might as well be with someone who makes you laugh and makes you happy." That sounded like the wisest piece of advice I'd ever heard.

Mom always had a sunny perspective for everything that went wrong and was a great problem solver. When we were small, she would read Oscar and me a children's book called *Could Be Worse!* about a grandpa who tells a tall tale of adventure where lots of crazy things happen. His response is always, "It could be worse!" and that was the motto my mother adopted whenever life didn't go as planned for us. I loved that book, and I loved listening to her read it because she always created the best voices for the characters. She was a natural performer and thrived in the spotlight.

Every Sunday morning at church, the music pastor would invite members up for what they called "special" song performances. Once or twice a month, Mom would sing a solo of her signature song, "My Redeemer Lives" by Crystal Lewis. Each time, she would have the whole church on their feet, clapping, dancing, shouting, and sometimes even running in the aisles because they were filled with the spirit of the Holy Ghost that she had called down from heaven with her glorious God-given talent. This is the same church where, 13 years earlier, my parents stood at the altar and shared their wedding vows (after a previous failed attempt where my dad was a no-show).

My mom would show me the photograph of this special day: my dad in a powder blue tuxedo, much thinner than I had ever seen him, surrounded by the familiar rust orange carpet and church pews that I would run through as a child during my mom's choir practice. My favorite part of the photo was my Aunt Loretta. She was several months pregnant with my cousin Alice and had fainted during the ceremony. And the moment was captured forever in this photo.

It was a wide shot of the scene, from the center aisle perspective. My mom is dressed in a classic puffy-sleeved early 1980s white wedding gown, holding her hands over her mouth and looking down toward the floor, where Aunt Loretta is sprawled flat on her back. The only visible part of her in the photo is her knees, ankles, and shoes popping out from behind the front row of church pews as if she's the Wicked Witch of the East after the house fell on her. Mom always said, "There is nothing more perfect about this picture," and I couldn't agree more.

When I was four years old, we lived in a tiny, one-story cottage in Columbus, Ohio. The house had three small bedrooms and one bathroom, where we all crammed together to get ready for church every Sunday morning. One morning in particular, we were all trying to brush our teeth at the same time, and I bumped my head pretty hard on the sink.

"Oh no! You've knocked your noggin', baby!" Mom comforted me as I cried. She spanked the sink and reprimanded it saying, "What a bad sink. Bad sink! Bad sink!" as if she were talking to a puppy who had just peed on the carpet. That made me giggle. "That's it; we need to get a bigger house!" she exclaimed.

Not too long after, we moved to a two-story white farmhouse—which felt massive in comparison—with a welcoming front porch that sat on two acres of land. This was the house where we had the sheep, where our neighbors had horses, and where Dad secretly grew weed in the basement. I loved this house because the entire upstairs was dedicated as a kids' space. We even had our own playroom and bathroom.

Dad said the house had problems because it used to be located at a different address, but someone had picked it up and moved it. He said that the house had settled wrong in the new location and that's why some parts of the house weren't level. I didn't understand how an entire house could be transported from one place to another, so I imagined a giant crane picking it up by the chimney and a helicopter dangling it over the city as it soared through the sky to its new location. I didn't notice the problems that seemed to fluster Dad. To me, the house was magical and offered so many opportunities to explore.

One of my favorite things about this house was the long hallway on the main level. The freshly refinished wood floors were everything. On rainy summer weekends, Mom would tell us to go get our sweatpants and socks on because it was time to "Pledge the hallway." We would race up to our rooms, find our fluffiest socks, and come back down to meet Mom, shaking a can of wood polish. She would hand us each a rag and squirt a generous glob of the cheerful lemon-scented product on top, and we would immediately get to work shining the heck out of that floor. Once we were finished, Mom would put her Paula Abdul cassette tape in the stereo, crank the volume up high, and we would each take turns running and sliding all over the slippery corridor.

In addition to being beautiful, like soap opera star Susan Lucci, my mom was also funny and quick-witted, like comedian Carol Burnett. She was exceptional at turning anything into a game, which meant there was never a dull moment in our house. She'd tell us, "People who say they're bored are just boring people," whenever we would hint at the notion of feeling the b word. Two phrases in particular had been outlawed in her presence: saying "I can't!" or "I'm bored" were considered criminal offenses that would either land us with extra chores or a lecture about how the word "can't" is not part of our vocabulary.

She even found a way to make the dull task of painting a closet feel more like a scene from *I Love Lucy*. After a couple hours of working, I turned to her to ask a question but instead got blasted in the face with a wet paintbrush. It turned into a full-on paint fight where we laughed and slapped paint all over each other as if Jackson Pollock himself were working his magic, drizzling and splashing a canvas in a chaotic frenzy. We were both the painter and the canvas, laughing until we cried at the sublime absurdity.

We spent the next several days picking white flakes of dried paint out of our hair and giggling about how silly it was. Mom was fueled by creating all sorts of these experiences that would make for great stories to tell later. But for every ounce of fun she provided and encouraged, she also had high expectations of me as her daughter, and I always aimed to please.

My dad could never be as wonderful and perfect as my mom was in my eyes. She did everything for me. She always gave me cool hairstyles in the mornings before school, she was fun and laughed a lot, and she cooked good food. She worked hard, was very stylish, and she let me join her whenever she worked out to Jane Fonda VHS tapes.

Dad was usually in a bad mood and watched a lot of TV (mostly professional wrestling, any of the *Rocky* movies, or NASCAR). He never wanted me around. He didn't like being interrupted, or hearing us talk about what we liked to do … He didn't even like to hear us laughing and having fun playing in the next room. We were always too loud, too much, or too needy. So Mom was my favorite. She never turned me away and always let me tell her about my school day.

When Dad moved to Washington, she told my brother and me, "I can't believe he is moving so far away. He couldn't get farther from his kids without leaving the continental United States." Her tone shifted to slightly judgemental when she said the next part. "I would never let anything get between you guys and me. If he had full custody and moved far away with you, I would follow you. Nothing would stop me from being a part of your life."

I knew she meant it when she said that. It was so comforting to me to know that even though my dad couldn't care less how far away he was from us, she would always be there for me. She would never abandon us. She was my safe place. She continued to illustrate her point about how much she loved us by telling and retelling this story about how the women she used to work in an office with would complain about their children.

"When I worked as a receptionist for the state, the other women who worked in my building would come in on Friday mornings, chatting excitedly about how they were looking forward to the weekend because they were sending their children away to a grandparent's house, and they were so ready to have a break from them." Her voice would shift again to that same judgemental tone she had when talking about my deadbeat dad.

"I could never relate to these women," she'd admit. "I could never understand why anyone would want to pawn their kids off on someone else for the weekend. What kind of mother doesn't want her children to be with her? I love hanging out with you guys, and I miss you every minute of the day when we aren't together. Even when you were a baby, and I would work late, I would come home and try to keep you awake as long as possible just so I could spend more time with you."

I remember thinking, *Wow, she really loves us.* I hoped that I would be a good mom someday who loved my own kids that much.

When I was in the seventh grade, my mom started to show me the ways of navigating the real world. She had been divorced from Dad for a whole year. She was always very open with me about her life and wanted to teach me how to use the wisdom that she had gained over the years. There was her standard speech about why you can't depend on a man and need to have your own education and career so that you never have to stay stuck being married to some loser, just because you need his financial support. And she also seized every opportunity to impart her skills of persuasion and negotiation to me.

One of my very first lessons in this came when I got in trouble for passing notes in Mrs. Harrison's seventh grade English class. This was when I got my first (and only) detention. I was mortified and felt so much shame. I just knew that Mrs. Harrison hated me now, and the thought of returning to her class felt like

I would be forever marked with a scarlet letter for breaking the "no note passing" rule. I came home that day in tears.

"Mom, Mrs. Harrison totally hates me. I was passing a note to a friend during her class, and she caught me. She gave me detention, and I had to go for 30 minutes after school today and sit with all the bad kids," I whined.

"Here's how we fix this," Mom schemed. "Next week, I will bring Mrs. Harrison lunch. On Monday when you arrive at her class, you tell her that your mom asked you over the weekend who your favorite teacher is. Then tell her that you told me it is her. Explain to Mrs. Harrison that your mother has offered to bring her lunch so we can all eat together one day. Ask her what her favorite lunch spot is and what day this week would work for me to bring her a meal. She will feel so honored that you have chosen her as your favorite teacher, and all of this will blow over."

Monday came, and I followed my mom's instructions to the letter. Mrs. Harrison looked quite pleased and impressed, gave me a day that she had open for lunch, and told me that she would love it if my mom would bring her McDonald's. Later that week when my mom and I sat down to eat with my teacher, my mom turned her charm level to 100 and carried the conversation, asking Mrs. Harrison questions about her life, her family, why she became a teacher, and what she loved about the students that year.

I watched in amazement as I nibbled on a french fry. I could not believe what I was seeing. Mrs. Harrison was eating up the attention and compliments, just as my mom had predicted. And the rest of the year, I was back in her good graces. Crisis averted.

My mom is so smart, I thought, feeling all the gratitude for this epic maneuver she had pulled off.

One year later, another opportunity for a big life lesson on persuasion and negotiation presented itself. This time, my mom was more explicit with her curriculum. My eighth grade class was having an essay contest that I desperately wanted to win. We were going to Washington, DC, for our class trip, and three students would have the honor of laying a wreath at the Tomb of the Unknown Soldier as part of the daily ceremony. Out of the whole class, I wanted to be one of the kids who got to do it.

"I've got to write this essay. It has to be perfect … but I don't even know where to start," I told her.

"You've got to tug on their heartstrings," she told me. "People want to know how you will carry this experience with you for the rest of your life. How it will completely and totally change the trajectory of your educational and personal life to be able to have such an honor. How proud you will be, how important this is, and how grateful you are for the service of these unknown soldiers who risked it all in the name of freedom."

"Wow, that's all so good … but I don't think I actually feel any of that," I admitted.

"Oh, that doesn't matter," she said dismissively. "People want to feel emotional and warm and fuzzy when they read these essays. If you want to win this contest, you have to give them what they want. Make them feel something. Make them stop in their tracks by illustrating what a life-changing experience this would be for you.

"Whether you feel it or not is irrelevant. People eat that bullshit up. The whole world only ever wants to hear what makes them feel good. So make them feel good about choosing you for this. If it's not you, it will be some other kid in your class, and you deserve this," she finished.

"Just write some emotional bull crap?" I asked.

"Yep, that's all you gotta do," she encouraged.

I went up to my room, found my pencil and paper, and

began to write exactly what my mom had outlined for me. An hour later, she proofread my draft, added her changes, and I typed it up.

A week after turning in the essay, I was awarded one of the spots, and a month later I was in Washington, DC, participating in the wreath-laying ceremony with two boys from my class—both of whom went on to join the military. One of them actually went to West Point on a full-ride scholarship. Two guys who meant what they wrote in their essays so much that they joined the military as soon as they graduated high school … and then me, the world's greatest emotional bullshit writer, who had learned exactly how to manipulate people, all thanks to my mom's elaborate scheme.

The summer after my freshman year in college, Dad offered to pay me to babysit my one-year-old baby sister, Jocelyn. I happened to be in town visiting on the day she was born but hadn't traveled back to Longview to visit her since. My stepmom, Monica, was working as a social worker, and their babysitter had recently moved away. They needed someone to fill in for three weeks so that they could find a replacement without causing Monica to have to take any time off work. I agreed to fly out for part of the summer. I wasn't too keen on the feelings of FOMO I had about leaving my mom and my boyfriend back in Ohio for so long, but my mom said it would be good for me to spend some time with my little sister. Once again, I did exactly as she said.

That summer in Washington, my dad would present a very different version of himself than I had ever experienced before. He made a serious effort to spend time with me and would pick up Jocelyn and me every day to join him on his lunch break. He now owned his own composting facility where he made cedar mulch, and he always wanted to tell me about what he did at the plant. He kept telling me how one day he was going to pass his business down to me and my brother, and we could move to Washington to help him run it.

"When you graduate college, you'll have a job here," he said.

"My major is fashion design; I don't think I am going to be qualified to work with dirt all day," I explained, trying my hardest to respectfully decline. Working with him sounded like complete hell.

"Sure you will," he said. "This is my legacy. This is important," he would add.

Every day at our lunch, his accountant joined us.

"This is Stacey," he introduced her. "She works for me and keeps my books. She'll probably be joining us a lot."

Stacey was a nice lady. Soft-spoken and smiled a lot. She laughed at everything my dad said, even when he wasn't being remotely funny. Mostly the two of them talked while I listened or helped Jocelyn eat her lunch.

After about a week of lunching with Dad and Stacey, he invited me to take Jocelyn to the park after work. She giggled and clapped as I pushed her in a baby swing. My dad suddenly got really serious and started to talk more quietly.

"Ash, I need to tell you about Stacey. I'm in love with her, and she's in love with me. We have never crossed the line or had sex, but emotionally, I feel so strongly for her. Monica is so mean, and Stacey is so nice to me. I think she is going to leave her husband soon, and we are going to try and be together," he confessed. "What do you think about her?"

I was speechless. *Oh my God,* I thought. *I am only 19 years old. Why on earth is he telling me this?*

I froze. I wasn't sure what he wanted to hear from me at that moment, but suddenly everything about his behavior toward me on this visit was becoming clear. He didn't actually want to spend time with me. He was using me as a buffer so he and Stacey could hang out without looking suspicious. I became extremely uncomfortable and still didn't know how to respond.

"I'm so sorry you and Monica have been struggling," I finally managed to nervously mutter, still pushing Jocelyn in the swing. "Stacey seems like a very nice lady." I did not want to get into the depths of this conversation because my convictions were that he was wrong to have an emotional affair, and I knew that was not what he wanted to hear me say.

I don't remember where the conversation went because my head started spinning. I felt so much guilt and sadness for my poor stepmom. She probably had no idea that this was going on. How could I look her in the eye now, knowing what I know?

I went to bed early that night, asking myself why he would tell me all about his feelings for another woman. Did he think I was such a religious killjoy that I would run to my stepmom and spill the beans, essentially helping him to get caught so she would leave him and he could be with Stacey? I knew that was not a position I wanted to be in.

The next morning after he left for work and the house was quiet, I called my mom.

"I'm not sure what to do now," I told her. "I already didn't like him, but this is just too much. Monica doesn't deserve this. And now I'm feeling so much guilt. I've got this terrible secret weighing heavily on my heart; I feel so used and dirty. I want to come home, but it's going to put Monica in a really bad spot because I don't think they've found a regular babysitter yet."

"Wow," my mom said. "I'm not surprised, but I'm so sorry that he put you in this position. It's not your job to take care of this for him, and if you want to come home, you should." She gave me permission to ask him if I could come home early, and when he got home from work that day, I asked him to come into my room because I wanted to talk.

"Dad, I'd like to go home early," I timidly said.

"Ummm, no. Why would you even ask that?" he retorted, slightly annoyed that I called him in for that request.

"I just really feel homesick. I miss my friends and boyfriend. I can't stay here anymore. I am not going to stay. I am going to go home. Nothing is going to change my mind. Mom said she could get me a flight back for tomorrow," I said in a rush. I knew if I told him the real reason, then I'd potentially risk Monica hearing us. I didn't want to be responsible for how she would discover that her husband was in love with another woman.

My dad's face got very red, and he had this deranged look in his eyes. He began screaming at me about how ungrateful I was after all he had done for me, ranting about how selfish I was for putting him and Monica in this situation where now they weren't going to have anyone to watch Jocelyn.

"Monica's going to have to miss work now. This is unbelievable. I can't believe you are doing this to me," he said as he began pulling my clothes out of drawers and stuffing my suitcase. I was sobbing and terrified. Monica came in to see what all the commotion was about.

"Ashley wants to leave because she's such a prude, and I told a raunchy joke at lunch that made her uncomfortable," he reported to Monica.

I didn't challenge what he said about the joke. Yes, he had told a dirty joke that I didn't think was funny a few days before, and I told him that day that I didn't like it. But that was definitely not why I was leaving. And even though I told him it was homesickness, he knew that wasn't why I wanted to go home. He knew his confession about Stacey was the reason.

Monica began crying and asked my dad why he was packing

my suitcase right then.

"She doesn't want to be here. I don't want her here a single second more than she has to be. She's going home tonight. Go get your stuff from the bathroom," he snapped at me.

I hurried past him and shut the bathroom door behind me. I turned the fan on and sat on the floor sobbing and hugging myself for a few minutes, trying to make sense of what was happening. After a few minutes, I dried my tears and gathered my things. He tossed my suitcase in the back of his truck, and I hugged my stepmom and sister goodbye. We spent the 45-minute drive from Longview to the Portland airport in complete silence.

As he pulled the truck into the departures lane, he handed me a $50 bill and told me to go into the airport to the airline counter and ask them to change my flight to whatever was first available out of town. I grabbed my suitcase and walked into the airport, eyes puffy and tears still flowing. The next flight to Columbus wouldn't be boarding for 10 hours. I called my mom once I knew when my flight would get in, and to tell her what had happened.

"Oh my, he is the worst. I'm glad you're not with him anymore. I'm sorry you have such a long wait. Try to get some sleep somewhere quiet in the airport tonight, and I will see you when you land tomorrow. Hang in there," she said. Hearing her voice gave me hope that I would be ok. Just a few more hours and then I would be back home and could put all of this behind me.

It will feel so good to be safe back with my mom, I thought.

There was something so soothing back then about the idea of my dad being the ultimate villain in my story, while my mom was the superhero who swooped in and saved the day. She was light, he was dark. At that time, I couldn't grasp that there is a duality to being human. That humans are capable of being a hero *and* a villain at any given moment.

I gave no grace to my father and didn't think he deserved it after how he treated me that day. I allowed it to deepen the wedge between us and was moving through life as the wounded girl with "daddy issues." I was content to be the victim of his behavior and used it to further my narrative that my mother was the savior of my world. In reality, it was all smoke and mirrors with her.

chapter five
TOO YOUNG TO DIE

"They say you die twice. One time when you stop breathing and a second time, a bit later on, when somebody says your name for the last time."

— **Banksy**

When I was five years old, I had an imaginary baby that I named Sarah. I loved her and cared for her and took her with me everywhere. She was perfect, with chubby cheeks and strawberry blonde ringlet curls that framed her sweet little face. No one else could see her, but I saw her so clearly, and I knew she needed me.

One Sunday after church at Nanny's house, I was holding Sarah while watching the women in the family bustling around the kitchen. Mom was working on the mashed potatoes and Aunt Loretta was setting the table while Nanny fried up a freshly picked bunch of green tomatoes from Grandpa's garden. Grandpa was sitting in his typical spot at the head of the dining room table, teasing all us kids as we stood around waiting for someone to say, "Food's ready!"

Grandpa noticed me holding Sarah and asked if he could hold her. I trusted him and said, "You can hold her, but please be careful with her head." I made the transfer as if I were holding a real, living baby. The moment she was fully in his arms, he pretended to drop her on the floor and then proceeded to stomp all over her, cackling loudly and smiling villainously as he pounded the floor with his church shoes.

I became completely hysterical as I was witnessing my baby being trampled, and there was nothing I could do about it. Nanny and Mom tried to calm me down by saying that it wasn't a big deal because she was "just an imaginary baby." But to me, to a five-year-old, she was so much more.

Both Nanny and my mom told me, "Ashley, don't be so dramatic. This is silly. Pull it together; she was not real."

My grandpa continued laughing in my face as I sobbed. No one seemed to care about the murder that had happened right before we said grace for our meal. They all just filled their plates and their bellies, while I tried to pick up the pieces of my heart. I believed that my creativity died that day with my precious imaginary baby Sarah. I stood in the kitchen at that moment and resolved to never imagine anything ever again. It would obviously only lead to destruction and heartbreak.

Not long after baby Sarah was taken from me, I found myself climbing a tree in my Aunt Loretta and Uncle Rhett's backyard, at Alice's ninth birthday party. The berries on the tree looked exactly like the ones on the mulberry tree at our house. I always loved climbing that tree and eating the berries while resting on a sturdy branch. So, I picked a few berries from my aunt and uncle's tree and started eating them. A few minutes later, my mom happened to notice that I was eating something, and she asked me about it. When I told her I was eating mulberries from the yard, Aunt Loretta came rushing over.

"Deb, that is not a mulberry tree. I think those berries might be poisonous."

Panic set in my mom's eyes, and I could see all the adults starting to worry.

"I'm calling poison control," my aunt announced.

I began to piece together everyone's frantic conversations. They thought the berries on this tree might be bad and make me sick—or worse, I might die because I ate them.

"Am I going to die? I can't die yet. I'm too young to die!" I sobbed and buried my face in my mom's lap. I could hear my aunt wrapping up the phone call with poison control.

"They said it didn't sound like she ate enough to cause any serious problems and to monitor her. If she starts feeling sick later, take her straight to the hospital," my aunt relayed.

"So I'm ... not going to die?" I asked, feeling a little less terrified.

As a kid, I was always concerned with death and dying. It seemed to me the most awful part about living. It was mysterious in a way that felt scary. Everyone at church always said that when you die you go to heaven, but I liked it on earth and didn't want to leave my family. Heaven sounded so lonely to me. I only knew a few souls up there, and they were mostly animals my dad had neglected and accidentally killed.

The real blow came with our family dog, Darth Vader, when I was seven years old. He was a stunning Doberman Pinscher that had been part of our family since before I was born. He was getting older, and Dad no longer wanted him to be an indoor dog, so Darth lived in the barn with Dad's hunting dogs. One day, I went into the barn and couldn't find Darth. I asked Mom about it.

"Darth was starting to get too old, so Dad took him out into the woods for his final walk," she told me.

I didn't understand exactly what that meant, but I knew I wouldn't be seeing Darth ever again, and that made me sad.

Years later, after Dad moved out and the divorce process had begun for my parents, I asked Mom what actually happened to Darth.

"Your dad," she said without hesitation, "didn't want to pay the $100 to have Darth put to sleep at the vet. Darth was very sick at that point, and we didn't have the extra money. So your dad got his rifle and took Darth into the woods to take care of it himself."

"Oh," was all I could muster in response. Dad was emotionless when it came to animals. He never expressed any remorse for any of the creatures that died because of his carelessness. I couldn't trust that any animal was ever safe in our home, so how was I supposed to feel safe and protected?

In 2006, every morning after my calls home to check in with my mom, I would sit on the F train headed to work and imagine the nightmare scenario of the day when she would call to tell me that Eric or Nanny had died.

I envisioned receiving the call at work and collapsing onto the floor, sobbing incessantly, unable to catch my breath or speak audible words aloud to my concerned coworkers, who were now dialing 9-1-1 and asking for an ambulance. I would be carried out wailing on a stretcher and taken to the hospital, and after being calmed down by some sort of medication, Conner would come and scoop me up with a rental car and immediately drive me back to Ohio where I would have to bury someone I loved but never got to say a proper goodbye to.

A version of this scenario played out in my sleeping and waking hours for a week straight, and I began to have a lot of anxiety about what if something actually happened and I wasn't there. I was also starting to feel like my mom could use the extra help and moral support. She had help with Nanny from Grandpa and Uncle Rhett, but with Eric, she was mostly on her own; plus she was taking care of Eric's elderly mother, Blythe, who we all affectionately called Bubby, the Jewish name for "grandma."

I knew at the very least that if I was back in Ohio I could offer my mom help with Bubby's doctor's appointments. And I would get a few extra weeks of visiting with Nanny and Eric before cancer consumed them both. I decided that when our lease in New York was up in September, Conner and I should move back to Ohio. Conner was hesitant but reluctantly agreed that being closer to my family during this difficult time was for the best. Even so, he never let me forget the sacrifice he made in leaving New York "too soon" so we could support my family.

Watching two people you love battle death every day really puts your life into perspective. When we moved back to Ohio, I was lucky enough to land a really great job as a denim designer at a mall brand that was based in Columbus. But the job required travel and long hours, which meant I didn't get to spend as much time with my family as I had hoped.

I spent hours, day after day, sitting in meetings, preparing for a bigger meeting that was coming up on our calendar, or attending a recap meeting about the meeting we just had. I would arrive at these assemblies of designers, merchants, and VPs, listening to everyone chatter, and suddenly I'd realize I was lost in my own mind. How much of Eric and Nanny's lives were slipping by, while I sat in this windowless room comparing an apricot thread color to an orange thread color?

THEY ARE LITERALLY BOTH ORANGE! Just pick one and let's go back to work so I can go home! I wanted to scream at them all and flip over the conference table. Instead, I sat there fully composed while screaming internally, pretending to listen and trying to remember to breathe. It seemed so bizarre to me that people I loved were dying while the rest of the world carried on without a care, unaware and unaffected, and I was expected to still show up every day as a functional and effective piece of the corporate machine.

The office campus was located within a series of three massive black buildings that were all connected by a system of underground tunnels as if the C.I.A. had designed a secret base below the fashion headquarters as a cover. As you walked deeper into the building, with its windowless corridors, everything felt dark. Beyond the lack of windows, something felt lifeless about the place. I felt it when I first started working there, but I was eager and fresh and not easily discouraged.

Eventually, the lack of positivity and the toxic culture wore me down, and I became just as jaded and apathetic as the rest of my coworkers. I often referred to the building as "The Black Building of Death" because most days the job felt more soul-sucking than a place to cultivate creativity and inspiration.

I made decent money but quickly learned that the job *had* to pay well to entice people to stay and overlook the awful hours and negative work culture. Some of my superiors had a legitimate *The Devil Wears Prada* vibe and would easily snap, throwing emotional tantrums and even the occasional desk telephone if sample delivery dates weren't being met. After a couple of years under their belt, most people working there had become un-happy shells of who they once were. It was a fast fashion zombie culture, with employees putting in overtime, trying to climb the corporate ladder, and curb-stomping whoever got in their way of ultimate glory.

And while the rebel inside my heart wanted to march into my boss' office and proclaim the injustices of the company and reclaim my purpose in life, it was easier to keep showing up and cashing the checks. Still, I felt called to do more with my life. I was watching Nanny and Eric slowly wither away, and when I looked into their eyes, I knew they wouldn't tell me to work harder. They would say, "Spend more time with the people who mean the most to you in the world. Follow your heart. Chase your dreams. Practice gratitude. Life is indeed too short."

Since quitting the fashion industry wasn't an option, I decided that I would look for ways to find purpose in my work that ran deeper than thread colors. I started writing myself miniature pep talks on sticky notes and putting them in places where I could see them as a reminder of who I really was. I would write things like:

you have a purpose that is bigger than this.

perfect is you being exactly who you are.

you are so loved.

Before long, my computer monitor at work had sticky notes all over it, and whenever I felt a little bit hopeless, these notes would help to pull my heart back into alignment with my purpose. I overheard my coworkers complaining enough to know that I wasn't alone in how I was feeling, so I began leaving these secret encouragements around the office for other people to discover. I would sneak one near the cash register in the cafeteria, tape a note to the bathroom door, and slip them into magazines in the lobby at every chance I got.

These notes gave me feelings of hope and light during a dark time, and I wanted others to feel the same. I discovered how good it felt to add a little kindness to the world and help people remember their worth. But I didn't know at the time the impact this seemingly small practice would have on my entire life.

Two months after moving back home to be close to my family, Nanny passed away. In the weeks leading up to her death, I spent as much time with her as I possibly could. I was so grateful to have had that time with her. The day she died, I was at work. My mom called and asked me to come to her house. Hospice had been helping my family for the past several weeks, and the nurse let my mom and grandpa know that the end was near. By the time I arrived, she was already gone.

After hugging and crying with my cousins for a good long while, I stood over Nanny's body, a shell of skin and bones on the rented hospital bed. I looked at her face. It no longer looked like her. Her hands were already cold. It felt so surreal to look at her because she was there, right in front of me, but *she wasn't there*.

I went to the upstairs bathroom flooded with emotion. I grabbed a handful of tissues to wipe my face and looked through the skylight, past the blue sky, and into the heavens. I raised both my hands, middle fingers in the air, and told God a fiery, "FUCK. YOU."

The sobbing overcame me. I fell to the ground, kept my middle fingers high, and prayed the most fervent prayer of my life, "I hate you. I hate what you've taken from me. I hate that I feel this loss so deeply." The words came tumbling from my mouth in a whisper between sobs. "I hate that you didn't heal her. I fucking hate cancer. Jesus, I fucking hate you."

A few days later, over 500 people came to pay their respects at Nanny's funeral, many of them sharing the various ways that she had touched their lives with her kindness. It was beautiful and healing to see how her small acts of love for people had truly made a difference.

We will never truly matter unless we reflect back to others that they matter to us. I thought about my secret encouragement project. *This is what it's all about.* I decided then to keep it going.

This had to be my life's mission.

Only six months after Nanny passed, Eric's health declined more rapidly. Soon we were inundated with more hospice nurses and another round of rented hospital equipment. Eric was agitated and spent his days and nights tossing and turning. He never fully allowed himself to rest. I think he was truly terrified of dying. It seemed to me that he thought if he went to sleep, he wouldn't wake up again—and he wasn't ready to die. So he would sit, heavily medicated, and catch himself as he started to doze off, jerking awake with a start. It was like watching him die and come back to life a thousand times a day.

He was with us, and not with us. He seemed to be having a very real spiritual and psychedelic experience. He was seeing all sorts of marvelous sights. He would describe what he saw to us: strings connecting each of us from our hearts to his; incredible light shows bursting with sparkly, vibrant color; music that only he could hear. He often looked at Conner, thinking he was using some sort of video projection or something to display these visions, and he would earnestly ask, "How are you doing this?"

My poor mother was exhausted because if Eric wasn't resting, that meant she was not resting either. We were taking shifts, but I still had my full-time job, so I wasn't able to be there long enough for her to get more than an hour or two of sleep.

"He just needs more morphine so he will settle down and his body can rest," the hospice nurse encouraged. My mom agreed to up his dosage.

The next day, they gave him a double dose of the medicine. His body finally relaxed, and the next moment, he was gone.

I wasn't very close to Grandpa Hurley, but when he got sick, I made sure to go visit him and Fat Grandma as often as I could. The familiar sights of hospice and tubes and rented hospital machinery didn't even phase me anymore. I'd seen this set up far too many times in the last few years, and it was starting to feel like every autumn, along with the leaves falling from the trees, someone was preparing to die. I did not enjoy the visits, especially when my dad was in town during my grandpa's final days. We never really recovered after the summer he involved me in his affair with his accountant, and I couldn't stand the sight of him.

The Hurley family, never short on drama, got one final surprise as Grandpa Hurley was beginning to fade away. A woman arrived at the house and identified herself as his estranged daughter, Karina. She looked to be in her mid-fifties, with ashy brown hair that was cut into a short bob. She was thin, unlike Fat Grandma and Aunt Rosie (my dad's sister), and her facial structure favored my dad's and Grandpa Hurley's. She was invited inside and sat on the edge of the couch next to the hospital bed.

She explained that while she was growing up, Grandpa—who she reported was her biological father—would send money to her mother every so often, but he rarely visited. Grandpa Hurley confirmed everything she said through weak nods and labored breathing. Everyone had a different opinion of her arrival. Fat Grandma was not shocked. She knew that her husband had been a "wandering philanderer" (her words) during their marriage. My dad embraced her and cried. He was elated and in awe of the fact that he had just gained a new sister at this stage in life. Aunt Rosie, always the jealous type, despised Karina upon arrival and did not take the news well. Since Grandpa Hurley was inching toward his final days, Karina wanted to come and meet him before he passed.

My dad and Karina became inseparable from that moment forward. Karina was going through a divorce, and my dad convinced her that she should move to Longview and work with him. After Grandpa Hurley's funeral a few weeks later, Karina made the move to stay with my dad and stepmom, who were somehow miraculously still together after Dad's emotional affair with Stacey. My sister Jocelyn said that Dad had been sleeping in his own room for months, supposedly because his snoring was so incredibly loud that he kept Monica awake all night if they were in the same room, but it seemed as though there might be a bit more to it than that.

Karina had her own bedroom at my dad's. He had a large, old northwestern split-level house with five bedrooms, so there was plenty of space for everyone to have their own room. But Jocelyn told me that, while Karina had her own space, she was actually sleeping in my dad's bed with him every night. "They are always together," Jocelyn said, sounding more than a little disturbed. "They kiss each other on the lips in front of me and other people. It's getting really weird."

Monica confided in me as well. "She works with him at the compost facility, so they're together every moment of the day. The guys who work for your dad jokingly call her his 'sistress' because it's like they're married," she lamented. "It's to the point that when Jocelyn and I go out to dinner at a restaurant with your dad and Karina, everyone there thinks that *Karina* is your dad's wife and not me. It's so bizarre and becoming a problem in our marriage."

"This sounds like some fucked up incestuous bullshit. I'm so sorry; he's terrible," was all I could say in response.

Monica divorced my dad not long after, and he put her through the same dramatic hell he made my mom endure to achieve her freedom. Jocelyn struggled in her relationship with him, just like I did. I tried to be there for her as much as I could, but it was hard with the distance and the age gap between us. I was in the stage of life where I had tiny babies of my own to take care of, plus a husband who was very demanding, almost more than our kids. Keeping tabs on my dad's stupidity was no longer something I had the time or energy for.

Jocelyn, being a minor, still had to deal with him regularly, visiting on the occasional weekend or staying with him if Monica had to go out of town for work. Once her mom had to be away for two whole weeks, and my dad took Jocelyn's cell phone away, preventing her from being able to stay in touch with her mom unless he gave her permission to have the conversation.

My dad's manipulative ways were striking again, and poor Jocelyn couldn't escape them either. Jocelyn had been saving money to put toward her future college education. She wasn't yet 18 years old, so my dad and Monica were listed as owners of the savings account with her. During the divorce with Monica, Dad's compost business started to fall apart. He owed a lot of people a lot of money and had no way to pay them back.

"I had $4,000 in my savings account," Jocelyn told me. "I had been saving that money for years—birthday money from my grandparents, money I earned working babysitting jobs every summer. He took it ALL, Ashley."

"What?!" This time he had finally done it. I was shocked, though I probably shouldn't have been. "Did he even ask or tell you why?" I couldn't make sense of it in my brain. What kind of father cleans out his 16-year-old daughter's bank account?

"When I asked him about it, he said, 'You're too young to be having that kind of money anyways. I needed it more than you.' Since he was one of the owners of the account, he could just walk right in and take it, and there's nothing I can do about it." She was fuming.

"God, Jocelyn. I am so sorry he did that to you. He hasn't changed a bit," I sighed. "I hate that he is our dad."

"Me too," she agreed.

Not long after the incident with Jocelyn, the entire compost company tanked. Dad sold all his big rig equipment and put the money in a bank account that belonged to Karina only so that Monica would not be able to access any money during their divorce process.

What he did to Jocelyn was more of the same selfish bullshit he had pulled with me time and again. Not to mention his alleged incestuous behavior—it was too much for me to want to keep the door open. So I did something I have never done before to anyone. I ghosted him without explanation. He and I had never had a solid foundation anyway, and I didn't see the point in carrying on a charade. I knew that even if I were to explain this to him, he wouldn't get it and would somehow twist my reasons for severing our relationship into something that made him out to be the victim.

That was 2018, and I don't regret the choice at all. That might sound ruthless coming from "the kindness girl," but I was finally learning the value of standing up for myself and setting boundaries.

In September 2009, I flew to New York to meet up with Conner, who was there for a work trip. I was so excited to see him because I had the most life-changing news: I was pregnant.

When I told him, he seemed happy. I couldn't believe we were going to have a baby. It felt so grown up, and yet I still felt like a 17-year-old girl, unsure of her future most days. We walked around the city, talking about this new human that would be joining our family, and stopping to window shop at any baby boutiques we passed.

Ten weeks later, it was time for my first ultrasound. We were both so excited. I nervously joked, "What if I'm not really pregnant and nothing is in there?"

As I lay on the exam table, the nurse squeezed cold jelly onto my stomach and began the scan. She was silent, and that made me nervous. I looked at the monitor. *What am I looking at here— It's just a big, black circle,* I thought. *Oh my God. I just made that horrible joke and now there's actually nothing in there.* My head was spinning with worries.

"What's happening?" I asked the nurse.

She looked down at me, wiped the jelly from my stomach, and said, "I'll be right back."

"What the heck is happening?" I said to Conner, who was leaning silently against the wall. "Something is wrong."

She returned with a box of tissues, which she basically tossed at me before sitting down and saying, "You're having a miscarriage. It happens to one in four women. Take a tissue on your way out."

And just as quickly as she so casually dropped the news, she got up and walked out of the room.

"I'm not sure what that was, but I am not just going to take her word for it," I said in a panicked voice, feeling hot, salty tears flowing from my eyes.

"Let's get out of here, and we will figure this out," Conner said.

I was in total shock and denial of this news and decided to get a second opinion. A close friend recommended her doctor. At the appointment, Dr. Archer explained everything thoroughly and with compassion.

"I'm so sorry to confirm that your baby is no longer viable," she said. "I know this is difficult news to hear, and I want to answer all the questions you may have." She sat with me and held my hand as I asked her how this might have happened.

"It's very common, and nothing is wrong with you. But we do need to outline a plan for your miscarriage," she explained. "Your body has to get rid of the fetal tissue inside your uterus. Sometimes this happens naturally, and sometimes we have to go in and perform an abortion to remove the tissue before it causes sickness and infection."

"An abortion?" I asked. "I don't want an abortion."

"I know that word comes with a lot of heaviness and is a bit taboo, but it's just what the process is called. Your baby is already gone," she gently reasoned. "I know it sounds scary and confusing, and you don't have to decide anything today. I can give you two weeks at the most to see if the tissue passes naturally. At that point, I would require you to have the procedure done so that you don't get sick."

"I want to wait and see what happens on my own," I said. I was still in shock, secretly praying that everyone was wrong and that if I waited, my baby would miraculously materialize inside my body.

"That is ok," she replied. "The longest we can go before taking action is November 1. We'll schedule the procedure for then, and if it happens naturally before that, you can let me know. I'm so sorry for your loss."

Conner and I sat in the car for an hour after that doctor's appointment, frozen with grief, sobbing into each other's shoulders.

While I was completely devastated, I was grateful for Dr. Archer's kindness, especially after the terrible experience I had with the nurse at the first appointment. I cried for the entire two weeks leading up to the first of November and begged God every day to let me pass this on my own without surgery. I felt that was the only way I would truly have peace and closure.

On the last day of October, I started feeling uncomfortably strange and went to the bathroom. There was blood in my underwear. A lot of it. I sat on the toilet, felt a pop, and suddenly blood was pouring out of me like a waterfall. I had never seen so much in my life. Terrified and shaking, I called for Conner. "I think I'm having the miscarriage right now," my voice trembled.

"What do we do?" Conner asked. I was annoyed that he turned to me for our next step instead of jumping into action hero mode to handle things, but even in my surreal state of shock, I knew I didn't have time to be annoyed. This was an emergency.

"I mean, this is a lot of blood. I think we need to go to the ER." I asked him to get me a towel to absorb the blood—there was so much. I did my best to breathe through the unbearable cramps and pain as we rushed to the hospital.

The emergency room is maybe the spookiest place you could be on Halloween. It felt eerie, seeing people in the waiting room dressed as Dracula or a pirate wench, looking worried for their loved ones. They ushered us to a room with a bed rather quickly because of the amount of bleeding I was experiencing.

A doctor came in and assessed the situation. I described the immense pain I was in, with cramps shooting through my lower back. "Those are actually contractions," she said. "Your body has to pass this like it would if you were in active labor. I can give you something for the pain."

A nurse came and gave me a dose of morphine, hooking me up to tubes and wires and showing me a button to push if I was in need of assistance. Soon the pain subsided, and then we were told we just had to wait. A couple of hours later, I passed the gestational sac that once held our baby, and I was officially no longer pregnant. I felt completely hollow.

My mom met us back at our house when we finally returned from the hospital. She was cooking a meal and had a spot prepared for me on the couch. She held me while I cried. She stroked my hair and wiped my tears.

"You will have as many children as you want someday. You will get through this," she said.

Maybe she sincerely meant it in the moment but hearing her words felt like a greeting card author's attempt at encouragement—addressing the theme with a positive spin that was useless to a broken heart. Nothing anyone could say would've made me feel whole. I felt like I might never recover from the pain and the loss.

"I'll be there to pick you up at 4:30, ok?" I asked.

"Yeah, we'll be ready," came the tired voice on the other end of the phone call.

I hung up the phone and walked into the dining room, looking toward Conner who was sitting at the table, hunched over his computer. The kids had pulled out a slew of their toys and upended every couch cushion to build a fort.

"Mommy! Help us!" they cheered.

"I can help real quick, but then I have to go get Miss Elizabeth. I'm taking her to look at her wedding dress today," I said as I quickly arranged the cushions into an A-frame shape and draped a sheet over it. "You guys be good for Daddy, and please don't destroy the house." I kissed them both on the head and walked toward my purse and car keys.

"How long will you be gone?" Conner sighed, turning just slightly in his chair to take a momentary pause from his aimless social media scrolling to make eye contact with me. "I'm not going to be able to babysit them all day."

Babysit. His. Own. Kids. *Wow, what a man I've scored here,* I thought. But I didn't dare say that out loud. Instead, I replied, "The dress shop is about 30 minutes from here. I'm picking up Elizabeth and her mom and driving them. We will probably be an hour or so at the fitting. I'm guessing it will be at least two hours. Can I take your car? I think it will be easier for her to get in and out of with how much pain she's been in lately."

"I don't know. I feel kind of weird about having her in my car. Like, after she dies, it's gonna be weird that she was in my car," he said plainly, as if it wasn't a completely insensitive, not to mention crazy-sounding, statement to make about your wife's dying friend. He continued, "Look, I know Elizabeth is sick and everything, but you can't keep inconveniencing your own family to help her out. You've already taken groceries to them multiple times—are they ever paying us back for those, by the way? All I'm saying is, there are plenty of other people who could be taking her right now. Why do they need you?"

I could feel my heart sinking. It was always a battle for me to step away from the house for any reason, and here he was criticizing me for wanting to help out one of my best friends who was dying from a rare form of kidney cancer.

Elizabeth and her fiancé, Brody, were forced to move their wedding date up by three months because Elizabeth's latest prognosis was that she wouldn't likely make it to Christmas. She asked me to drive her and her mother to her wedding dress fitting. It was such a beautiful honor for me to have that precious time with her. I loved her so much, and my heart was so heavy watching her suffer from this illness. I wanted to do everything I could to make her feel my love and support before she moved on from this life. And Conner showed no sympathy.

"Are you serious right now?" I finally replied. "She's my

friend, and she's *dying*, Conner. I'm sorry this is such an inconvenience to you. I'm taking your car. I'll be back in a couple of hours."

I walked out of the house and got into his car, repulsed by the selfishness I had just witnessed. *This can't be the man I chose to marry*, I thought as I escaped down the driveway.

Elizabeth and I had been friends for a little more than four years. I met her when we were both pregnant with our youngest children. She had Evan six weeks before I had Milo, and so we would often find ourselves in the nursing mothers' room together at church on Sunday mornings. We clicked immediately. Both of us struggling to get our boobs out to feed our impatient, screaming babies created a lasting bond, it turned out.

Since our kids were similar ages, we would often meet up for play dates during our lonely days seeking human connection as stay-at-home moms. She shared with me over Chick-fil-A nuggets and waffle fries that she had discovered her husband, Rylan, had cheated on her. This was the final straw, and she was making plans to divorce him. He had several previous offenses, and she was done. She had no family in town and no income other than her husband, but she was determined to free herself. I hugged her and told her that she had my full support and that I knew she could do this.

The next few months I watched her grow in confidence and strength as she fought to get free from Rylan. He didn't let her go without unnecessary drama, and she handled everything with so much grace. When she was finally free and met Brody, it seemed she could now build the life and world she'd always wanted. She was a true and beautiful diamond. I was so thrilled for her to finally be with someone who wholeheartedly appreciated and celebrated her sparkle. And then, the cancer arrived.

I pulled into Elizabeth's driveway. It was mid-August, and

the air was thick and hot in Nashville. The cicadas buzzed loudly in the trees above us as I helped them both into the car. While I drove, we chatted about wedding stuff. She was three weeks away from the wedding day, and the bridal shop we were going to had agreed to do a rush order for her so that everything would be ready in time. When I saw her in the dress, my heart wrestled between happiness and sorrow, thinking of the wonderful day she had ahead of her while knowing that her remaining days were numbered.

The next day, I helped Elizabeth pack some boxes. After the wedding, she and Brody were going to move to Chicago with the boys, to be closer to Elizabeth's parents during her last days. It was hard, sorting through my friend's stuff as if she was already gone.

On her wedding day, Elizabeth looked stunning and so happy. She was surrounded by loved ones, family, and friends doing their part to help make this day special for her and Brody. All of our kids were running around the property giggling as they explored. I knew that so many people there wanted time with Elizabeth, so I hung back to give everyone else more space with her.

I thought about how overwhelming it can be when you're at your own wedding and everyone wants to say hello to the bride and groom. I imagined there was a lot of added pressure with everyone clamoring to be around her because this might be the very last time they ever got to see her before she passed away. *I've had such sweet moments with Elizabeth driving her to the dress fittings. I don't need to insert myself here today*, I thought.

After the ceremony, there was a huge reception in an old barn that had been converted into an event space. People were eating and dancing and drinking in true celebratory fashion. Suddenly, Conner approached me and handed me our son, who was shaking and crying hysterically. "What's going on, buddy?" I asked Milo, trying to calm him down.

"I'll tell you what's going on," Conner huffed. "This old man over there just yelled at MY son. He grabbed Milo's arm to shake a rock out of his hand that he had picked up off the ground. I'm fucking PISSED right now. I have to do something." His nostrils flared as he spoke, and he started to walk away.

"Wait, I'm so confused," I said, stopping him. "You seem really angry about this. I'm not sure what happened, but you need to calm down. I don't want to make a scene at Elizabeth's wedding tonight," I urged.

He completely flew off the handle. "You weren't there; you didn't see it. This man touched our kid. What don't you get about that? I will not calm down. He is gonna pay for what he did. He's one of the owners of this place. I'm going to write a review that will destroy them. How's that for justice?" Justice and revenge can look really similar when you're angry. I continued to try to diffuse his emotions, but everything I said only made him angrier, and he now directed his anger at me.

"Ashley, I don't care that they gave Elizabeth this venue for free! That man crossed a line and won't apologize to our son for what he did. Now he has to pay for his actions. I have to defend my family." Conner rattled on, telling anyone who passed by what happened, while I tried to calm Milo, who was still crying in my arms because Conner was creating a chaotic scene that was now drawing a crowd. I was mortified.

"Please, Conner, let's just take a beat here," I begged. "I really don't want Elizabeth to know about this. Not today, ok?"

"Once again, you put everyone else before your own family, Ashley. I'm going to handle this myself," he scolded me and stormed away.

A few moments later, I noticed Elizabeth's dad and Conner

talking in a dimly lit corner of the barn. I walked over to hear her dad begging Conner to not leave a bad review or cause problems for the owner of the event space.

"As a father, I'm asking you to please not pursue this any further," he implored Conner. "I'm not discounting or excusing what happened to your son, but these people have given Elizabeth the greatest gift today, allowing us to have the space for free so that we can celebrate with her on her terms before the cancer consumes her. Please, can you find it in your heart to let it go?"

"As a *father*, you know I have to protect my family," Conner said coldly. "I can't just stand here and let that man hurt my son. What if he did this to other kids? That would not be ok. It needs to stop, and they're going to pay for what they did." He wasn't budging.

"I think we need to leave," I whispered to Conner.

"That's fine. We'll go, but I'm going to write a review on social media and destroy them tomorrow."

The drive home was torture. Thankfully our kids had quickly fallen asleep, so they didn't have to be subjected to any more of Conner's ranting. I, however, got a 45-minute lecture on why I was a terrible and unsupportive wife.

"You should've backed me up regardless," he said. "We're supposed to be a team. I was trying to protect our kid, and you opposed me in front of everyone. That's so disrespectful."

I just listened. Inside, I was shutting down. It made no difference what I said; he was as mad at me as he was at the old man. I was envious that the old man was free of Conner's wrath, while I was stuck in a car with it. My heart ached for Elizabeth as we drove on. All I could think was, *That may be the last time I see my friend alive, and he completely destroyed the memory of this beautiful night with his behavior.*

I cried myself to sleep that night, thinking about Elizabeth. Thinking about all the sorrow and grief I had known. About how precious life was and how foolishly Conner behaved. I felt a sadness settle deep into my heart. *I think I chose the wrong person.* I prayed silently to God, *How do I fix this? Help me fix this. Please.*

chapter six

THE PRICE
OF BEAUTY

"The seeds of beauty are in humility."

— Maxime Lagacé

My first serious relationship was with my high school boyfriend, Matteo. We met at the Fellowship of Christian Athletes (FCA) retreat in the fall of my senior year. FCA was exactly what it sounds like: a faith-based student-led organization where once a week on Friday mornings before school, students of Christian faith gathered to read devotionals and build community. The retreat was held at a campground in southern Ohio where several schools in our region brought their FCA groups for a weekend of friendly competition, youth-group-style church services, and lots of Jesus talks.

When I first spotted him in the multipurpose room that we used as our church sanctuary, I thought he was the most gorgeous boy I'd ever seen. My cousin Alice was a camp counselor, and she was hanging with him and a few of the other counselors, goofing off and laughing while we all filed into our seats for the first session of camp.

As I found a seat, Alice approached me. "Ashley, come over here! I want to introduce you to Matteo."

"Matteo, this is my cousin Ashley who I was telling you about. Ash, Matteo is into a lot of the same artsy things you are. I figured you two should meet."

"Hi," I said quietly, wondering how the heck I was going to manage an entire weekend trying to look as cool as possible so he wouldn't think I was lame.

"Hey, it's good to meet you," he said with a smile. His dark, curly hair swayed when he nodded his head at me. We made small talk for a few minutes, and then I walked back to my seat, eyes wide, thinking, *Oh my God, oh my God, oh my God ... He knows who I am!* I had never had the attention of anyone this good-looking before. Boys at my high school just didn't look like him.

Every so often when all the campers would gather, I would catch his eye and smile or wave. He'd smile and wave back. By breakfast the next day, he was stopping by my cabin's table to say hello. I liked having his attention; it made me feel special.

By the end of the two-day retreat, we were all packing our cars and getting ready to leave. I was riding home with Alice, so I stayed behind to help the other counselors clean up.

"So, Matteo's kinda cute, isn't he?" Alice pressed. "What do you think of him?"

"Of course I think he's really cute," I said. I could feel my face getting hot with embarrassment.

"He likes you," Alice said.

"Excuse me, what?" I said, totally shocked.

"Yeah, he told me he thinks you're really pretty. I think he's a nice guy, Ash. You should talk to him more," Alice encouraged me.

As I slammed the trunk shut, I saw Matteo walking toward us.

"Hey! A few of us are going to stop and grab a burger on our way home. Would you two like to tag along?" Matteo asked.

"Yeah, totally!" Alice replied.

"Cool, just follow us out then!" he said as he jogged off to another car.

Everything about that meal was a total blur. I was so nervous but grateful to have a buffer in Alice and a few of the other camp counselors from the weekend.

"You don't seem like a high school kid to me," Matteo said as we gathered our trays and walked them to the trash can. "Usually high school girls are all giggly and loud, but you're so mature acting ... I like it," he said.

"Thanks," I replied, unsure how to respond to that compliment.

"So ... can I call you sometime?" he asked.

"Absolutely. I'd love that," I said with a huge smile that made my face tingle.

Alice and I did squeal and act all giggly and annoying the whole way home from the restaurant, though. This was just too exciting for both of us.

When I returned home, I chatted with my mom for a bit about the weekend and then took a long, hot shower. When I got back to my room, my phone's answering machine had a message (this was 2000, when everyone still had landline phones).

"Hey, Ashley. This is Matteo Garcia calling. Please call me back when you can talk! Ok bye!"

Oh my God. He already called me. I couldn't believe it. *Do I call him back now? Yes, I definitely call him back now.* My hands were shaking as I dialed his number. He answered on the second ring, and we talked for over an hour. Not only that, but he asked me out at the end of our chat, and we had a date set for the following Friday.

Soon Matteo and I were officially an item, and things got

serious fast. That year at Christmas, Matteo encouraged me to come over and help his mom bake cookies. Every year she baked for days and assembled cute Christmas tins filled with baked goods to give out to everyone she knew. I spent a day with her in the kitchen, learning how to sift flour and use a KitchenAid mixer. I had fun working with her in the kitchen, and Matteo seemed to really like that I was getting involved with his family. That year for Christmas, he gifted me my own KitchenAid mixer.

"That's the weirdest gift to give your girlfriend who is still in high school," Eric noted when we walked in the door with it, and I asked where I should store it.

"I'm investing in my future," Matteo said. I liked hearing that he was thinking long-term for us. I thought being his wife would make me the luckiest girl. (Now, this sentiment makes me want to puke a little. But I digress.)

We had been dating for a few months, and my Senior Prom was coming up. I brought it up with Matteo one evening when he called. "Do you want to go to my prom with me this year?" I asked, trying to gauge if he felt too old to go since he'd already graduated.

"Ah, you know how I feel about all that high school stuff … But, I don't want you to have to go alone … " he hesitated.

I tried to mask the disappointment in my voice with a happy and carefree tone. Keeping it casual, I lied, "Okay, I mean, it's not a big deal …" It was actually a huge deal to me.

I think he could sense that I really wanted to go. "Okay, we'll go. It'll be fine. I can't have you there dancing with other guys," he teased.

"Alright, great!" I was screaming internally with excitement.

Finally, prom day had arrived. Matteo brought me a corsage to wear that matched my dress. He seemed a little agitated, but I didn't think much of it as we drove off toward the venue.

"I'm so excited because my name is on the list for Prom Court this year," I told him.

"That's nice," he said in a less than enthusiastic voice. "Hope you win."

We arrived fashionably late to the party. Music was playing while colored lights darted around the room, casting orange and pink and blue sparkles on the faces of my friends and classmates. A fog machine added extra atmosphere to the party, and I was really excited to dance the night away with Matteo.

"Let's put our stuff down at a table and then we can go dance," I suggested.

He followed me to a table where I found a few of my friends had saved us seats. We all hugged and giggled as we twirled around showing off our fancy dresses.

"You go ahead with your friends and dance. I'm gonna sit here for a few minutes, and then I'll join you later," Matteo mumbled as he sat down at the table.

"Ok, yeah," I said as I scurried off with my friends.

After three or four songs, he still hadn't come to join me on the dance floor, so I went to check in. I sat in the chair next to him and asked, "Hey, what's going on? You haven't come out to dance with me yet."

"Yeah, I'm just not feeling it right now. Sorry," he said as he sat with his arms folded across his chest.

"Ok, well do you plan to dance with me at all?" I asked.

"Maybe. I don't know yet."

I sat there for a moment, a little disappointed that he didn't seem to want to be there with me. The music stopped and our Prom Committee supervisor, Mr. Hayley, began calling the Prom Court's names to step onto the dance floor.

"Ok I'm gonna go do this thing real quick ... Can we keep talking about this when I get back?" I asked.

He nodded but didn't budge from his seat.

"Now that everyone's here, we're going to announce your 2001 Prom King and Queen," Mr. Hayley continued. "But, truly there are no losers here tonight. You all look like royalty." He paused and the room fell silent.

"This year's Prom King is Mr. Jayce Graham!" Everyone cheered and clapped for Jayce, the school wrestling state champion, while Mr. Hayley handed him his King's crown and bedazzled Prom King sash.

"And of course, a true King needs a proper Queen!" Mr. Hayley was loving building the suspense of this moment. I looked over at the table where Matteo was still sitting, arms folded.

"Your 2001 Prom Queen is Ashley Hurley!" I heard my name, and suddenly someone was pinning a sparkly tiara onto my head and helping me put on my own bedazzled Prom Queen sash.

"And now, this year's King and Queen will share a dance," Mr. Hayley announced while "Hero" by Enrique Iglesias played over the sound system. I found Jayce on the dance floor. We made small talk as we danced under the spinning lights of a giant disco ball. Finally, the song ended, and I headed back to the table.

"Hey, are you ok?" I asked.

"No, I shouldn't be here," he answered. "You knew I wasn't into all this high school stuff. You shouldn't have asked me to come to this with you."

I sat down, quickly deflated from the royal victory I had just experienced.

"Well, let's just leave then," I offered after sitting through another song, the tension building between us. He finally got up from his seat, and I followed him out the door.

He drove me back to my house in silence. As he pulled into my driveway, I asked, "Are we going to be ok?"

"I don't know," was all he said.

We sat there for a minute more in silence, then I gathered my things and got out of the car. I felt the tears welling up in my eyes before I could get to the front door. I blinked them back so Matteo wouldn't see me cry. It was 10:00 p.m. on prom night, and instead of happily dancing with all my friends, reveling in my Prom Queen victory, I was standing on the front porch in shock, watching my boyfriend drive away. I shut the front door, leaned back against it, and slid down to the floor sobbing.

"What is going on?" my mom asked as she rushed over to me.

Through tears, I told her everything that had happened. "I think we're going to break up," I said. "My heart literally feels like I'm being stabbed a thousand times."

"I don't think he deserves to keep you, honey. It sounds like he was a complete jerk tonight," she said as she rocked me in her arms. I felt safe again there. After a good long while of me sobbing into her lap, my mom finally suggested, "Why don't you go upstairs and get ready for bed, and we can talk about this more tomorrow, if you want."

Monday after school, he stopped by my house.

"I ... I wanted to say I'm sorry," he lamented. "I should not have said I would go to your prom with you because deep down I knew I didn't want to go. But I'm your boyfriend, so I also knew you expected me to go. That's why I was in such a bad mood that night."

"I wish you had told me this beforehand," I said. "I forgive you but that really hurt my feelings."

"I know. I did not mean for that to happen. Do you think we can work this out?" he asked as he took my hand.

I looked into his eyes. "Yes, I'm willing to work through this with you. But will you promise to always tell me from now on when you don't want to do something?"

"I promise," he said.

That fall, I was starting my freshman year at art school, and Matteo had enrolled in an art education program close by. In the evenings, we hung out, working on our art assignments and making out.

"You know trophy wives don't have to go to college," he said to me one day when I was stressing out about a homework assignment.

"What's a trophy wife?" I asked.

"It's when a guy marries a beautiful girl and gets to show her off like he won the Heisman trophy," he explained. "You're going to be my trophy wife someday, and you'll stay at home with our kids while I go to work to take care of you," he added as he grabbed my waist and pulled me close to him for a kiss.

I thought about the idea of having that life and how easy it sounded. Then I remembered my mom's advice. "Get a good education so you never have to depend on a man." But I could see the future Matteo was describing, and I was so in love with him that I couldn't see how he was changing and starting to control me little by little, literally sculpting me into his version of the perfect girlfriend. Manipulation is sneaky like that.

"I don't like it when you wear nail polish. You should take it off and go natural," he would suggest.

We worked out together, and he started designing my workouts, putting together schedules for leg, arm, chest, and back days.

Once while I was standing at the kitchen sink, he came up behind me and pinched my hips, grabbing a small handful of skin on both sides. "I can tell you haven't been to the gym in a few days," he noted.

"Yeah, I've been busy with school this week," I said sheepishly. Was he suggesting I had put on a little weight?

We were starting to argue more and more. And every time, I caved, apologizing and begging for his forgiveness, even if I had done nothing wrong. I was aware that our relationship wasn't working, but I continued to stay because I thought my love was strong enough to get us through the issues we were having.

But when I looked at him, I started to see ugliness where I once saw beauty. His good looks became overshadowed by his nasty attitude and controlling behavior, and I finally called and told him I wanted to break up. I still loved him, but I knew that my love was being wasted, and I didn't like how awful and insecure he was making me feel.

"You're going to throw away two years of our lives over a few stupid things I've said? Well, I don't want to break up. You've got me crying now ... I'm coming over. We need to talk face to face," he said.

"No, please don't come here. I don't want to see you right now," I said.

Ten minutes later, he was knocking on my door and asking my mom to send me outside.

"Ash, Matteo is here. He wants you to go out and sit with him on the porch," she said.

I knew he wouldn't leave until he saw me, so I walked outside, arms folded in defense. He stood up when I opened the door, wiping his eyes.

"Ashley, I love you. I don't know what you think is happening right now, but we are not going to break up. We just need a little space is all," he urged.

I felt my heart go cold as I stuffed all my emotions toward him into a lockbox so I would not cry in front of him. I knew if I showed any weakness in this moment, he would see it and convince me not to break up with him. I had to flip the switch and detach from my feelings toward him to protect myself.

107

"How can you sit here with me crying and have no reaction or feelings? That is so heartless," he said.

We sat on the porch for a long while, as he processed that I was actually serious about ending the relationship. Finally, he was ready to leave but said he wanted to keep talking about this.

"I really don't think that's a good idea," I said, as he got in his car. I turned around and walked back into the house, finally allowing the tears to stream down my face.

I dated a lot after breaking up with Matteo. I needed to get more people between him and me so that I could move on. I wasn't great at being alone, so I scheduled a date for every weekend I could.

We were at Nanny's house one Sunday to celebrate Uncle Rhett's birthday. A few of us were playing a card game called euchre, beloved by Ohioans statewide, when somehow my love life became the topic of the table. My grandpa got in on the conversation and took every opportunity he could to tease me.

"Ashley, I have something for you," he said as he reached into his pocket. He placed a nickel on the table and slid it toward me. "I want you to have this, and whenever you're out on dates, I want you to put this between your knees and hold it there tight." He cackled.

"Ok ... ?" I said, confused at what he was getting at.

"He means like when you're making out with boys, keep your knees together," my mom chimed in.

"Oh, haha," I said awkwardly. *Why is my grandpa even talking about my sex life right now?* I wondered. It seemed really inappropriate that he would essentially tell me, his 20-year-old granddaughter, to "keep my legs closed." I abruptly changed the subject and tried to move on. I wanted to die of embarrassment.

Since he was my elder, I was afraid to tell him I was un-comfortable with this conversation because there was a chance it would be viewed as me being disrespectful to him. I knew the reality was that *he* was being disrespectful to *me*, and I couldn't even do anything about it in my "respect your elders no matter what" dysfunctional family.

There used to be a commercial for diapers that depicted a happy couple going out dancing at a club and then cutting to that same couple swaying in their living room with a tiny baby swaddled in the mother's arms. They brought the point home with their emotional tagline, "Having a baby changes everything."

Having a baby does change everything. In the best ways. And it can also make everyone around you fucking crazy.

When I got pregnant again a few months after my mis-carriage, our families were so excited. I went into labor at 8:00 p.m. on a Tuesday night, and we called to let everyone know and asked them to sit tight until we had more information. I had a strong desire to labor with only Conner and the hospital staff in the room. I didn't want anyone else there for what felt like it would be a very private and sacred moment for me, entering into the first moments of motherhood.

No one listened. Everyone from Conner's dad, George; his stepmom, Cora; his mom, Florence, and her boyfriend; my mom; and my dad (who just happened to be in town) all filed into the hospital waiting room that night.

Conner's mom texted him, "We're all here! Let us know when we can come back and see you guys."

"We told you to stay home. Why are you here? It's 10:00 p.m. Ashley is still in labor," he replied.

I'm not sure what they were expecting, but every 20-30 minutes someone was texting from the waiting room, asking for an update.

"Can't you come out here and tell us what's going on?" his mom was texting, again. It was now midnight.

My contractions were intensifying, and I was already so tired ... when I started to vomit. Adrenaline was rushing through my whole body, I was trembling, and I couldn't make it stop. The puke was not something they warned me about in birth class, and I was regretting the Chipotle burrito bowl I had eaten for dinner that night. Unexpected vomiting scared me, and as a result, my entire mental game plan for dealing with my contractions was now tossed out the window.

Conner and I had discussed having a natural birth without using an epidural to avoid all the risks that we read about in the pregnancy books, but what I was experiencing wasn't this beautiful and peaceful process of welcoming a new life into the world that I had planned for, and I was scared.

The nurse came in. "You look like you're in a lot of pain, honey. Would you like to have an epidural? It would help you to be able to rest a bit before it's time to push later," she urged.

"No, she's not doing one of those," Conner replied abruptly as he texted his family. "Ash, everyone's on my case because I haven't been out there to see them yet. I'm going to just go for like 10 minutes to get them to chill for a bit. I'll be back."

"That's fine." I sighed as I tried to reposition my body to find a little relief from the pressure of what felt like a thousand pound wrecking ball trying to push out of my vagina.

When Conner was out of the room, the nurse returned. "You know," she said gently, "You're the only one in this room who is feeling the weight of this labor. You are the one who has to do the work of bringing your baby girl into the world. I'm not trying to tell you what to do, but I am going to tell you that you are allowed to change your mind about whether an epidural is right for you. I see women get them all the time, and I know it would help you to have more of the peaceful labor experience that you were hoping for."

I think I was just waiting for someone to give me permission to have an epidural. My mom had rattled on for years, even before I ever got pregnant, touting her strength and grit because she had both her babies without an epidural, like a fucking warrior princess. She had me convinced that I didn't need an epidural, and being the people-pleasing, obedient daughter I was, I wanted to do everything like her.

"Okay," I said reluctantly. "I think that an epidural is actually a good idea for me at this point." My entire body was still shaking with adrenaline.

The nurse ordered the epidural as Conner was returning from the waiting room.

"Did I just hear her ask for an epidural to be sent to our room?" he asked.

"Yeah, I'm sorry, this is way harder than I thought it would be." I heard the defeat in my voice as I spoke. "When I puked, I got thrown off, and now I can't calm down. I think this will help me," I explained apologetically to him.

"Well I guess there's not a lot I can do about it now," he said as he sat on the couch by the window, phone in his hand.

The sweetest relief came when the epidural set in. I was finally able to relax and even got a tiny bit of sleep before giving the final pushes as our daughter entered the world.

They placed her on my chest, and I felt … nothing. I felt *nothing*. Where was the intense rush of love every other new mom wrote about in their Facebook statuses and "birth story" blogs? What the fuck was wrong with me? Why didn't I feel love for this tiny human? All I could think was, *There's a crying baby on my chest, and I've got to figure out how to make this thing survive.* This. Thing. I called her a thing. *Oh my God, I'm going to be the worst mother in the history of mothering.*

Conner texted our families to announce that the baby was here, safe and sound. "When can we come in and see her? We're all so tired from being here all night and want to go home now," his mother reported. (As if we asked them to come and sit in the waiting room for hours ...)

I asked that Conner hold off our visitors just a few more minutes while I tried out nursing our daughter for the first time, and to give us time to get settled in our recovery room. Everyone entered before I was ready to see them, having grown impatient while waiting for 14 hours. Our baby was in the middle of her first bath when they arrived. She was wailing mad and hated the cold air and water as the nurses washed her clean of all the labor and delivery funk.

The nurses asked, "What's her name?"

"We haven't decided yet," Conner answered.

I wanted to pick her name before she was born, but he insisted that we needed to see what she was like before attaching a name to her. So once she was born, the nurses nicknamed her "Tank" because she weighed just over nine pounds when she came out of the oven.

"I can't have them calling our baby 'Tank' any longer," I said.

Finally, he agreed, and we decided on Elianna.

We were released from the hospital on Thanksgiving Day, and I put my firstborn in her going home outfit as the Macy's Thanksgiving Parade played on the television in our room. The nurse came with a wheelchair and pushed me out to meet Conner with our car.

As we drove home, I couldn't believe they just let me leave

with this kid and no instruction manual, and no one coming to check on us at home. I sat in the back seat, staring at her in the car seat, desperately looking for the overwhelming love I was supposed to be flooded with. Still, I felt nothing.

Those first few days navigating motherhood were so raw for me. I mostly sat in a rocking chair, trying to figure out how to nurse properly, and every time she would latch onto my breast, my toes literally curled with the pain. It was awful, but I wanted to make it work, so I just sat and sobbed while this tiny human destroyed my nipples.

She was crying a lot, and I was running on minutes of sleep. I became frustrated and unable to figure out how to calm her. I sobbed as Conner stood by offering suggestions. "I need to step away," I said as I handed her to him and retreated to the bathroom. I splashed cold water onto my face and sat on the side of the bathtub, breathing deeply and wondering if I'd ever figure out what the hell I was doing as a mother. *I've been in here for too long. I should go back and check on her*, I thought.

I expected to still hear crying when I returned to the bedroom, but what I saw instead was the most peaceful and beautiful scene. Conner, looking like the most patient and loving father, rocking our daughter and speaking to her gently while she rested peacefully in his arms. Tears welled up in my eyes. *This is so great, but how is he already so good at this?* I sat on the bed and watched them, happy and grateful that he seemed to be embracing his new role as a dad.

A few days after being home, we were due to take Elianna to her first doctor's appointment. Trying to get her safely in the car seat turned into a battle that I was not emotionally prepared to handle. Apparently, Conner wasn't either. We were getting frustrated, and our voices became more and more chaotic. In a moment of total panic when he couldn't get the buckle properly fastened for the eighth time, he turned around and punched the sofa cushions.

I collapsed onto the couch, stunned and sobbing, again. *How are we going to make it to this doctor's appointment, and where is the calm, cool, and collected dad from two days ago? We can't even buckle this baby into her car seat! We're going to ruin this kid*, I worried inside my heart. By some act of God, we got it figured out and made it to the appointment.

By the third week of her life, I was finding my rhythm as a mom, and finding the love, too. But my nursing experience was still hell. I didn't know what to do. My nipples were scabbing and cracking, and no amount of cream was bringing me the relief I longed for. I was told not to try pumping until the fourth week, and I wasn't even sure I would be able to successfully do that when the time came.

Conner's mother was visiting us that afternoon. She was holding Elianna, who was crying and couldn't be consoled. "Florence, I think she's crying because she's hungry," I said softly. "This is usually the next feeding time for her."

"Well, if you would pump, I could give this baby a bottle and feed her," she coldly snapped at me.

I reached and gently retrieved my baby from her grasp, and hurried off to the safety of the rocking chair and a door that I could close for privacy as I sobbed and fed my little girl. Was I being selfish by not pumping yet? I felt so much pressure to make my mother-in-law happy and give her the grandmother experience she so desired. That night while Elianna slept, I decided to try pumping for the first time.

I read the instruction manual and attached the pumps to my chest. I turned it to the lowest recommended setting since I had never done this before. This hurt just as much as actual nursing. My nipples were so badly scabbed at this point, and after about 15 seconds I looked down to see hot pink, bloody milk filling the containers. *Oh my God, I've been feeding my baby bloody milk.* I panicked. I took the pumps off and sobbed, laying on the cold bathroom tile, unable to breathe and feeling completely worthless.

I called Alice. She was an expert mom with three kids; she would know what to do. I told her everything.

"Oh, sweet girl," she said empathetically from the other side of the phone. "Listen, Elianna is getting everything she needs from you. The pumping—it's a machine. It's not organic, and it's rough on you ... especially when you've got unhealed wounds on your body. I promise you that your baby is not getting the same milk that you saw when you pumped. Don't you worry about that.

"What you do need to worry about," she continued, "is why are you trying to do something you're not ready for, just to please your mother-in-law? I want you to realize that you get to call the shots. You are the mom. If she or anyone else doesn't like it, that's too bad. Elianna is your baby. You know what is best for her. You can totally do this."

I took a few deep breaths as she spoke these healing words. I've got to start thinking about what is best for us first, and not worry about how other people are feeling, I repeated in my mind. I decided that if I had to become the bitchy daughter-in-law for the sake of my baby and my boobies, then that's what I had to do. I would no longer put my nipples on the line for the gratification of someone other than my firstborn.

Two weeks after we brought our daughter home, Conner flew out to New Zealand for a 14-day video shoot to work on a documentary for a ministry he was starting to travel with more often. We were actually planning a move to Nashville in a few weeks so that Conner could work more closely with this ministry. He felt "called by God" to be a part of it, and I was ready to get some distance between his family and us.

When we finally moved to Nashville, Elianna was 12 weeks old. Conner's parents were so disappointed we were moving away with their only grandchild and planned to visit us as often as possible.

Whenever George and Cora would visit us, Conner complained. He didn't seem to like spending time with his dad as much as he did with his mom. Still, he respected his dad, so he just chalked it up to not having a super close relationship and didn't talk much more about it.

I usually felt uncomfortable during their visits to our home in Nashville for other reasons. Our house only had one bathroom, so before I would go take a shower I would announce to everyone in the house, "I'm about to shower if anyone needs to use the restroom before I lock the door." I'd give fair warning and when everyone was square, I would take my 15-minute break from being a mother. Without fail, if Conner's dad was at our house, a couple of minutes into my shower, I would hear a knock at the door, and a muffled voice saying, "Ashley, it's George. I need to pee."

"Ok, I'm sorry … I'll just be a few minutes." The first time this happened, I didn't think much of it. But then it started happening at least once every time he visited us.

"Hey, you know your dad always asks to come in and pee when I'm in the shower?" I mentioned to Conner one night as we lay in bed. I was noticing a pattern after the fifth time it happened, and felt like I needed Conner to address it.

"No he doesn't," he replied.

"Yeah, he does," I insisted. "It's happened five times now."

"Well he has to go pee, I guess. What's the big deal, Ash?"

"It's just that when I ask if anyone has to pee before I get in the shower, he says he doesn't, and then five minutes later when I'm in the shower, he is asking to come in. It feels kind of weird is all," I reasoned.

"Ok, well I don't know what you want me to do about this. If he has to pee, he has to pee," he said.

"Yeah, ok … I guess." This conversation was obviously going nowhere.

I never let him in the bathroom while I was in the shower, but his knocking on the door while I was trying to get clean always really annoyed me. If a grown man legitimately can't hold his pee for 15 minutes while I finish my shower, he should go get his prostate checked. Several years into this ridiculous charade, while I was showering and his dad was visiting, Conner unlocked the bathroom door with the key, entered, and shut the door behind him.

"Uh, hello??" I said loudly.

"Hey, it's me," Conner said as he stuck his head into the shower. "So, my dad really needs to pee. Can you just let him in here? He won't look at you."

"No fucking way," I said harshly. "He is absolutely not coming in here while I am naked on the other side of a piece of plastic. He can hold it until I get out."

"No, he can't. He said he really has to go."

"I literally asked him seven minutes ago, and he declined to pee before I showered. No, he has to wait. Please make sure to lock the door on your way out," I said firmly.

"Oh my gosh, you're being so weird. Fine. I'll tell him to go pee in the backyard. This is ridiculous," Conner said as he shut the door.

I already felt like no one respected my personal space, and this violation solidified that. And yet somehow, as I rinsed the frothy shampoo bubbles from my hair, I was feeling like the disappointing bad guy.

When our daughter turned five, George and Cora came to Nashville to celebrate Elianna's birthday. We had made arrangements to not only do the standard school birthday cupcake delivery but also to have George read a book to Elianna's class. George was a retired teacher, and this seemed important to him, so I made sure to set it up with the preschool teacher.

Elianna asked for two things for her birthday that year: to have a sweet treat delivered to her class and to build her very own bear at the famous mall store of the same name. We also planned a fun dinner with everyone that evening, since Conner's family was in town for a visit.

The morning of her birthday was like any other birthday morning. She awoke to balloons covering every inch of her floor. The Birthday Balloon Fairy (me) had blown up balloons while she slept and filled the room so that when she woke up, there would be a colorful surprise waiting for her. I do this every year, and the kids love it. We have to seize every opportunity to create a little joy and magic in life, especially when everything else feels like it's falling apart.

We ate breakfast, then I packed her lunch, got her ready for school, and dropped her off. "What time will you be back with cupcakes?" she asked excitedly.

"Your teacher said we could come by about 30 minutes before school dismissal to share cupcakes, and also Grandpa is going to read to your class today!" I answered.

We hugged, and she went into her class. When I returned from school drop-off, Conner's parents had just arrived at our house, and they were eagerly awaiting us, as I had our three-year-old with me. Conner had asked for "a few minutes of peace and quiet" before I dropped him off to work that day. On top of that, I would be left to entertain his parents the whole day (as I usually was whenever they would come to visit), while he went to a trendy co-working space that we couldn't actually afford.

Most of the time when Conner's family visited, I found myself trying to stay out of the way and allow them to have as much one-on-one time with their grandkids as possible. Once we had kids, it was obvious that no one really seemed to value a relationship with me beyond the fact that I was the gatekeeper to the babies. This visit felt much the same. Truth be told, I did enjoy the break from being touched 24/7 by sticky, tiny child hands.

Less than 30 minutes after we had returned home from school birthday fun, Conner's dad, Elianna, and Milo were sitting on the floor playing with blocks in the living room. I sat less than 12 steps away at our dining room table. Our house was tiny, so even if I was in my bedroom with the door shut, I would still know everything that was happening under our roof.

I was paying a few bills online when I looked up and observed Cora darting into the room from the kitchen. She held out her iPhone, the screen at full brightness, and angrily pointed it directly in George's face and said, "What is the meaning of this?"

He stuttered, "I-I-I-I ... I don't know, Cora."

She continued to hold the phone in front of his face. The kids, mostly unaware of the awkwardness of the moment, thankfully got up to go get a new toy from one of their bedrooms. I sat at the dining room table behind my laptop screen, watching the terrible scene unfold.

"What do you mean you don't know? You know exactly what this is." She pushed the phone even closer to his face. "How do you think *this* got on my phone, George? I don't look at things like this, so how do you think it got there?"

I could see the phone screen, in plain view. There was a naked woman with bright red, curly hair that reminded me of Merida from the Disney movie *Brave* that I had recently watched with my kids. Not a correlation I wanted to make. My eyes widened. Should I get up and leave the room? Should I ask them to take whatever this was outside? I was paralyzed with discomfort and anxiety. I was barely breathing, watching this trainwreck explode before my very eyes.

He took a deep breath. Finally, after a pause that felt like an eternity, he replied, "I'm telling you the truth, Cora. I have no idea how that got there."

A little backstory. George had an iPhone for approximately three months before he suddenly got rid of it to go back to a flip phone that didn't have internet capabilities. When he announced that he was going back to the old-school phone, Conner asked why, and his dad told him it was because he felt he was spending too much time on it, researching random things on the internet. After that conversation, Conner told me about it and added, "That means he was looking at porn and got caught by Cora. She probably made him get rid of the phone. He used to have all kinds of dirty magazines hidden under his mattress when I was younger, so this is pretty on brand for him."

So there I was, stuck at my dining room table, watching a grown ass old man try to explain to his wife why there was pornography on *her* iPhone.

Finally, she stormed off, unsatisfied with his lackluster lies, and he retreated to the bathroom for 45 minutes (our only bathroom, remember?), talking to himself loudly under his breath, saying, "I really messed up this time ..." over and over again.

The tension in the house after this explosive confrontation was thick, and I felt every ounce of it. To say I was triggered would be an understatement. Cora had taken their car and left, without any indication of where she was going or when she would be back.

When George finally came out of the bathroom, I could barely look him in the eye. What woman wants to learn that her father-in-law has such a severe porn addiction that he couldn't resist sneaking to the hotel bathroom to jerk off with his wife's iPhone? Jesus fucking Christ.

It was time for me to go get Conner from his co-working space, so I escaped with the kids and headed in that direction, leaving his dad to his own misery and trying to figure out how to break the news to Conner.

"So things got weird with your parents this afternoon," I said once he got in the car.

"What do you mean?" he asked.

I went on to describe what happened, and he could not believe what I was telling him. We returned home, and it was still just Conner's dad. No Cora waiting at the house.

"Uh, Dad ... where is Cora?" Conner asked.

"I don't know right now," he said sheepishly. "I tried calling her, but it went to voicemail."

We were supposed to leave in 30 minutes with the birthday girl to go get dinner and take her to Build-A-Bear. "Do you think we should wait to see if Cora comes back?" I asked.

All I could think was that my daughter only turns five once, and now my memory of what was supposed to be a fun day has been hijacked by this knowledge of my father-in-law's indiscretions. I felt sick to my stomach.

We waited a while and then right as we were getting the kids ready to leave for dinner, Cora returned—and brought with her a frigidity that made my skin crawl. She and George whispered a few unpleasantries to each other, and after I got both kids safely buckled into their car seats, I told Conner that I needed to take a minute to go to the restroom.

I came back into the house and closed the bathroom door. I sobbed as I sat on the side of the bathtub, thinking about how awful and awkward I was feeling, and how terrible they both were, behaving this way on their granddaughter's big birthday. I decided that I would not give them the power to ruin this day for her. I would not let her know that things were awful. I would go to dinner and take her to get her very special bear with a big happy smile on my face because I love her so much and she deserves to have a fun birthday even if the adults in her life are acting like idiots.

I tried to collect myself and wiped my eyes as Conner came knocking on the bathroom door to tell me we had to leave (apparently I was taking too long). I opened the door, and he could tell I had been crying. He asked why.

"Seriously? Conner, today has been awful. You have no idea how horrible I have felt trying to navigate whatever bullshit is going on between your parents. It has been incredibly uncomfortable for me. And you weren't even here."

"Just ... come out soon, ok?" He pleaded. He hated being alone with his parents almost as much as I did.

When I got into the car, I decided I would ignore the two senior citizens with bad attitudes, and only talk to my kiddos and Conner. It was the only way I knew how to move forward with the evening. Of course, if one of them asked me a direct question,

I would reply, but it was difficult to even look in their direction.

The entire time we were at Build-A-Bear, Cora and George stood in the middle of the store, mostly silent and looking miserable with their arms folded. I was embarrassed to be in public with them. It was obvious to anyone nearby that they were in a massive argument.

Finally, the evening was over and his parents left to go back to their hotel. I had never been more relieved to get away from anyone in all my life. The next morning, his dad called to say that they were heading back to Columbus early.

Conner took that opportunity to tell his dad how uncomfortable their behavior the day before had made me. His dad's response really sealed the deal for me. "Well, Ashley made us feel very unwelcome. She didn't even talk to us or anything all night when we were at the mall or at dinner."

Gaslighting at its finest, right? Never mind that they had a huge argument, and I had to see a naked woman on a phone screen while my kids were steps away. Never mind that Cora drove off without telling anyone where she was going or when she would be returning. Never mind that they nearly ruined their granddaughter's fifth birthday.

Me. The daughter-in-law. I'm the reason they were leaving early. Good. Fucking. Riddance. I was now entering the era of IDGAF energy when it came to my in-laws. All of them. I was no longer going to give two shits about what they thought of me or wanted from me. They had such little regard for me, why should I continually set myself on fire to keep them warm and cozy? I remembered the promise I made to myself during the anguish of my bloody nipples. Time to refine my boundaries. I would no longer base my self-worth on what other people thought about me.

Conner wasn't completely unhelpful during the labor and delivery process with our firstborn. He *did* manage to do the bare minimum of holding one of my legs while I pushed our daughter into existence ... But most of my time laboring, he spent pacing the room or on his phone. It wasn't exactly the scenario of a beautiful partnership that I had imagined as we sat in child-birth classes together.

So when I found out that I was going to have a second baby, I immediately knew that I wanted to have someone in the delivery room with me who would be more helpful. I needed a doula. I found a fantastic doula-in-training through a friend at church, and she was the most supportive friend I could have had during my pregnancy. Conner objected at first, but when I told him it was free because she was still learning, he easily agreed.

On the day I went into labor with our son, I decided to wait as long as possible before going to the hospital. I felt that I might have gone to the hospital too early with Elianna, and so I wanted to be in the comfort of my own home for as much time as I could before round two. The sterile environment, fluorescent lights, and constant noise and disruption that are unavoidable in hospital rooms just added anxiety to the waiting between contractions.

But this time I waited almost too long, and as we drove through the night toward the hospital, my contractions were less than two minutes apart, and I was in terrible pain. Every bump in the road was a stab in my uterus, and every stoplight lasted an obscene amount of time. I rolled down my window on the passenger side and felt the cool April air on my face.

A car full of drunk college kids blasting "Fancy" by Iggy Azalea pulled up next to us, and a girl in the back seat rolled her window down, leaned out, looked me in the eyes, and said "Whoooooooo!" before they sped off. I pressed my back against the passenger seat, trying to alleviate some of the intense pressure I was feeling in my lower half, contemplating what a very different night we were having than the car full of party animals with no responsibilities.

When we finally arrived at the hospital, our doula, Joanna, texted that she was on her way. I waddled into the building to start the admission process. The nurse working admin that night asked me to sit and fill out paperwork, and I scribbled through it while Conner sat in the chair next to me. I felt like the baby was pushing his own way out, so I tossed the half-finished paperwork on the desk and announced, "This is my second baby, and he is coming NOW."

"Ok," replied the nurse. "I just need you to pee in this cup and then we will have a delivery room ready for you."

"No, you aren't listening to me," I said, this time with more force. "If I sit down on the toilet to pee in your cup, this baby will fall out of me and into the toilet."

Before I knew it, I was in the hospital bed begging for an epidural. The doctor was on his way, and Joanna had just arrived as I was nearly crawling up the wall in pain from the strongest contractions I have ever felt.

"I want to push now," I begged.

"We're waiting on the epidural and the doctor. Be patient with us and hang in there," the nurse said. I was certain the baby's head was crowning, but I didn't tell them that because I was afraid they wouldn't give me the epidural if they knew.

Joanna squeezed my hips with every contraction, trying to counter the pressure. It was sweet, briefly blissful, relief. At the height of my pain, she was right there with me, and I heard her say under her breath, "You've got to be kidding me." I looked at her, and she was staring at Conner, who was half asleep on the couch in the corner of the room, completely disengaged from the birth of his son.

Finally, I got the epidural, and Dr. Bentley arrived. "Look at you, ready to go!" he said, wasting no time getting all up in my business. "Let's do this!"

Seven quick pushes and 45 minutes after stepping through the hospital doors, I was watching Conner snap photos of our son with his iPhone for his Instagram announcement that Milo had arrived. A swirling cocktail of hormones surged through my body, and all I could think was, *I am in this game with a partner who makes me feel as though I am actually alone, and only wants to engage with the world on social media.*

I stuffed those thoughts deep down, slapped a smile on my face, and grabbed my emotional shovel, ready to dig deeper inside myself for the love and support I so longed for. *If I love everyone around me more fiercely, maybe I'll feel that love in return,* I thought. But that's not how it works here on planet Earth, and sometimes no matter how much effort you put into loving someone, it isn't enough.

After the required 24 hours in the hospital after our son was born, I insisted I was ready to go home, and since this was my second baby, Dr. Bentley agreed to sign me out. I hated the hospital rooms ... They never feel restful, and I missed my daughter.

Once my mom got the news that I was in labor, she drove down to Nashville from Columbus and was planning to stay a few days to help me adjust to life as a mom of two kids. When we arrived home, she and Elianna were playing. We had dinner and then my mom decided to take Elianna shopping at Target with her. They returned 90 minutes later, and my mom was visibly frustrated with Elianna.

"She had a full-on tantrum in the middle of the shoe aisle, and it was so embarrassing and unacceptable," she reported.

"What happened?" I asked from the couch, an hours-old baby attached to my breast.

Elianna was cranky, but it was past her bedtime, and this had been a huge couple of days for her. She just met her new baby brother, and she had been navigating a rotating cast of visitors and babysitters, including her grandma who seemed to be extremely upset with her.

Hearing the commotion, Conner came out of our bedroom and into the living room. "What's going on?" he huffed.

My mom rehashed her story and added more details about how other people were staring at her and said, "*My* kids never would have behaved that way. I never would have allowed it. She was totally disrespectful. You guys should discipline her more."

"Now, hold on a second, Deb. You're telling me your toddlers never cried and acted up in a store? We both know that they most certainly did. That's what kids do when they are tired or aren't getting their way," he pushed back.

"No, they *never* did. *I* didn't allow it. And honestly, I think Elianna's too spoiled and gets to call all the shots with you guys. She's going to be such a brat if you don't get it under control. Plus now you've got two of them ..." she groaned condescendingly.

"No way. Kids have meltdowns. There's nothing wrong with her other than she's got a lot of adjustments and new things happening today. That's a lot for anyone. Cut her a break." He wasn't wrong, and I had never seen him so passionate about sticking up for anyone or anything before.

Conner continued to push back, as I sat bewildered watching my mother and my husband face off. I wasn't sure what was happening, but I couldn't get involved. I was nursing my son and felt trapped there. Something about the scene unfolding before me took me back to when I was six years old again, seeing my mom and dad fight. It was that same feeling of helplessness that overwhelmed my entire being.

The next thing I knew, Conner was storming out of the house saying he was going to pick something up at the grocery store, and my mom was fuming. Elianna was playing in her room, and I had finally finished nursing. I laid Milo in his crib and went to get Elianna ready for bed. My head was throbbing as I revisited the argument I had just witnessed, and tried to make sense of it all. My mom came into Elianna's room.

"Ashley, I don't know how you guys are going to make this work," she said discouragingly.

"I'm not sure what you mean," I timidly replied. "We'll be fine. There's just a lot of change happening right now." I tried to remain neutral yet positive.

As I got Elianna situated and cozy in her bed, my mom left the room, and I said bedtime prayers with my daughter and sang her lullabies with tears streaming down my face. What a terrible first night home with our new baby. I was exhausted and it wasn't even over yet. I knew that when I stepped outside of the safety of my daughter's room, I would have to talk to my mom more about how embarrassing it was for her to be disrespected in the middle of the store by a two-year-old.

When I finally emerged, my mother was gone, and so was her stuff. I called Conner.

"Hey, so ... my mom isn't here anymore. I went to put Elianna to bed, and when I came out, she was gone. And she took her bags with her."

"What? Are you serious? I know we were having a disagreement but why would she just leave like that? Did she tell you she was leaving, or write a note or anything?" he asked.

"No, she's just gone," I repeated.

By 10:00 p.m., I still hadn't heard from my mom, so I called her to make sure she was ok, and see if she was coming back or not.

"No, I won't be staying somewhere that I don't feel welcome. Conner was so rude to me," she seethed through the phone.

"I can't believe you left me like that," was all I could say in response. We hung up the phone, and I sobbed until I didn't have any tears left in my body to cry.

Conner was apologetic for upsetting me but added, "I'm not sorry at all about how I defended my daughter. I will always, always defend my family."

I agreed with him and felt relieved to know that he was engaging with our family unit in a way that I hadn't seen in ages. I was, however, heartbroken at the way this incident had ended. It seemed to me that my mom was becoming more and more of a crazymaker in my life, and I was shocked that she had such a negative reaction to whatever happened in the Target shoe aisle that evening.

And, not for the first time, she had hopped in her car and abandoned me without saying goodbye. I knew at that moment that my relationship with my mom was shifting; she and I were on a ship that was slowly being swallowed up by the darkest ocean.

"Ouch! You're being too rough," I whined as my mom brushed out the tangles in my hair from my wild night of restless flips and flops in bed that produced the worst kinds of knots at the nape of my six-year-old neck.

"You have to hold still," she replied, slightly agitated.

I notoriously had monster tangles in my hair, and it was always an event to brush them out. But leaving the house with a stringy, tangled rat's nest was not acceptable. "You can't go around looking like no one loves you," my mom would say.

But the way she jerked the brush through my long mess of hair always felt like she was actually taking off my entire scalp. My head was so tender, and sitting still while I was in so much pain was almost impossible.

"You wanna look beautiful, don't you, Ash?" she asked me.

"Yes," I would moan through the pain.

"Well, this is the price of beauty, my dear. No pain, no gain!" she exclaimed as she knocked the brush harder into my skull and yanked it down my back. "If you want to look a certain way, you have to go through the process to make it happen."

I wanted to be beautiful like her, and so I pushed myself to sit as still as possible, my eyes filling with tears while she pulled and twisted and surrounded me in a thick cloud of hair spray. *Beauty is pain*, I thought.

chapter seven
A LIFETIME OF ADVENTURE

"You, of all people, deserve a happy ending."
— Sylvain Reynard

Six months into our marriage, we were living in Columbus, and I was invited to a girls' night with several old high school volleyball friends. My friend Katie hosted us. We had been friends since seventh grade, and we were bridesmaids in each other's weddings.

As I drove up to her house, I began to notice the stark differences between her cute suburban life and mine. We got married the same year, but her life appeared to be way more put together and grown up. She had a big, beautiful house in a gated suburban development. All her furniture was purchased new and color-coordinated. She had a fucking cheese board—I didn't even know that was a thing. Her flat-screen television was hanging on the wall, and there were no cords in sight dangling below it. She had a guest bedroom that was beautifully decorated and equipped for whoever might want to visit for a night or two.

Gosh, I don't have any of this stuff … I must be behind, I thought. I knew that material things don't bring happiness, but I was unaware until that moment that people my age could even own any of these things. And in my competitive nature, I suddenly felt as though Katie was beating me at adulting. I went home that night and shared with Conner how nice and put together Katie's house was. He listened intently to everything I was saying as we sat in our duplex rental with secondhand furniture and a box television that sat in an entertainment stand on the floor, cords knotted and exploding from behind it like fireworks.

"Look," he said after a long pause. "I know we don't own a house or any of those fancy things that Katie has filled hers with, and I can't promise you that we can have all those things right now or even anytime in the near future ... but what I can promise you is that we will have a lifetime of adventure together." He looked me in the eyes and held my hand.

"That's all I want," I replied. I knew we didn't need any of that stuff to make our love great, and his thoughtful response gave me hope that all my fears on our wedding night were simply post-wedding jitters. At that moment, I was so proud to be Conner's wife. I felt seen and heard. I felt validated and cared for. And I believed we were on our way to so many beautiful adventures.

When we moved to Nashville, our parents on all sides fought over where we would stay when we were back in Columbus for visits. Conner's parents wanted us to give each grandparent (three houses total) equal time on each visit so that everyone would get to see the baby and it would be "fair." But the idea of staying at three different houses for a six-day trip with young kids and all the equipment that has to come with you—pack-n-play, car seat, stroller, diaper bag, breast pumps, and so on ...

It seemed like a ton of work to pack it all up every two days just so that grandparents were getting equal time. I shared with my mom how stressed I was feeling with all the pressure from Conner's parents. "Conner doesn't even want to stay with his dad and Cora," I told her. "He gets really annoyed staying there even just for short dinner visits."

To be honest, Conner and I had been married for seven years at this point, and I still wasn't even comfortable enough in their home to help myself to a glass of water. The house was always so quiet and felt cold and gloomy, even on beautiful sunshiny days. I was relieved when Conner said we would never stay there, and I didn't have a clue how to handle the fact they were now suggesting that we do. My mom's bright idea was that we stay at a neutral house so that no grandparents were getting more time than another.

"You should stay with Alice and Matt," she said. "They have three kids, so they have toys and baby things that would save you from bringing your whole house every visit."

It wasn't a bad idea. We would never have to stay with grandparents, including my mom, whose third husband, Garth, was really rubbing me the wrong way. (How do you tell your mother that her husband is a creep?) Since it was her idea, I knew she was ok with it. And while I knew Conner's parents wouldn't love this news, once Alice graciously agreed to host us anytime we came to town, I told Conner it was his responsibility to break it to his pushy parents.

Our system worked out great for us and our kids, who adored their older cousins and the time they got to spend there playing with them. Leaving Alice's to go visit our parents so they could see their grandkids got increasingly harder because it was obvious that our kids enjoyed their cousins more than their grandparents. Occasionally we would allow the kids to stay the night with one of our parents, and I should've known that would be a mistake. Conner's dad would literally count the minutes that each grandparent got with the grandkids, and if my mom or Conner's mom got even 10 minutes more, he would have something to say about it.

On one visit in particular, Elianna was being extra clingy and was having a hard time leaving my side to let anyone else engage with her. Travel can be really hard on a toddler. While we were visiting my mom, she picked Elianna up to hold her, and Elianna screamed and cried and reached for me. As she passed Elianna to me, she said in a condescending and irritated tone, "She treats me like I'm some kind of monster. She doesn't recognize me so she screams and cries, and she only wants you."

I felt my heart sink deep into my chest at that moment, feeling as though I had let my mom down somehow because my little girl was overtired, overstimulated, and over being passed around from person to person. I spent at least an hour every night during our visits just holding her while she cried because she was too overwhelmed to lie down and go to sleep. I would rock her and sing to her while Conner and my cousins hung out one floor above me laughing and drinking.

The next day, we'd have to be up doing it all again to visit someone else who was counting the minutes we spent with them versus the minutes we spent somewhere else. It was exhausting trying to jump through all the grandparent hoops being thrown at me, but I wanted our kids to have a good relationship with their grandparents, so I did everything I could to give equal time to everyone.

Conner began slowly checking out of the communication with his parents about our visits. They knew that I was the one in charge of the schedule, so as soon as Conner would even mention the possibility of us coming to visit, they would text me asking for details and days, telling me how they believed it would be best to spend our time.

I loathed being in this position. When I had to say no, I would get relentless pushback and then if they didn't let up, I was soon begging Conner to step in and communicate the plan. I was usually exhausted from planning the trip before we had even left Nashville, and trips to Ohio continued to be a major source of stress and anxiety for me from each side of our families. I was beginning to hate our visits there.

After our daughter was born, there were adventures, but they weren't the dreamy kind I had pictured when Conner made me that romantic promise of a lifetime of adventure in the early years of our relationship. Somewhere along our journey as husband and wife, I had taken on the role of "submissive wife" in a very toxic way. It was my own misinterpretation and religious upbringing that led me to believe that a "good Christian wife" was one who fully gave up herself to serve and support her husband.

It was such a distorted perspective of love: fully abandon every hope and desire you have because you no longer matter, and make it your life's calling to be a "help-mate" to your husband. No one ever came out and said this verbatim to me, but the underlying vibe of my upbringing confirmed this belief within me. If the Bible was a roadmap for a life worthy of heaven, then it was also the authority on my marriage and how I should fall in line and be a good little woman.

Especially since becoming a mother—a stay-at-home mother—I felt I owed him every part of me. Always giving him my attention or affection, he had me at his full disposal any time he wanted or needed me. At one point I even joked in response to his demands, impersonating an Igor character made famous as an assistant to the mad scientist in classic horror movies. Dragging one leg behind me and squinting one eye, I slurred, "Yesssssssssh, Masssssthhhher" when he called for me. Conner laughed, but I wasn't joking. I actually felt like his assistant most days.

He would come home from a guys' poker night and share with me that all the husbands there were discussing how often they had sex with their wives. The average answer was once or twice a week. I did not want to hear how frequently our church friends were getting it on.

"When the women have a ladies' night, do you guys talk about this stuff?" he asked.

"No, we never really discuss sex," I quietly mumbled, turning my head away. These conversations always made me so uncomfortable because I knew that every time I saw my friends and their husbands, I would think to myself, *They only do it once a week. She's so lucky.*

"Well, don't ever talk about me to your girlfriends," he said. "We should keep the intimate details of our life to ourselves."

At that time, Conner and I were having sex four or five nights a week because I never said no, even though I wanted to. I had learned my lesson about saying no to him, and it was easier to give him what he wanted than it was to argue about it for 45 minutes and then still have to give it up. I gave in to this dysfunctional sex-life hack after a colossal argument one evening following an expensive date night.

Conner always enjoyed eating at the trendy and expensive restaurants in town. I enjoyed the food, but I always knew we were going to drop more than $150 on dinner alone whenever we went out, and the reality was we didn't have that kind of cash to be tossing around so frivolously. But he wanted to try the new cool spots and snap pics of his food for Instagram, or a shot of me with a caption like, "Date night with the wife." Most of the date was him talking at me about his work issues and asking my thoughts on how to navigate certain problems he was having with coworkers or clients. We would usually stay out until 10:30 or 11:00 p.m. and then make our way back home to relieve the babysitter.

I was friends with most of our babysitters, so when we returned, we usually chatted for a bit before they left our house. Avery was our babysitter that night. Our kids loved it when Avery came to play with them. Elianna thought that Avery was so cool that we named a messy bun after her. In the mornings before school, I'd ask, "Elianna, how do you wanna wear your hair today?" With all the excitement she could muster, Elianna would reply, "Give me an Avery bun!" Avery is a total diamond.

Avery didn't have a car, so I would usually take her home after Conner and I returned from date nights. She lived close by, and it was easy to drop her off. I also really enjoyed the eight minutes of solitude I had in the car driving back home. I took a moment to make a payment to her on Venmo; it was now 11:45 p.m. I would have to rise with the kids the next morning by 6:00 a.m., and I was doing the math in my head. *If I get home, wash my face, and get their school clothes ready for tomorrow, I can still get to bed before 12:30 a.m., and I'll be able to score about five and a half hours of sleep,* I reasoned as I pulled into our driveway.

I dragged my tired body into the house and made my way through the kitchen to hang up the car keys. Conner was laying on the couch watching *Bar Rescue*. I walked past him as he sat up and stared at me. He followed me into the bedroom, where I was changing out of my clothes and looking for my favorite comfy pants. I brushed my teeth and washed my face, and headed toward the bed. I was exhausted. He walked into the room and said, "Ok, so you're just going to bed now?"

"Yeah," I said sleepily. "It's late, and I have to get up early with the kids tomorrow."

"Well, that is so selfish," he snapped.

"Excuse me?" I said.

"Do you know how many women would *kill* to have a husband like me, to take them out to fancy dinners and dates? And you won't even give me sex now? You know that I'm stressed out and that sex helps me clear my head," he pushed back.

We talked in circles for 45 minutes, me explaining why I didn't want to give it up and him on the constant loop about my selfishness. Then I noticed the time. It was now one o'clock in the morning, and he was not relenting. I knew if I wanted this conversation to end, I was going to have to give him what he wanted. Suddenly, I heard myself apologizing to him, "You're right, I'm sorry. Let's go ahead and do it."

Tired and empty, I took my clothes off and lay beneath him while he did his thing. I never understood why people called having sex "making love." Being intimate with him never felt like that to me.

"You're not acting like you're enjoying this," he said between heavy breaths and thrusts.

I wasn't enjoying it. I wanted to be in bed asleep instead of being violated in the middle of the night. But I knew better at this point than to say anything more. I felt myself slip deeper into my body, falling into the blackness of myself while outwardly I managed a few flat moans and grunts. I felt nothing, just numbness as I counted the minutes until I could finally get him off of me and go to sleep.

I thought of the scenes in *Game of Thrones* when Emilia Clarke's character Daenerys Targaryen was given to Jason Momoa's character Khal Drogo to be his wife, and how he would force himself on her, knowing that she didn't want to be with him. The shot would often go straight to Daenerys' face as Drogo was raping her, and you could see the darkness in her eyes as she would fall away from the present moment and into herself to escape her traumatic reality.

I recognized that look in her eyes as the look I saw in my own eyes after Conner had finished, and I was in the bathroom cleaning up. I caught a glimpse of my reflection in the mirror and thought, *You look absolutely miserable*, before climbing into bed next to an already asleep and snoring man who had gotten exactly what he wanted.

For years I kept a prayer journal. I would write in it almost daily, asking God's blessing on my marriage and begging Him to help Conner find more freelance work. "Make me a better wife to this man. Help me to be there for him and to support him in every way. Bless the work that he is doing and help him to have favor with his clients. Help his work go smoothly and ease his stress …"

Rereading these journal entries now makes my stomach queasy. I can feel the sadness in each of them as I pleaded with God. Sometimes, I could only write the words, "Please help," over and over again. These desperate prayers were showing up more frequently now.

"It only takes one phone call to change the entire trajectory of your business," I would encourage Conner when he began to stress out about the lack of jobs coming his way. Inevitably, he would arrive at the realization that a family living the freelance lifestyle usually experienced the "feast or famine" of living paycheck to paycheck, and to add insult to injury, often his clients were late making payments. When things would get really bad, he would sit me down to explain to me how all our financial problems were my fault.

Over dinner one evening, he yet again brought it up. "If you would get a job, we would have more steady money. Even something part-time would help us out a lot."

"Ok," I said hesitantly. We had been down this road before. I had done the math. If I got a part-time job somewhere, we would need to hire a babysitter, and that would cost at least $15 an hour to cover our two kids. So to make it worth paying someone to watch the kids, I would need to make at least double what the babysitter was making, and part-time jobs at the time did not usually pay employees $30 an hour. You may be wondering why on earth I would even need a babysitter. You're probably thinking, "Why can't Conner tag team with you and watch the kids while you're working?"

That is a very valid question. He often worked from home, and his schedule was extremely flexible, but he couldn't be bothered with taking care of his own children. Usually, the pattern looked like this: He would realize we were running out of money, and he would blame me for the fact that we didn't have any money. I would apply to jobs and have second or third interviews, and then when he would realize that my having a part-time job would mean that I would be away from home most evenings and weekends which would require him to do dinner and bedtime with our kids. He would then say, "Oh, I really don't want you to have to work, Ash. Don't take that job; I will figure it out."

And "figuring it out" usually meant he was making a phone call to his mom to ask her if he could borrow some money. She would bail us out, and then the pattern would reset the next month when funds would inevitably dry up again. We might've been broke but we always looked like we had money. He upgraded his iPhone every time they announced a new release, he wore expensive raw denim, and packages of sneakers or clothes for him were delivered to our house almost weekly. "I need to look good on these shoots, Ashley," he would explain. "The client is a fashion brand. I can't show up in uncool clothing."

But somehow, I was the reason that we didn't have enough money.

I could never leave him alone with the kids for more than an hour or two—even on the weekends. When I would be invited to go out with friends, it always felt like I had to ask his permission to go, and this particular night was no different.

"Conner, Teagan has invited me out to dinner and drinks with a few friends on Friday night. Are you cool to stay here with the kids for a few hours so I can go?" I asked timidly.

"How late will you be out, and can you make us dinner before you leave?" was his typical first reaction. He wasn't directly saying "No," but he was letting me know that he couldn't—or didn't want to—handle any of the major responsibilities with our children.

"Yes, I plan to make dinner for you and the kids before I leave, and everyone's meeting at 7, so I'll probably be home by 10:00 or 10:30 p.m. at the latest. All you'll need to do is get the kids in bed by 8:00 or 8:30," I explained, trying to make this as easy on him as possible.

I made dinner, got the kids to the table, kissed everyone goodbye, and left as they were eating. "Please don't destroy the house, and clean up after dinner for me!" I said as I swiped up my purse and keys, rushed out the door before anyone else could ask me for anything, and hopped in the driver's seat, letting out a huge sigh of relief to be out of the house.

When I returned home at 10:30 p.m., I could hear the sounds of kids' TV shows blasting from our television and noticed the kids and Conner's plates still on the table, the food hardened and extra sticky. Conner, who was sitting at the end of the table on his computer, didn't look up from his favorite pastime of either scrolling Facebook or browsing for new sneakers. Our children, still very much awake, were sitting on our cushionless couch with two bowls of Goldfish crackers, surrounded by every toy we owned. It looked like an actual tornado had dumped all their shit out in the living room.

"Hey guys, aren't you so sleepy?" I said in my nicest passive-aggressive tone, trying to indicate to Conner that they were not supposed to be awake at 10:30 at night. Milo reached up for me, and I took him to his bedroom where I spent 20 minutes rocking and singing to him so he would know that it was now time to go to bed. Once he was asleep, I quietly left his room and then help-ed Elianna get to bed. Another 15 minutes had passed before I finally stepped out of Elianna's room at 11:00 p.m., and was then greeted with the mess of toys scattered about and dirty dishes still left on the table.

I took a very long, deep breath and reached for the plates. "So, I thought you'd have them in bed ..." I started with the most important of the trinity of unhelpfulness that he piled on me and planned to address the rest later.

"Yeah, they weren't tired, and then they just wanted you. They aren't used to me doing bedtime with them, so I gave them a snack and put on the TV so they could wait for you."

OH. MY. GOD. ARE. YOU. FUCKING. SERIOUS?!?! I screamed inside my mind as I scraped hours-old food off plates and rinsed them for the dishwasher. Another deep breath. "Ok, well it's just that they're still really little, and being up late like that will mess with our whole schedule tomorrow, and they're probably going to be extra tired and cranky."

"I don't know what you want me to say, Ash. Sorry. They didn't want me; they wanted *you*. And I had work to do, so I let them chill. I don't see the harm in that." He was still sitting at his computer, and it didn't look like work on his computer screen, unless "work" involved watching Alex Jones conspiracy theory video rants.

"Can you at least come and help me pick up all these toys?" I said. "It's really not fun to get home after 10:00 p.m. and see this giant mess AND still have to put our kids to bed."

He slowly and reluctantly got up and started putting toys in the toy basket. I couldn't even look at him, I was so frustrated and disappointed.

"Hey … when we finish this, you gonna reward me for letting you go out tonight?" he asked.

"You think you deserve a reward for *this*?" I countered. "I'm so tired and every time I go out for even an hour, when I return, the house is completely destroyed, and it appears as if you did nothing but sit at your computer while the kids ran amuck through the house. Then I end up with extra work to do." This was the first time I was saying a firm "no" to his sexual advances.

"Wow, real cool, Ashley. I'm doing the best I can here. I am super stressed out with work and you knew that and left me here with the kids."

"Yeah, I thought you'd be able to manage your own children for a couple of hours, but I guess I was wrong." I stood up and carried the toy basket to the next room and started getting ready for bed, where I would lay fuming until he came to bed two and a half hours later. He tried to talk to me, and I pretended to be sound asleep so that I didn't have to rehash the previous events or get guilt-tripped into giving him sex.

Similar situations continued to happen any time I would

make plans to be away, and I began to understand that the price I was paying to go out with my friends was not worth the amount of work and disappointment I would come home to after being gone. I pointed out my frustration with him one afternoon over coffee.

He looked me straight in the eyes and said, "Well, you just need to know that you can't really count on me to be with our kids if you have to be somewhere else."

I was appalled. I couldn't imagine ever saying this to him. About *our children*. He was gone all the time, traveling for work or out at meetings. Why was he so disengaged from our family and unwilling to pitch in and help more?

"Let me repeat what you just told me. As the father of our kids, I can't count on you to step up and be a responsible parent. Do you realize what you're saying right now?" I asked, shocked at his nonchalance.

"Yeah, I'm telling you that I am too busy with work—trying to *feed* and *clothe* our family—and that if you want to go out for a fun hang with your friends, you're going to have to find a way to do that without depending on me."

At this point in the conversation, I shut down emotionally. He was still talking, but I couldn't even hear what he was saying. Lost in my own thoughts, I felt a heavy sadness that my husband, the father of my children, couldn't be depended on to help out with our kids. Didn't *want* to help out with our kids. I was at a loss for words.

Never was the dysfunction in our relationship so obvious as when Conner would become uber paranoid that I was cheating on him. It was in these all too frequent moments that I learned how to navigate uncomfortable situations and diffuse his obsessive thoughts on the subject. Sometimes the accusations would become so outlandish that I would feel compelled to write them down in a secret note on my phone. Like ... for proof. I couldn't believe he was saying such awful things to me.

"If you ever cheated on me it would be completely over between us," he would threaten.

"Ok, well good thing I'm not a cheater and that won't ever happen," I would reply, hoping that would be enough to end the conversation.

"No, Ash, I mean it," he would add. "I mean ... The only way I would be ok with you cheating on me would be if you cheated on me with a girl. It would still be over between us, but I would be ok with it if you gave me a parting gift of a threesome with you and your lesbian lover." He would then smile wryly.

In complete shock, I would ask, "Are you serious?"

"It's every guy's fantasy," he would say, attempting to excuse his perspective as if it were the same as telling his wife that every man picks their nose. "And also, you should know that if you ever do leave me for someone else, I will absolutely be going and having sex with as many women as possible, since I never got to sow my wild oats in my 20s."

This conversation happened at least five times during our marriage. The last time I found myself hearing him say that he would be entitled to a sexual parting gift with me and my unnamed nonexistent lesbian lover, I finally got fed up enough to say, "Conner, if I EVER cheat on you, I can promise you that it will be because I want nothing to do with you, and so you will NEVER receive a threesome as a parting gift from me."

Another time that he accused me of cheating in the most over-the-top way was when he burst into our son's bedroom while I was nursing him one October evening in 2014, our six-month-old baby attached to my breast, and me sitting in an old mustard yellow rocking chair in the dim light. Conner's frustration raged as he towered over me. "I know you are having an affair," he said.

"Do you even know who I am?" I retorted. "I'm not capable of that. Now, or ever."

"Something is off, and I know you are cheating on me," he added.

"Well, I'm not. With what time do you think I would be able to manage any other relationship? You are always here working. I am always here with our kids. I am sitting in this chair nursing our son. How on earth do you even think I have the time to be unfaithful?" It was late, I was tired, and these accusations were totally bogus.

I pushed back more, asking him what he saw as an indicator of possible infidelity. He couldn't even name one thing, just kept repeating how things felt "off" with us.

"Ever considered that things are off because I am now a mom of two, one of whom is still nursing and the other who isn't even three years old yet," I said, attempting to bring him back down to reality. It was exhausting always having to jump through hoops to keep him grounded and justify my existence, but I was willing to do it because, at that time, codependency was my toxic trait.

We talked in circles for what felt like an hour, and then he eventually left the room, and I was alone with my baby in the dark. I continued to hold Milo, even though he had stopped nursing, while I sobbed quietly. I felt so hurt that my husband didn't know me well enough to know that cheating wasn't something I would ever consider. I had watched my parents cheat on each other all throughout my childhood, and I knew how it affected me as a child.

I made a vow to myself that loyalty to my husband was going

to be the number one priority in my own marriage. But it didn't matter. Conner didn't trust me. He said because my parents cheated so much, it made me all the more likely to follow in their footsteps. *Maybe he's right,* I thought. *I'll need to be even more deliberate about my resolve to be a good wife so that I can prove him wrong.*

Each time he would spout off an accusation of infidelity my way, I was compelled to develop new ways to avoid any and all contact with men so as not to put myself in any compromising situations. I stopped making eye contact with my friends' husbands and avoided looking in the direction of the shirtless guys jogging down the street. Everyone was fair game and could become a topic of discussion between the two of us any time Conner felt threatened.

"Do you like that guy? I saw you looking at him. Do you like him? You like the way he looks?" he would press. "I definitely don't look like that with my shirt off. Would you be more attracted to me if I looked like that?"

"I didn't notice any guy, who are you referring to?" I would say flatly. I learned that the less emotion or reaction I would give him, the less intense the argument. If I saw anyone who looked like a man running down the street in the distance, I would turn my whole body so that I was not facing their direction at all. I would either look directly at Conner or at our kids in the back seat, offering them a snack or a drink from their water bottles. It was so much easier to look away than it was to have to explain repeatedly that I was not looking lustfully at another man.

I was starting to gather all this information about our relationship and my husband's insecurities, and I began to create a set of unspoken rules that I had to follow in order to avoid conflict and make him feel a sense of safety and security in our relationship. I wasn't walking on eggshells, I was walking across a tightrope of wet toilet paper. I learned how to behave and followed these rules as closely as possible, and when I could execute the rules perfectly, he was nicer, and it was easier for me to manage his emotions. Messed up, right?

At the time, I thought that I was solving the problem, but all I was doing was deeply enabling his insecurities, control, manipulation, and sense of entitlement. But all I could think about was the advice of my mom from my college years, "If you don't take care of your man, someone else will." I was doing the very best I knew at that moment in time. I had no idea how my actions and desire to avoid conflict were the direct cause of my misery.

Somewhere in this messy world from miscarriage to motherhood to my totally fucked up marriage, I decided to find my purpose in the one space where I knew there was a gaping hole in my heart. Because words of encouragement are my strongest love language, I was inspired to begin writing tiny pep talks on post-it notes (this was before I took this idea to my place of work) and putting them on my bathroom mirror to help me get through the day.

I was able to translate every sad thought I had into a contrasting positive affirmation, and every time I saw the note, I was reminded that true hope and love exist within me.

One night at a women's Bible study, I shared with our group that I had been doing this, and everyone got so excited about it and wanted to join me. The enthusiasm from my friends helped me to be more intentional about what I was already doing, and my friend Raina said the idea reminded her of this quote from Mother Teresa: "Spread love everywhere you go. Let no one ever come to you without leaving happier."

Something about the words "love everywhere" really connected with me as exactly what I was trying to do: put kindness out in the world everywhere I could so that other people would be encouraged and see love where they didn't before. I decided to officially call this project Love Everywhere, and my friends joined forces with me for a weekend service project to share the love, passing out bumper-sticker-style encouragements on cards that I had designed to make it easy for us to share a little kindness in our community.

That day, we scattered kind notes all over our neighborhood. We left them on car windshields, in the greeting card section at Target, and tucked away in the self-help books on the shelves of the public library. It was the most fun and inspiring thing I had ever been a part of, and then the unexpected happened.

These postcards also had a website address to a blog where a few of us were writing posts about our experiences and how we were finding hope in darkness. People began sending us messages through our blog, explaining how discovering one of our cards had transformed their entire day. I was hooked. I knew I had to keep this project going. It was the bright spot I had been longing for, and it made me feel good to remind others of their inner sparkle.

Not long after moving to Nashville as a new mother, Love Everywhere lost momentum. All my friends who were doing it with me back in Ohio were having babies, too, and the distance made it almost impossible to keep it alive. By the time Milo was born, I was finding myself with that old feeling of lacking purpose once again—this time coupled with postpartum depression. I didn't know I was depressed; I just assumed that was how everyone felt. I was lost, trying to stay afloat in a sticky sea of peanut butter crackers and orange juice, and I could not see the shore.

I still don't know if it was simply to shut me up so he could talk about his own issues again or if he actually had a sincere moment of thoughtfulness toward me, but as I shared how I was feeling one evening over dinner, Conner looked at me in a rare moment of generosity and said, "Why don't you start up your Love Everywhere thing again? That should give you a creative outlet while you're home just being a mom, and you should make an Instagram for it so that you can document what you're doing."

Wow, that's actually not a bad suggestion, I thought. Plus, the fact that he suggested it made me feel like the project had his blessing and would be ok for me to put energy into. He even helped me create the website and logo design.

A few months into having an Instagram account, Love Everywhere had gathered a couple of thousand followers, and I was feeling so good about the fact that I was able to share so much kindness in the world. People were even reaching out and asking if they could join me and share a little love in their own cities.

Before I knew it, I had given away 5,000 Love Everywhere cards. I never asked any of these people to pay even so much as shipping because, to me, this work felt like a calling—almost like my ministry. And I couldn't bring myself to ask people to pay for kindness. But after mailing 5,000 cards, Conner came to me and said, "I think this project is cool, but you can't keep sending people cards for free. You need to consider selling them."

I was uncomfortable with the idea of asking people to pay me for a few stacks of cardstock but eventually landed on the idea that I could use my experience in the world of fashion design to create my own merchandise and sell the products, not the cards. Every purchase would then receive a free gift of a pack of Love Everywhere cards so that others could join the cause and support what I was doing, and I could keep kindness free.

I launched my store with one pre-order item to help fund the production because I had almost no money to start a business and build inventory. Thankfully, I had lots of well-connected friends, so several of them with larger followings on social media generously agreed to share my project, and soon I had over 50 orders for my first item. I was elated and felt so proud of this new community I was building.

It felt so good to be validated in work that meant so much to me. Things felt as though they were turning around. Maybe I was finally on the right path, and maybe all this positivity and good karma would start to trickle into my marriage that was so broken. Maybe I was finally standing on solid ground and the sun would shine on my face again.

chapter eight

BLOOD IS THICKER THAN WATER

"Blood is thicker than water but you can drown in both."
— **Colin Swan**

Baby experts everywhere will tell you that when you have a newborn you should sleep when they sleep. So, as a new mom of two, I tried my best to take that advice the first few days of being home with our son. My daughter was just over two years old, and we were working on potty training with her. In retrospect, it wasn't the best idea to potty train while also navigating a new baby at home, but these are simply the delirious choices we make sometimes.

I had just finished nursing Milo, who was finally asleep. I knew I would have at least an hour to get some much-needed rest, so I asked Conner (who was supposed to be taking a week off work to help me adjust to our new situation) to spend time with our daughter while I went to get a little sleep. He agreed, so I went to our bedroom and drifted off. Forty-five minutes later, I awoke and, after laying in the bed for about five more minutes, I decided that it was a better idea to get up so that I could relieve Conner.

When I emerged from the bedroom, I was shocked at what

I saw. Conner was sitting at the dining room table on his computer, the movie *Gremlins* was playing loudly on the television, and our daughter was hiding behind the couch in a corner with a massive poop in her underwear, playing with her Barbies. I didn't know what to be more upset about: the fact that a scary movie was on the TV, or the fact that our daughter had a massive torpedo of shit poking straight out like a dog tail from her ass.

"Conner, what the heck are you doing right now?" I asked, annoyed.

"I'm doing some research for my next shoot," he replied, unbothered.

"Ok but you're not supposed to be working right now, you're supposed to be watching Elianna," I said.

"She's fine. I put a movie on for her, and she's playing over there," he said without looking up from his screen.

"Ummm, no, she is NOT fine," I snapped back. "She's got a giant turd in her undies, and you're playing a scary movie," I reached for the remote and turned on *Yo Gabba Gabba*.

"That movie is not scary, and I didn't know that she had pooped," he said.

"Seriously? *GREMLINS* is not acceptable for a two-year-old, Conner. And you should be paying more attention to her, especially because we are potty training," I tried to reason with him.

"It's not that big of a deal."

"Yes, it is," I groaned as I helped Elianna get into clean underwear.

"Sorry, Ashley, I actually have to work and provide for these two kids now, and if I don't work, I don't get paid. That's how freelance works. I can't believe that you don't get that," he said condescendingly.

"I asked you for *an hour*. So I could sleep while our son was sleeping. Do you think that my request was asking too much from you?" I could feel my blood boiling, and I could hear Milo starting to wake up on the baby monitor. He had nothing left to say as I hurried to go retrieve Milo from his crib.

This was the first time that Conner showed one of our kids a scary movie that was inappropriate for their age, but it wasn't the last. Three years later, he decided to introduce our kids to the *Cult of Chucky* movie trailer. While I was getting both kids ready for bed, he called for Milo, "Hey buddy, come in here! I want to show you something."

Milo went running to his dad without hesitation because occasionally Conner would show him something about *Star Wars* when he called for him in this same way.

As I was brushing Elianna's hair, I could hear Milo starting to express that he didn't like whatever Conner was showing him on his computer. I could hear Conner saying, "It's not real, buddy. It's just a doll. None of this is real."

But Milo had seen enough and came running into the bathroom to find me. Conner got up and followed after him. As soon as Milo saw his dad, he started screaming and crying and tried to squeeze his tiny body behind the toilet of our very small bathroom.

"What is happening right now? Why is he acting so scared?" I asked.

"Oh, well, I was just showing him the new *Chucky* trailer," he replied. "Milo, it's not real," he repeated.

"You did WHAT?" I asked as I reached for Milo and tried to console him.

"It's not a big deal, he likes *Star Wars,* and this is just like that," he said, excusing his behavior.

"Clearly it's not the same if he's so afraid of it right now and crying," I said. "I'm taking him to bed. Ellie, you can go into your room, and I will be there as soon as I get Milo settled. Ok, sweet girl?" I was trying to not make a big deal of it in front of our kids, but Milo's total terror was obvious to all of us.

That movie was just entering theaters, and the posters were on billboards all over town. Even if we were going to the movie theater for a kids' movie, Milo would see the poster and cling to me, burying his head in my chest so that he didn't have to look at Chucky. He developed a sudden fear of the dark and would often tell me that he had scary dreams about Chucky. He couldn't even say his name; he only could say, "that bad kid."

I was furious with Conner, but he made every excuse for why it was ok and how it wasn't his fault. He was my husband, and the father of my children ... I wanted to respect him and let him be the leader of our family, but it felt like the direction he was headed was going to take us all completely off the path into the darkest scary woods.

After I finally got both kids to sleep, I tried to explain (once again) why Chucky is not appropriate for a three-year-old. Conner wasn't getting the message, and he offered an insincere, "Ok, sorry. I'll stop talking about Chucky." But the damage was already done.

I was realizing more and more that we were not the parenting team that I had envisioned we would be.

Late August in Nashville feels oppressive. The heat and humidity are like a hot, wet towel that slaps you in the face when you open the door to go outside. Conner's dad and stepmom were in town for another visit, and Conner was out of town on a shoot for work. I was taking advantage of having the extra help with the kids and decided to go to the YMCA to work out completely and totally alone while the kids stayed at the house with their grandparents. It was going to be glorious.

As I pulled into the parking lot, my phone rang. It was my cousin, Birdie, and her tone was more serious than I have ever heard her before. "Hey, Ash. I need to talk to you about something; do you have time now?" she asked.

"Yeah, what's up?" I said, concerned.

"Well, I need to tell you this, and I want you to hear it from me before you hear it from anyone else." She paused to collect herself. I was breathless, listening. She continued, "Bridget has pushed and pushed me, and everyone wants answers about why I still don't come to family stuff. And it's because of Arthur."

This conversation with Birdie requires some context. Birdie had been calling our grandfather by his first name (Arthur) for a while. After Nanny died, Arthur almost immediately married Nanny's cousin Marina, and when he did that the entire family split. Marina had been living with them while Nanny was sick and was helping Arthur and my mom take care of her during her final days.

When they suddenly announced that they were in love just three weeks after Nanny had passed, the tension was as thick as the Tennessee air in August. No one liked how they jumped right into being married. It felt really weird to me, and it did to Birdie and Alice, too. So much so that Birdie stopped coming to family gatherings if Arthur and Marina were going to be there.

No one questioned Birdie at the time because everyone just assumed that she had such a hatred for Marina that she couldn't bear to be around her. Then, like Nanny, Marina became terminally ill just a couple of years after they had married, and soon passed away. Nanny's lifelong best friend, Bridget, had recently become a widow. I bet you can guess what happened next.

When Bridget heard that Marina was sick, she came to help Arthur care for his second dying wife. Arthur, who was never good at being alone, immediately fell in love with Bridget, and as soon as Marina was six feet deep, Arthur married his first wife Connie's best friend. Bridget was appalled at the state of our family and the fact that Birdie refused to come to any family gatherings, even now that Marina was dead.

"Connie would not want this for her family," Bridget would say, and she made it her mission to fix it. She pushed and prodded and pressured Uncle Rhett to get answers, and after several weeks, Birdie had to finally speak up, which brings me back to this phone call.

There I sat in my parked car on the phone with Birdie as she shared her story, her voice strong, but tearful. "When I was eight years old, I stayed the night with Nanny and Arthur. They had me sleep in the bed with them. Nanny was on one side and Arthur on the other. I woke up to him touching me—sexually—and then he told me not to tell anyone, that it had to be our secret.

"I have been in therapy for the last 10 years over this. I don't want to address this with Arthur, but I also don't want to be forced to see him anymore. When Nanny died, that was my opportunity to step away, and I do not plan to ever see him again." She went on to detail more of the experience, but as I was hearing her talk, my whole body began to shake.

Four years before this phone call with Birdie, as I was buckling my daughter into her car seat, I had a very strange feeling and memory of darkness and the sound of a belt buckle jingling. I remember thinking, *Was I sexually abused by my grand-father? No way. I must be dealing with some weird postpartum mental health thing or something. I can definitely never tell any-one about this, and I need to just stop thinking about it because everyone will think I am nuts.*

I convinced myself that I was crazy for thinking this and put these thoughts into a lockbox in my brain and did not dare to reopen the box. But this phone call with Birdie took a sledge-hammer to the lockbox and suddenly a flood of memories came pouring into my awareness. I sat there holding the phone, completely breathless, in total panic.

"Ashley, I think that this happened to you, too, because you guys lived with them when you were around that same age as when it happened to me." Birdie's voice sounded like she was underwater. She pulled me back to the conversation. "Do you have any memories of anything?" she asked, gently.

"Oh my God. I do, but they're all kind of dark and fuzzy," I stuttered. Then I told her about the strange flashback I had while buckling Elianna into her car seat all those years ago. I was spinning out. "I think I need to talk to my mom about this," I said. "Does she know?"

"I have only told my mom and dad so far," she said.

"Okay. Thanks for telling me. And I'm so sorry," I replied.

I sat completely paralyzed in my car, unable to move, unable to drive, unable to breathe. Thoughts raced through my mind. Mentally, I was standing in a giant office space full of filing cabinets of my memories, and I was sifting through folders and files full of every moment in my childhood, trying to see if I could get more clarity.

What actually happened to me? I kept asking myself.

After some time spent processing my conversation with Birdie, I called my mom. My hands were trembling, and I felt my vocal cords tighten. She answered. "Hey," I said quietly. "I have to talk to you ..." and I went on to explain what Birdie had shared with me. "Mom, I believe Birdie, and I have my own memories that feel kind of confusing and foggy that I'm trying to make sense of."

Before I could even complete my last sentence, my mom

began screaming at me. "This is unbelievable. My dad would NEVER. He needs to have the right to say, 'No, I did not do this.' You have no proof other than a CHILD'S memory. You are thinking of no one but yourself.

"I am the only one who is there for him." She had barely taken a breath. "I have no support. His kidneys are failing, he's going to die. Why don't you and Birdie take a lie detector test, and we will see what's true. You're making all this up because your dad was a piece of shit, and you have a crush on your grandpa."

"Oh my God, are you fucking serious? I came to you because I have questions, and I wanted your support as my mom. I cannot in my entire being imagine saying the things you just said to me to my own daughter if she ever came to me about an issue like this. I don't want to talk to you unless you are willing to be more supportive," I said through my tears as I hung up the phone.

I collapsed onto the floor sobbing. My whole body felt cold and numb, and I kept hearing her screaming at me in my head. I couldn't believe that she responded the way she did. I was truly shocked and heartbroken.

Later that night, I was planning to hang out with my friend Teagan. She graciously listened as I shared and cried, and then she said something that I didn't know would change my life. "Ashley, I am so sorry that all this is happening. It sounds like you need a professional to help you figure all of this out. I'm texting you my therapist's phone number. Please reach out to her and consider setting up an appointment. I love you."

The next morning I texted the therapist, and soon I was on a phone call with her to discuss what I was interested in working on in therapy. Conner said that we couldn't afford therapy, and I told him I couldn't afford to not be in therapy at this point. While we couldn't afford a weekly therapy session, I was meeting Valerie once every two weeks to work through everything that happened.

We tried everything from talk therapy to EMDR to inner child work. The inner child work was the most painful for me. I could not connect to this little girl version of myself. I told Valerie the story of how my grandfather had stomped on baby Sarah, and how I felt that was the moment I unplugged from my inner child. She asked me what I saw in my mind when I thought of my inner child.

"I see a little girl with tangled hair and dirt on her face, wearing a striped and tattered dress and no shoes. She's got a small suitcase and a floppy teddy bear in her arms. She is a foster child that someone dropped off on my doorstep, and I do not know what to do with her or what to say, because I didn't even want to be a foster mom," I replied.

Valerie didn't say anything for a moment. After what felt like an eternity, she said, "That's incredibly sad, and I'm so sorry that you see yourself that way. We will work on getting you the tools you need to start bringing that little girl into conversation with you. I think you'll find that she is going to help you so much in your healing journey."

One Saturday after lunch, I decided to put a movie on for the kids to watch while I did some cleaning. Elianna chose a Disney movie called *Tangled*. We had never watched it before, but I knew that it would keep them entertained and buy me some time. I found myself listening to the story and the songs from the other room, and then it hit me like a punch to the gut. If you haven't seen the movie (highly recommend), the basic story goes like this:

When Rapunzel's mother was pregnant with her, she fell extremely ill and the only thing that would cure her was a rare and magical glowing flower, and this caused Rapunzel to be born with the flower's magical powers in her hair. Mother Gothel was using the flower to keep herself looking young and beautiful, and she knew she could steal the magical powers from the little girl.

Mother Gothel would have to visit the flower often to maintain her youthful look, and singing a special song would activate the powers (and also Rapunzel's hair magic). She kidnaps Rapunzel and takes her into hiding in the famed princess' tower, where Rapunzel is held captive, never allowed to explore the world outside her window.

Mother Gothel periodically leaves Rapunzel in the tower alone while she travels to the market. When Rapunzel is nearing her 18th birthday, she devises a plan to nervously ask her mother if she can finally leave the tower to see the display of lanterns that always happens in the kingdom on her birthday.

Upon hearing this question, Mother Gothel initially brushes off Rapunzel's request using humor instead of fully hearing her pleas to be allowed to finally see the lanterns. While Mother Gothel is being followed around by Rapunzel, who is trying to ask her permission to explore the world, they pass a mirror and what happens next stopped me dead in my tracks.

Mother Gothel, pulling Rapunzel close to her so both of them are standing in the center of the mirror, says, "Rapunzel, look in that mirror. Do you know what I see? I see a strong, confident, beautiful young lady. Oh look, you're here too!" she adds, pointing to Rapunzel.

I was floored. I had lived this exact scene before. My mother actually said those very words to me as we looked in a mirror together once when I was a teenager, and she laughed just like Mother Gothel after dropping the punchline.

It was like Disney had taken a snippet of my life and put it in their movie. I stopped cleaning and joined the kids on the couch to finish the movie. The parallels in the personality of Mother Gothel to my own mom opened my eyes to so much about my own childhood that I never fully understood until finding this animated character. My mom was a bit of a witch.

About two weeks after that awful phone call with my mom, my dog Roger suddenly got extremely sick and had to be put down. I had so much sorrow in my life at the time. I was confused and filled with grief over the things that my mother had said to me, and now I was losing the very best dog I had ever known. Roger was kind and gentle. He was a massive comfort to me when I was going through my miscarriage and stuck close to my side. He was always there when I needed him most and offered his best snuggles when he knew I was having a hard day. As soon as he got sick, I called Conner, who was out of town on a video shoot.

"Something is wrong with Roger," I reported. "I'm really concerned. He's not keeping anything down and he's puking a lot."

"He'll be fine, Ash. He's been sick before," came Conner's unbothered voice from the other side of the phone.

"This seems different," I said.

Two more days passed before Conner got home, and I had to quarantine Roger in the kitchen to keep him in a spot where if he vomited, it would be easy to clean up. He looked miserable and so sad to be separated from the rest of us. My heart was breaking for him, and I knew that it wasn't just a regular "my dog puked once" situation.

As soon as Conner saw him in person, he knew it, too. I called my friend Teagan to stay with our kids, and Conner and I took Roger to the vet. He told us there was a very large mass under Roger's rib cage.

"We can do more tests. We can even do surgery. But I'll take off my doctor hat for a moment and tell you that as a dog owner, I wouldn't put him through all that torture if he were mine. Even if we do surgery, we'll only be able to buy him a small extension of life, and it won't be a quality life. If it were me, I would put him down. I'll give you some time to think about it," the vet said sincerely.

I was sobbing and lying on the floor next to Roger, who hadn't moved since we arrived.

"I'm really sorry but we can't afford surgery and testing for Roger, Ash," Conner said. It was the first time I had heard that kind of sorrow and sincerity in his voice since our miscarriage.

"I love him, and I wouldn't want to put him through all that unnecessary suffering anyway," I said. "But I'm also not ready to say goodbye to him. This is so hard." I knew that this was going to be the last time I would get to hold Roger and tell him I loved him.

Conner left the room to go tell the vet that we were ready to put Roger down. We had about 10 minutes alone together while they gathered all the things they needed to peacefully end the life of my very best friend. I cried and told him how sorry I was. I wrapped my arms around him and thanked him for the gift he gave us by being a part of our family. I told him how special he was and what he meant to me. Even writing this now, years later, I am sobbing. That dog was so incredible.

The doctor returned to the room with an assistant and a tray of lethal injections. He explained the steps he was about to take, and how it would all affect Roger's body, and I watched as he faded into an eternal sleep. I wailed, holding his head in my hands and kissing the bridge of his nose. One moment he was there with me, and the next he was not.

I couldn't let go, and I couldn't contain my grief. It felt like I was grieving every death of everyone I had ever loved. The ache in my heart tore into a gaping wound, and I was bleeding out emotionally. So much heartbreak had consumed me of late. It felt like everything in my life was being blown up, and I couldn't do anything about it.

I didn't stop crying for weeks. The house was lonely without Roger, and everything reminded me of him. Explaining to the kids that he was gone was so difficult. We got a couple of children's books that were helpful to explain where Roger had gone since he was not with us anymore, but I now understood why some parents opted to tell their children that they sent the family dog to live on a farm to be happy forever herding sheep or cows.

If only all of life could be as easy as going to live on a farm. I wished I could have crossed over to whatever is after this life with Roger. All these problems and heartbreaks were starting to feel like too much for me to handle.

"Hey," I answered the phone. It was Conner.

"This is fucking stupid. These people wouldn't know talent if it pissed on their doormat," Conner fumed. "I need you to come and pick me up."

We had shared a car for 10 years, so every morning I would drop him off at work and then pick him up at the end of the day. But it was highly unusual for him to ask me to come get him early.

"It's 12:30 p.m. on a Tuesday ..." I said, confused. "Are you sick? Aren't you needed at your office?"

Conner had only been working at this media start-up company for about three weeks. Before that, he had spent a year at another start-up company, but he was let go as part of a round of layoffs before the company fully folded. He took a couple of months off looking for new work before he landed a job as a creative director at this new media start-up.

"They just fired me. I'm so pissed. I walked out, and I'm at this diner on the corner. Meet me there."

I loaded up the kids into our minivan and headed toward Conner. I was praying the whole way there that God would help Conner to calm down and guide us during this mess. I sighed, feeling stress bubble up in my chest. *He literally just got this job, and he's already lost it,* I thought, my mind spinning. *This can't be good for him since it was only recently that he was let go from the last company. Losing two jobs in less than six months is definitely not good.*

We pulled into the parking lot of the diner, and Conner was outside on the phone, pacing back and forth like he always did. He got in the car, and I could tell he was talking to his mom on the phone. As soon as they said goodbye, he barely took a breath before he started ranting to me. I took a deep breath and held the metaphorical bucket so he could fill it up with all the word vomit.

I kept thinking, *How can I best support him right now? What can I say to help him through this?* but I was coming up short on answers. I decided to do my best to keep a calm and positive attitude for the sake of our family and encourage him as much as I could by affirming his skills and work ethic.

"I'm so sorry this happened. We will figure it out," I said as we pulled into our driveway.

He decided to go back to freelancing, and for the first few days, he took some time to process his feelings. He was back to working from home, which meant that he had 24/7 access to me. Yippee. He immediately started utilizing me to read through and proof his pitch decks and written video treatments.

I was a sounding board on everything from how to reply to an email to "What do you think of these boots? Or this fleece? Or this shirt?" He was shopping if he wasn't supposed to be working, and he was consuming every free moment of my day. I was literally never alone. I tried to be understanding but eventually, I was getting overwhelmed, and I asked him to give me a break.

"Ok, Ashley. I'm just over here trying to survive and feed our kids. But don't let me bother you," he snapped back at me. "Actually, I don't think you're doing enough to contribute to our family's finances."

Here we go again, I thought.

I knew what was coming next. We were certainly due for an "Ashley doesn't make enough money for the family" conversation. He was twice fired and stressed out. But he was also unwilling to help more with the kids, so my hands were, once again, tied. I wasn't unwilling to work. I *wanted* to work, desperately. But Conner made it almost impossible to even consider because I couldn't count on him to pick up the slack as my partner in parenting our kids.

So I braced myself for the emotional roller coaster of being told why I'm a terrible wife for not contributing financially while simultaneously being held back by the very person telling me I wasn't enough.

\\|/

chapter nine

TRUTH TELLER

"You own everything that happened to you. Tell your stories. If people wanted you to write warmly about them, they should have behaved better."

— **Anne Lamott**

Most of my first memories come from when I was six years old. I've been in therapy for years as an adult because of so much that happened during that time of my life, which feels extremely dark. It's funny how as a child you just accept certain things that are fucked as completely normal behavior because you don't really know any better yet.

When I was six years old, in the darkness of night, my mom snatched up my brother and me and took us to a convent. There was a family that had been living with us for a couple of months— Laney, Cole, and their seven-year-old son, Bryson. We weren't Catholic, but they were, and Laney had instructed my mom to take my brother and me to the convent after a massive argument between my mom and dad.

The place was foreign to me. We were handed over to a nun who lived on the property, without much explanation, and told that we would wait with her until Nanny was able to come and get us. It felt very late in the evening, and I remember being extremely tired. Sister Julia took us inside to a dimly lit room where we played the board game *Trouble* and watched the local news.

I felt confused and scared. I was too afraid to ask why we were there, so I just tried to survive the moment, hoping Nanny would arrive sooner than later. The sun was rising on the horizon when Nanny finally arrived. I had fallen asleep on Sister Julia's couch and awoke disoriented, unsure of where I was or why I was there.

I remember getting in Nanny's maroon Buick and sitting on the velvety seat in the back, looking out the window at the convent now illuminated by the first morning light as we drove away. No one—not me, my brother, my mom, or Nanny—ever spoke of this moment again.

Nine weeks after that unthinkable phone conversation with my mom in which she accused me of having a crush on my grandfather, she finally reached out and offered to attend a therapy session with me. I had been working hard in therapy to uncover my foggy memories, to understand what happened to me, and to work through the feelings of abandonment I'd been experiencing most of my life.

With the guidance of my therapist, I wrote a letter that I would read when my mom came to town for our therapy session. When the day arrived, we awkwardly sat on the couch, and my mom took that opportunity to crack a couple of jokes to my therapist as we all settled into her office.

"Thank you for coming in today, Deb," Valerie began. "I know you and Ashley have been having some difficulty in your relationship, and I've been working with her for several weeks now." As she went on to explain a few confidentiality statements and other quick housekeeping items with my mom, I could feel my heart pounding. I was overwhelmed with anxiety as I waited for the cue to read my letter. Finally, Valerie said, "I know Ashley has prepared a statement because there's a lot to say, and she doesn't want to leave anything out. Ashley, are you ready to share?"

I nervously shifted in my seat, clutching my phone and staring at the letter sitting boldly in my Notes app. My voice was shaking as I replied, "Yes," and began reading:

Watching our family crumble has been incredibly difficult. I know that you know this and feel the heartbreak that we have all been feeling. I am not diminishing your feelings in this AT ALL, but I have felt throughout this situation that you have been making it more about you than showing love, support, and concern for what Birdie has come forward with, and ultimately my own questions surrounding this situation.

I'm not sure whether or not I was abused, but based on my uncomfortable memories that have resurfaced after being buried for years, and because I believe Birdie's admission, I am inclined to believe that it more than likely happened to me, too.

I may never know for sure exactly what may or may not have occurred, and I have to figure out how to be ok with that fact. But I have not even really been able to wrap my head around how I feel about all of this since it has surfaced, because when I came to you to share my distress and confusion and ask for your support and love, I was left feeling orphaned. I didn't recognize you at all. Your response to me in my time of need was to attack me and imply that I was lying. At that point, I realized that you are blind to any perspective but your own. You would rather go on shoving problems under the rug than have to deal with the actual issues within our relationship and family.

As an adult, I have felt completely let down by you as a mother, specifically once I became a mother myself and started making decisions outside of what pleases you, which was always my main goal growing up. To make you proud and have your approval on my report card, my college major, moving to New York ... I did all of that because that's what you wanted me to do.

Growing up, I always thought you were fantastic, and in many ways you were. But both you and Dad overshared personal information about your relationship, as well as exposed me to some traumatic experiences (certainly unintentional at best, but still not something that any child should see). This set me up to believe love and marriage are full of dramatic exits and unhealthy sexual behaviors.

I've never told you this before, but as a first- or second-grader, I actually walked in on you cheating on Dad with that guy Cole who worked at the car dealership with him. I stood in the bathroom doorway of your bedroom and saw you in a white thong, rolling around on the waterbed with him. You didn't see me—at least I don't think that you did—and so I turned around and went back up to my room, knowing I wasn't supposed to see that, and vowing not to say anything about it because I was sure I would be in trouble. I have carried that with me all these years, not knowing what to do with such a traumatic memory. Later in life, when you and Dad were getting divorced, you overshared with me about how the two of you would cheat on each other—him first, then you as an act of revenge on him.

I heard and watched the two of you fight constantly. I saw you both engage in horrible divorce games—domestic abuse, jail, custody, etc. Every chance Dad had, he would try to tell me messed up stuff about you. But of the two parents I had, you were the most stable so I always defended you.

Now as an adult, I'm piecing together the truth, and you're both guilty of trying to manipulate me and pit me against the other parent by telling a child inappropriate information. So, we are here now because of how you have hurt me and then refused to hear, support, or love me in the ways I needed you to as my mother.

I do not want any of this to affect my children. I don't want them to grow up questioning my love for them or wondering whether I would support them in a hard time. I especially NEVER want them to feel unsafe with me or another family member who is supposed to love and protect them. And I certainly don't want them to have questionable memories regarding sex or be exposed to unhealthy sexual situations that would impact how they handle intimacy in their adulthood—as I am now.

You said so many hurtful things during our last phone call in September, and I need some clarity regarding these statements. We cannot move forward in our relationship without some sort of closure or resolution.

I poured my heart out, and I was terrified to put my true feelings out there. I cried and trembled as I read the letter, and my mom was stone cold. Her face was completely blank and there was no light in her eyes. When I finished reading, there was a long silence. Finally, my therapist stepped in and asked my mother to respond, "Okay. So Ashley just shared some really big things. Do you have anything to say in response to everything she said?"

She sat up straight, adjusted her fake boobs, and said, "I don't know what you want me to say here. I was a good mom. I went to all your volleyball games, and you and your brother had everything you needed."

Emotionally drained, I sank deep into the corner of the couch and looked at the clock. We still had 80 minutes left in our 90-minute session, and she was completely closed off to everything I had just shared. At that moment, I realized she was incapable of truly hearing and supporting me. She wanted to go through the motions of showing up to therapy so she could say she made this grand gesture of driving all the way down to Nashville to meet with me, but she didn't actually want to do the hard work that was necessary to help us move forward in a positive direction.

At the end of the session that went absolutely nowhere, my therapist graciously tried to help us define what we wanted from our relationship. "We have just a few minutes left here today, and I would like both of you to set some expectations on how you'd like to move past this. What do you want your relationship to look like?"

My mom perked up. "I'll go first!" she said, as if she was winning a gold star for participation. Facing Valerie, like a contestant answering a question at a beauty pageant, she said, "I want to laugh and watch movies and eat popcorn with Ashley like we used to." Then she quickly turned her head to me, awaiting my response.

I hesitated. Not because I didn't have an answer, but because I was so astonished at hers. I took a long, hopeless breath and quietly said, "I want to be supported, loved, heard, and believed." I finally understood that she was never going to be capable of being the kind of mother I so desperately needed and wanted her to be. My idea of who she was (or what I thought a mother should be) did not align with who she actually was, and this reality filled me with grief and sadness. I had to make a decision on how we could maintain our relationship, knowing that everything between us would be forever changed.

I was stunned at the lack of realness I had just experienced in this therapy session, and while I became even more discouraged in having any trust that our relationship could be truly mended, I was not a quitter. I didn't want to give up on her or discard our relationship. I wanted to try to find a way for us to heal. It pains me to say it now, but I still wanted her approval. But nothing I could do, no amount of slapping on a smile to eat pop-corn and watch stupid movies would ever be enough, because loving someone who isn't safe will never cultivate an atmosphere of trust and security. It only prolongs the inevitable: more disappointment and sorrow.

In seventh, eighth, and ninth grades, I tried out for cheerleading, but I did not actually make the squad until my sophomore year of high school. Every year that I didn't make it, I would come home from school in tears because I wanted so badly to be a cheerleader like my cousins, Alice and Birdie.

My mom, seeing my disappointment and sadness, would try to help me by saying things like, "You're way prettier than any of the girls that made the team. You know what we're going to do instead of cheerleading that will be way more exciting? I'm gonna put you in modeling and get you an agent." With my mother, it was beauty first, always. And if you can succeed at something "cooler," you can beat the losers who didn't choose you. That'll really show that cheerleading coach what a mistake she made by not picking me for the team (hashtag sarcasm).

Over time, this felt more and more like an empty promise to get me to forget my problem. She offered me this weird con-solation prize three years in a row, and by my ninth-grade dis-appointment, I decided to ask her why she never actually fol-lowed through on the idea.

Since I called her out, she said, "You're right! Let's look up a local modeling agency and see about getting you an appoint-ment." One day, she noticed an ad in the local paper for an open call for aspiring models, so she clipped it and showed it to me. "There's an open call on Saturday at 11:00 a.m. We're going!" she announced.

We arrived a little early and walked into a room full of young ladies my age with their parents. We found our way to a couple of free chairs where brochures and questionnaires on clipboards awaited us. My mom quickly filled out the forms just before the official start of the open call. A tall man wearing glasses who worked at the agency kicked things off by introducing himself and making a welcome announcement.

"Welcome everyone to the agency's open call for models. I'm Davis, and I'm going to take some time to share a little bit about our modeling program." He went on to explain that the agency offered modeling classes so we could all learn about posing and walking a runway. He said anyone would be eligible to enroll in classes, even if we did not get a call back after today's open call.

My mom opened her brochure, where she reviewed the various classes that were available.

This is so cool. I'm gonna get to learn how to pose like a real model! These classes will be so interesting. No sooner had I finished that thought when my mom leaned into my shoulder, put the brochure in my lap, pointed at the line that said, "Bundle Both Professional Modeling Courses for $1,299!" and whispered, "This is a scam, let's go." She stood up and walked confidently toward the exit.

When we got to our car, I asked, "How do you know it was a scam? I thought all that sounded good."

"Any legitimate modeling agent isn't going to make you pay for classes. They make money off you by taking a percentage of your rate when you get jobs. I heard on the news that if an agency asks you to pay big money like that upfront, it's a scam. And after you take their stupid classes, they don't actually find you jobs."

I trusted that she knew what she was talking about, and we drove away.

When I tried out for cheerleading again my sophomore year, I finally got it! I was overjoyed. The thing I had wanted for so long was finally mine. I had practiced for hours and hours at home and with friends until I became good enough to make the team. I had not given up. I rushed home to tell my mom the exciting news. She was in the kitchen, chopping vegetables for dinner.

"You'll never believe it!" I exclaimed.

"What's going on?" she asked curiously.

"I made the squad. I'm officially a cheerleader!"

"Wow, Ashley!" She stopped cutting the potatoes and looked right at me. "That's really great. I can't believe you did it. You've tried out so many times. If I were you I would've quit after not making it the very first time." Her tone as she spoke seemed to me just slightly less excited than I had hoped for, and in my memory, it has a slight bend toward sarcasm.

I was so proud of myself for finally making the team, and nothing felt better to me than working hard and finally seeing it pay off. After that, I forgot all about modeling, but it was just like my mom to try and "fix" a problem with a superficial solution or a promise she didn't keep. It was all a show to keep up appearances. Putting in the emotional work was not her strong suit. Slapping a quick fix Band-Aid on my emotional wounds was easier and probably made her feel as though she was doing enough, even though the message I was receiving was that my problems weren't worth much more than a cheap drugstore bandage.

The last day of fifth grade felt like one of the most epic days of my life. I waited impatiently for the dismissal bell to ring and signal my summer freedom. As soon as school was over, my mom and Aunt Loretta would be waiting for us in the car to drive all of us straight to Florida for summer vacation. My uncle had to work, and my dad had some class finals at the community college he was attending.

Mom was giddy at the fact that Dad couldn't join us. My aunt drove the first shift of our 14-hour drive down to Orlando. The plan was to drive nonstop so they could maximize our time, only stopping for the occasional rest-stop bathroom break. While they drove, Birdie, Alice, Oscar, and I all slept or played road trip games to pass the time.

We arrived at our vacation rental condo early the next morning. The house was covered in pretty pink stucco and there was a beautiful swing on the front porch, swaying slightly in the breeze. I was seeing real-life palm trees for the first time ever, just hanging out in people's front yards, as casual and common as buckeye trees in Ohio. I couldn't believe how beautiful it was, and I'd only seen one random neighborhood so far.

Exhausted from the drive, we all fell out of the car, dragging our bags inside to claim our beds. The sun was beginning to rise, and I was blown away to see that there was an awesome swimming pool right outside the back door. This place seemed so fancy to me. I couldn't believe we were going to be staying here for a whole week.

The first day, we took it easy and hung out at the pool, swimming and laying in the warm Florida sunshine. Around lunchtime, we made up a bunch of ham and cheese sandwiches, grabbed a few cans of soda and a bag of BBQ chips, and headed to the picnic table poolside. My mom, holding a paper plate full of food in one hand and a can of Diet Coke in the other, slowly began to back away from the table to get a better look at the neighbor's pool and patio.

Before we knew it, we all heard a massive splash and looked over to see my mother coming up out of the water for air, a large chunk of ham stuck to her forehead, the Diet Coke unharmed.

She kept her arm up straight and didn't take it down with her. We laughed about this all week as we continued to find pieces of ham and chips floating in the water, and also because the way she saved that soda felt like it could have been a scene from the perfect summer Diet Coke commercial. Mom thought it was so hilarious that she reenacted it a few times to get us laughing again.

The next day we had planned to spend the day at the beach. This was my very first time seeing the ocean, and I was blown away when I looked out and saw endless water as far as what looked like the end of the earth. It was captivating. I sat on the shoreline and watched the waves as they rolled in and out, feeling my body sink into the sand just slightly every time the water would engulf my legs.

Mom and Birdie prided themselves on their ability to worship the sun, and Mom would often tell me that "Sunscreen is for the weak," as she would pass me the suntan lotion that was designed to attract the rays and had no actual SPF.

We had been there for a few hours, snacking and watching seagulls fly off with entire Ziplock bags of sandwiches and other delicious treats that the families around us were trying to enjoy. These birds were relentless scavengers and would swoop down and take the sandwich right out of someone's hand as they were about to take a bite. When we were all ready to eat our lunch, we were told to eat fast so we didn't become their next victims. We were unsuccessful. Seagulls were bombing us left and right. Those birds were not fucking around, and nothing was going to stand between them and our Publix deli sandwiches.

After lunch, the sun was really beaming down on us, and soon everyone except Birdie and my mom were huddled under our one umbrella, sunburned and shivering, trying to get a little shade for protection. We were all begging them to stop tanning so we could head back to the condo, but my mom was not having it.

"Guys, we are never near the beach. We need just a little more time here," she said.

So we all had to wait. But we kept complaining and eventually there was no way to relax and soak up the sun with four other people hurling complaints and constant pleas to leave.

I was shivering and pretty sure I got sun poisoning from our day at the beach, but I loved the ocean more than anything I had ever seen. It felt worth the pain and blistered peeling skin to be able to see it in person. We gathered our things and piled into the car. We were all annoyed at my mom and Birdie for making us stay there an extra 45 minutes.

The ride back to the condo was blazingly silent until we pulled up to the driveway and saw our red Jeep Cherokee parked in the shade. "What the heck is Louis doing here?" Aunt Loretta said under her breath.

My mom's face turned gloomy. "He isn't supposed to be here," she said as Aunt Loretta put the car in park. Waiting on the porch was my dad, smiling and wearing what we called "witness wear"—clothes that would inspire people to salvation. His T-shirt had a cartoon graphic of a man lying dead on his back, next to a dropped neapolitan ice cream cone with chewing gum stuck on the bottom of one of his sandals. Above the image were the words "DON'T BE CAUGHT DEAD WITHOUT JESUS" in bold green letters.

None of us were happy to see him. He was technically not invited on this trip, yet here he was, having driven 14 hours in our Jeep all by himself, ready to slather on the sunscreen and share his unwelcome opinions about how we should vacation from this point forward.

He and my mom took a sidebar to talk when he arrived.

Although I wasn't privy to the conversation, I can only imagine how it went: My mom expressing concern that he drove all the way to Florida when he said he couldn't come. My dad explaining that he was having a serious case of FOMO so he skipped his finals to come down to the beach.

Mom had been sleeping on the pull out couch the past couple of nights, but when Dad arrived, he refused to sleep there, so we all had to switch rooms so that he could have a room with a door, which meant that Oscar and I were forced to share the couch. I was not happy about this at all, because I had been sharing a room with my cousin Alice and was loving life so much as her roomie.

The next day we decided to stick around the condo and swim. Dad kept doing cannonballs into the pool which caused the biggest splashy waves, and no matter where you were outside of the water, you were in the splash zone. If he wasn't making waves, he was floating on his back like a starfish, raft-free, his toes pointed up and out of the water, toward the sun. On this trip, both of these things were highly offensive to me, especially the splashing.

It must've been annoying to my mom as well, because after a few jumps she looked at him and said, "You're making huge waves like you're Moby Dick or some giant whale." Every time he would jump, she would clap and cheer, "Moby! Moby! Moby!" until everyone in the pool chimed in. I knew it wasn't the nicest thing to do, but he was so irritating, and at 11 years old, I idolized my mom. If she was doing it, so was I. And since his mere presence on this vacation basically ruined the whole vibe, I didn't feel bad about being mean to him at all.

When I was 16, my mom won a trip to Amsterdam in the Netherlands for selling the most insurance policies at the agency where she worked. She took me with her, and I was so excited for my first trip abroad. When we landed, I fell in love with the canals and the landscape and history that was visible on every corner. We were told that marijuana was legal, and to stay away from the Red Light district. But my mom, ever the adventurous spirit, landed us exactly there, after curiously following a trans woman wearing a leather outfit with the ass cheeks cut out and her whole bum exposed in the crisp Dutch air.

"Whoa, look at HER! Let's follow and see where she goes!" Mom said excitedly as she darted into the street to chase after her. We followed casually down the street, and as we got closer to the Red Light district, I began to notice the shift in the types of people hanging around. This must be what Harry Potter felt like when he suddenly found himself in Knockturn Alley after traveling by floo powder to the wrong fireplace.

Suddenly there were girls wearing almost nothing, standing in windows and waving at passersby to see if they were interested in coming inside to partake of their services. I had never seen a sex worker on the clock before in real life, and I wasn't sure if it was ok to make eye contact. I kept my head down. Eventually, we lost track of the woman we were chasing and Mom said, "That was fun! But I can't believe I got so caught up in the chase that I didn't even look before crossing the street!"

Later that day, we met up with the rest of the insurance company sales winners to tour the Anne Frank House. This was such a transformative experience for me. I had recently read *The Diary of a Young Girl*, and seeing her living space was haunting. I was so grateful to have had this experience, and the contrast between the two major activities of the day was not lost on me. Going from a district where just about anything goes, to a house that felt like holy ground—that was my mother for you.

Christmas of 2017, we went back to Ohio with the kids to visit family. Like always, we stayed with Alice and Matt and spent the days split between our parents. This usually meant a nine-hour day at both Conner's mom and dad's houses, and me going out to a chain restaurant with my mom and the kids, leaving Conner behind at my cousin's to "work." That December, he had an obsession with sneakers, and every time I turned around, he was asking my opinion on various shoes he was considering buying with his Christmas money.

It was so generous of his parents to think of us each year, and Conner always asked for money because he said he never liked any of the gifts his parents got him otherwise. "This way I don't have to bother you for the receipt to return it," he'd say, as if he were being extra thoughtful about not bothering them, versus his actual attitude of, "I'm too cool to wear any clothing item from The Gap."

That year, when his parents asked me what I wanted for Christmas, I told them that I wanted to take improv classes. I needed a hobby, something to get me out of the house where I could make friends that weren't the moms of my kids' friends at school. I thought that having an actual class to go to would be a good enough excuse to leave Conner home with our kids for an hour every Tuesday night for eight weeks.

Plus, I thought it would be fun to learn to be a quick-witted thinker and tap into my funny bone. The class was $250, and I knew I would never be able to convince Conner to let me spend *his* "hard-earned" money on something so frivolous. I was so grateful that Christmas to have received the exact amount I needed to enroll in the class.

When it was time to visit my mom, we engaged in the superficial connection that had become customary since that dreadful therapy session. I was still trying my hardest to give her the fun, silly, popcorn-eating daughter that she said she wanted, and in order to do that, I had to drop my own expectations for her role in my life. I had already stopped going to her house a few Christmases ago because Garth made me feel extremely uncomfortable. He was very awkward toward me and my kids whenever we were around, and I had to endure my mother's tears on more than one occasion when she would run away to our house in Nashville because they'd had another fight.

This particular Christmas, she suggested we meet for lunch at a chain restaurant in town called O'Charley's, and the plan after that was to take the kids shopping at Target, where it had become a tradition that she would fill up an entire cart full of toys for them as her gift to us. While we waited on our food to arrive, she and Elianna were talking as I attempted to keep Milo entertained with a dinner roll and a few little toys from my purse.

"Hey Ellie," my mom said excitedly. "Did you know that your daddy is a magician?"

"No way!" Elianna answered, her eyes growing wide because she had recently taken an interest in learning magic tricks.

"Yeah," my mom said snarkily. "He made your mommy disappear." She paused, and I looked up from my menu and made eye contact with her. She added, "I mean, from Ohio. He made her disappear from Ohio."

It's funny how in one split second, the human brain can fire off 8,000 thoughts and play out a variety of scenarios and outcomes, depending on your reaction and choice of words. I knew that if I reacted at all, it would feed into whatever pot she thought she was stirring. I wanted to scream at her, "Are you fucking kidding me right now? WHO says THAT to their granddaughter? Why would you do that? Are you that fucking passive-aggressive?"

Instead, I thought to myself, *You have 90 minutes left with her. Ignore her comment. Stay calm for the kids. Let it go. You can do this.* I wasn't going to give her the satisfaction of a fight.

And so I opted to bite my tongue and power through, as I took a mental note and slapped another Band-Aid on the wounds of my heart that she was constantly reopening. *It is impossible for her to be who I need her to be as a mother. I need to let go of my attachment to this outcome,* I resolved in my mind. I felt my spirit turning inward as we arrived in the Target parking lot and entered the building, but my face kept smiling.

Each year we finished out our Ohio visit with Alice and Matt's New Year's Eve party—dancing the night away while our kids rang in the New Year with Conner's mom. This was always a night I looked forward to because we got dressed up fancy, and I got to spend the evening with my cousins and friends dancing in a hotel ballroom. Most people at the party booked a room at the hotel, so they could drink and party late into the night and then stumble back to their rooms.

I didn't even drink alcohol during the first few years that we attended this party. I wasn't trying to be straight-edged, but I was not interested in losing control of myself because my *self* was the only thing I had control over. Even though I was totally sober, most people at the party assumed I was completely smashed because I loved dancing and could have a fantastic time without alcohol. The last few years we attended this party, our marriage was not in the greatest place, yet the expectation from Conner was that we would be having tons of sex since we had this hotel room and were kids-free.

The pressure to give him what he wanted became a lot to manage, so I was now discovering that a vodka and cranberry helped me not to think so much about the sex part of the night. I finally understood why most people enjoyed drinking. It was so that they could escape their anxieties, their insecurities, their pain, even their lives, just for a few minutes.

185

This was the one night of the year that I gave myself permission to get a little loose, but I never allowed myself to have more than three drinks throughout the entire night. Conner, who was so irritated that I wouldn't drink with him on our honeymoon at the all-inclusive resort in Jamaica (this was pre-Michael Scott in *The Office*, but still hits me as hilarious every time I see that episode), loved that I was now open to consume an occasional adult bevvy, and he made sure to keep a drink in my hand all night.

I wondered what was wrong with me. Why didn't I want to have a night of crazy sex with my husband? He seemed to always want it, and I could have gone the entire year without it. Clearly, he wasn't the problem. I was. Right?

But the drinking helped, and I decided to embrace the "fake it till you make it" mindset with him. I did everything I knew to do to let him know I was enjoying it, even when I wasn't. Because the few times I decided to not play the role of a satisfied wife inevitably led to a back-and-forth game, where I would end up having to explain my "selfish behavior" and literally beg him to come back and finish. It was degrading and exhausting, and I felt so empty and unfulfilled. Maybe I wasn't the problem after all.

We headed back to Nashville on January 3, and as soon as we returned to our reality at home, Conner opened his computer, leaving me to unpack all the suitcases, put away the massive pile of new toys the kids had been spoiled with, and do all the laundry from the trip.

From the laundry room, I heard Conner say, "Fuck this."

I took a deep breath and entered the dining room to find him in a total panic. "YOU didn't remind me to pay the mortgage payment in December, and now it's a month late. It's going to show up on MY credit report, and all of this could've been avoided if you would have reminded me to pay it."

"You're saying that you forgot to pay it and that's my fault

... how, exactly?" I asked.

"You know how busy and stressed out I've been, and it's your job as my wife to remind me to pay the bills."

"Um, it's your responsibility to pay the bills. We agreed that you would manage that when we moved to Nashville since you wanted to be in charge of our finances," I reminded him.

"Well, it's still your fault because you should always ask me if I paid the bills. I've been working nonstop and you knew that. The least you could do is help me out here, Ash." He refused to accept any responsibility for this missed payment.

"Conner, the entire month of December you kept calling me over to your computer to ask my opinion on a plethora of sneakers you wanted to buy with your Christmas money. I assumed that if you had time to look at shoes all day, you had time to remember to pay our bills."

"Listen, it's more than that. My latest check hasn't been delivered yet and now we are really strapped for cash because we spent too much money in Ohio. I'm gonna need to use that money you got for Christmas to pay a couple of bills," he urged.

Of course, I could not object. I didn't want our water or electricity to be shut off, so I handed over the envelope with my $250 for improv classes, and then we never had the extra money for me to enroll in the class after that. I also took a few minutes out of my evening to go into our shared family calendar and add reminders that would alert Conner when bills were due. I would be damned if he was going to make his lack of responsibility my fault, and this was the only way I knew how to stay on top of it all.

He wanted to have monthly family finance meetings, and I agreed. But those "meetings" were me watching him fumble around a Google Sheet where he copied and pasted bill totals and prioritized how he wanted to pay them, and then lectured me on how I wasn't helping enough in this area.

When I offered to help out more by taking the duty of making sure the bills were paid, he would say, "I don't trust you to pay the bills properly since you are the reason we missed that mortgage payment in December." Delusional. I learned that what he expected during this financial planning time was for me to sit in misery with him while he looked at a spreadsheet.

I tried to keep quiet so that I wouldn't say something that would set him off, but not so quiet that I seemed uninterested. I tried to be engaged, but not so much that I would have any actual control or say over where the money was going. No matter what I did, it was never good enough, and we would ultimately end up fighting because the kids kept pulling my attention away from him.

Walking the tightrope of his demands and emotional state was a balancing act by itself. How massive the weight of being his wife was. I felt powerless. I was expected to sit back and support him silently while he mismanaged our finances, and I was also not allowed to give our children the attention they needed when he was around because every one of his needs trumped anything and everything else.

The cycle of inner self-talk was mostly a constant loop of me beating myself up for ever partnering with someone so controlling. It was a miserable existence, and I was finally waking up to the truth of my reality. I knew that we were becoming a toxic combination, but the big question yet to be answered was whether I would find the confidence and courage to do something about it.

chapter ten

I WANT MY WIFE BACK

*"Love yourself first and everything else falls into line.
You really have to love yourself to get anything
done in this world."*

— **Lucille Ball**

Immediately after my terrible therapy day with my mother, having spilled my guts for what felt like absolutely no positive forward motion, I fell into a dark and deep cave of depression. The morning after our session I was unable to get out of bed, and my entire body stung and throbbed as if I had been hit by a semi-truck and left on the side of the road to die, slowly being picked apart by turkey vultures.

This feeling will go away, I thought. But it didn't. We were supposed to take our kids to the Nashville Christmas Parade that day, but I couldn't get out of bed. My body was lifeless and everything hurt. It took every ounce of energy just to hold myself upright. I love parades and was really excited about going downtown to see all the floats and giant character balloons through the eyes of my children. But my heart was deflated.

I was paralyzed and felt incredibly guilty for not being able to rally like I usually could. I knew I was ruining the fun day my little family was looking forward to, and we would not get another chance to make great holiday memories with our kids until they were a whole 365 days older. *What if this doesn't go away, and I ruin Christmas?*

In my worst moments, while I glumly sat on the couch trying to bring my heart back to life, my daughter would come and hold my face in her hands and say, "Mommy, please get up!" and I would gather my strength to power through, feeling emotionally weighed down by what felt like heavy concrete cinder blocks. Smiling felt impossible. It was as if 20-pound dumbbells were attached to the corners of my mouth, but I tried to smile at my children while I played with them.

I loved them, but my heart was far from them. My heart was far from everything. I had shut it down while my mind sifted through endless memories of my relationship with my mother, trying to figure out where it all went so wrong. I was lonely, thanks to a husband who didn't seem to notice my existential crisis, yet never physically alone, thanks to two kids who needed me.

I longed for someone to see my pain and show me a tiny bit of empathy. To hold me close. To tell me everything was going to be alright. I was lost in thought constantly as I tried to pull myself together each day to continue my duties as a mom and wife. Cooking dinner was a battle and always took everything I had in me. One evening while washing dishes, I could hear the muffled sound of our children laughing and being rambunctious in the next room.

I felt the hot water rushing over my hands, but I was somewhere else. I remember thinking, *How did I end up here? Why has all this happened to me?* My eyes were brimming with salty tears when suddenly I was brought back to the present moment by two hands clapping violently in my face, and a voice yelling, "I WANT MY WIFE BACK!"

I turned slowly and found my husband, fuming, standing behind me and spouting off about how the kids were out of control. "I'm trying to work. I'm so stressed out. You need to handle these kids; they're too loud. I can't think," he demanded.

I had no words. I just looked at him and realized that there was no space for me to have a crisis. I was not allowed to be wounded, to need support, or to ask anything of him, but I was expected to be fully available to meet his every need. It was clear that he believed he was more essential than me in our relationship. He had important work to do and money to make, and that eclipsed everything else.

My job was to manage our children and take care of things around the house. And at the end of the day, I was expected to sit with him so he could process his stress and work drama. But what about how I was feeling? Did my feelings matter to him at all?

I no longer had the room in my heart or mind to tolerate or care about whatever he was going through like I used to because I was on fucking fire. I longed for him to check in on me, to care about how I was doing with all that was going on in my life, to just say, "How are you handling life right now?" But we were not equal partners in our marriage.

He only wanted me to help him edit videos, reply to emails, and give myself to him sexually when he felt the need to "clear his head," as he always put it. I desperately wanted to be a good wife and give him what he needed. The only way I knew how to do that was to mentally pack my feelings into a box and lock it up tight. To go numb to my inner chaos and focus on meeting his expectations.

I didn't know what else to do. He was my last person. I needed this relationship to work. I couldn't handle losing another person I loved.

My friend Raina had become such a rock for me during the latest family crisis with my mother. She checked on me almost daily. "I'm sending you a Venmo payment for a follow-up session with your therapist," she said, knowing Conner would give me push-back on the cost if I asked him for the money for more therapy so close to the last session I had not even a week ago with my mom. "You're going to need this time to process everything with your therapist. That session sounds like it was really rough, and you can't hold all that in for another month until your next scheduled visit."

She was right. I felt like I was dying, and I needed someone to talk to. I thanked her for her extreme generosity toward me. I felt so helpless, but having Raina in my corner felt like everything to me. Someone actually cared. I was sad that we were in two different cities but grateful for her constant support and en-couraging text messages.

I sat in my follow-up appointment with Valerie on the same couch where my mother and I had imploded a week prior. Once I got settled, Valerie confessed, "I'm probably not supposed to say this to you, but I have never in all my years as a therapist seen anyone who has as many walls up as your mother. That was painful for ME, and I'm not related to her. How are you doing?"

"I was honestly so shocked at how it went. It wasn't how I had hoped it would go at all. I was so terrified to share, and then when I did, I wasn't even sure she heard me. It felt like the lights were off in her eyes. She was just going through the motions to be able to say that she showed up and did therapy with me, and that this one session should have been able to fix all our prob-lems," I lamented.

"I'm frightened about how I have been feeling since meeting with her. I'm also wondering if something happened to her with her dad when she was a kid, and she just hasn't ever been able to deal with it, based on how she responded to me when it all came out. I'm struggling on so many levels. I'm not myself. I am sad and unmotivated. I am in agony and can't find any joy or happiness. My whole body hurts, and I cry all the time. I feel like I am grieving her as if she has passed away," I confessed.

"I can see that grief all over you even right now," Valerie observed. "How are things at home if you're feeling this way?"

"Not great," I said, starting to feel hot tears pouring out of my eyes. "I don't think that there is any space for me to be crazy because Conner is crazy enough, and we can't have two crazy parents in our house right now. The kids need someone who can show up for them," I said. I went on to tell her about how Conner had clapped "I want my wife back" in my face, and how I knew that I needed to get it together because he wasn't going to magically start thinking of how I must be feeling having to deal with all this pain.

"Have you ever considered getting on medication for depression? I think it would help you so much right now to find a baseline and get you functional in your house for your kids so that we can start working through everything that you've got going on." She was gently helping me see that I could get some relief from the horrors of my heartbreak.

"Well, my mom has always said that people who need to be medicated are weak," I said. "I'm not closed off to it. I don't even believe that she's right in this way of thinking. But it's like I can hear her saying these words to me and so the thought is in there, even though I know it's not true."

"I would encourage you to consider it. I think it could really benefit you and help you get back up after being knocked down so hard. Here's the number to a psychiatrist who you can see to get a prescription."

I called the psychiatrist. Her rates were astronomical—$325

for one visit—and we were waiting on checks from Conner's last freelance job. We were always waiting on checks. By some miracle, I was able to convince him that I absolutely needed this appointment and to get on the medication so that I could get better. I worded it more like, "so I can get better and be there for you," that way it was clear that he was going to benefit from this, and I could return to our normal scheduled programming of being at his beck and call.

The psychiatrist was kind and listened to me explain what I had gone through, what I was feeling, and what my therapist thought might help me. "I think I'm only comfortable with a very low dose of Lexapro," I told her when it came time to discuss my medication options. Valerie and I had talked about this option, and I trusted her. I nervously looked out the window at the gray December day, a few leaves clinging to a tree branch, unwilling to let go for fear of falling, I imagined.

Moments later she was writing me up a prescription. Walking out of her office and back down to my car felt like a weird mix between finding a golden ticket to the Willy Wonka candy factory and living in a dismal post-apocalyptic world. I got in the car and took the most expensive square of paper I'd ever seen to my local pharmacy. Why is it so costly to get mental health care in America?

With a fresh prescription, I wasted no time and took it immediately when I got home. The very next morning I felt slightly more like myself (even though I was told it would take a week or two to really kick in). Whether or not it was a placebo effect, I woke up and sat with my children and felt a genuine smile and sincere gratitude for that moment. That was enough of a boost from the dark cave for me to see a sliver of sunlight. Hope was possible, and I was not completely lost. Thank God for Lexapro.

Conner's uncle owned a condo in Grant Park in Chicago that he and his wife were only using part of the year, so, much of the time, it sat empty. He offered it up to us to use whenever we wanted to visit Chicago, so every October for a few years we would spend a weekend in the city. Conner loved it because it was the perfect opportunity for him to get Instagram content and look like a badass visiting all the coolest restaurants and bars in Chi-town. I was happy to tag along and fell in love with the city more and more every time we visited.

But I was still finding it difficult to connect with Conner, as our relationship was so lopsided with him constantly dominating what we talked about when we were alone (and it was rarely asking me what I was dreaming of or how I was doing). We had been married for more than 10 years now, so this felt normal, and I was used to it.

This particular year, the musical *Hamilton* was playing in Chicago, and I had fallen in love with the soundtrack (ok, I was slightly obsessed) and thought that Lin-Manuel Miranda was a complete genius. Conner was repulsed by all musicals, so even when we lived in New York, he never went to a Broadway show with me.

But *Hamilton* had a "cool" factor because (1) It was really hard to get tickets, and (2) The Roots and heaps of other cool celebrities and influencers had shared how amazing they thought it was. So, as we boarded our flight, when I said, "How incredible would it be if we could go see *Hamilton* while we're in Chicago?" he was actually listening.

We got settled in our seats on the airplane, and he turned to me and said, "I bet I could find us last-minute tickets online."

One 90-minute flight and $800 (that we definitely couldn't afford) later, he had secured us tickets at the show that evening, where we would be sitting in the eighth row. "This was more expensive than I thought it would be, but this is how much I love you," he said. "I wanted to make this happen for you."

Maybe we aren't completely hopeless in our relationship, I thought. It seemed he had actually put real effort into something I was interested in for a change, and that felt really nice. I wondered if we could be on the same team again. I longed for balance in our relationship, and I wanted so badly to fix what was disconnected. Was this a turning point for us? I sincerely prayed that it was.

As soon as we landed, we went to dinner and then I found myself seated in the theater, watching as excited people filed in with their programs and high expectations.

"Want me to get a pic of you in front of the stage with your program?" Conner asked.

"Oh, that's ok," I declined.

"Ash, we came all the way here, and I paid $800 for these tickets. Let me take a photo of you," he insisted.

"Ok, but can we do it from my seat and not like, up there where everyone can see me?" My introverted heart was flaring up, and I was feeling flush with embarrassment.

"Yeah, fine," he agreed.

He took the photo and as I sat back down in my seat, an exuberant woman vibrated into her seat next to me. She was so high on life and what she was about to experience that her brown hair and white dress were almost glowing with a fluorescent aura. I could tell she was there alone, and since we were about to experience the *Hamilton* magic together for the next few hours, I decided to strike up a friendly conversation with her.

"Hey there! I'm Ashley," I said as I stuck out my hand for a handshake.

"Oh, hi!" she replied. "I'm Rachel."

"Is this your first time seeing the show?" I asked.

"Oh, no ... This will be my eighth time seeing the show. Wait, is it *your* first time?"

"Yeah. We just flew in from Nashville this afternoon. My husband actually got these tickets last minute only a couple of hours ago."

"Oh my God," she exclaimed. "I've had these tickets for eight months."

"Wow. That's crazy. What else are you going to do while you are in Chicago?" I asked.

"Literally nothing. I flew in today for the show, and I will leave tomorrow morning to head back to Florida." She paused for a moment and then asked, "Are you like a real fan or were you just looking for something to do tonight?"

"Oh, I'm a fan. I've listened to the soundtrack on repeat forever," I answered, feeling a bit like I was being interrogated about the legitimacy of my fandom.

"Have you read the book?" she fired back.

"Yes, I loved it," I said, proud of myself for passing that prerequisite for seeing the show.

"Did you watch the PBS special?" she asked sharply.

"Absolutely! It was fascinating." Again, my heart swelled with pride that I was totally nailing this *Hamilton* pop quiz.

"Ok, we'll probably get along just fine then," she said.

At that point, the lights dimmed in the theater, and a hush came over the audience as we heard the announcement that the show was about to begin. Moments later we heard the first notes from the famous opening song, "Alexander Hamilton," and my excitement quickly turned to utter bewilderment as Rachel had not only begun singing along, loudly, with the performers but was also doing what appeared to be a suppressed and seated version of the choreography that was happening on stage.

"What the fuck is happening with her?" I leaned over to

whisper to Conner. He glanced and said, "Oh no, it looks like the two of you are not on the same level of superfan as you thought. Hope she doesn't ruin this for us."

She, unfortunately, did kind of ruin it for me. She was so distracting the entire performance, from her sing-alongs to her outrageously loud sobbing at all the sad and emotional parts— especially when Eliza burns all of Alexander's love letters. I was continually pulled out of the story and into the drama that was unfolding in the chair next to me.

At the point where he began to hear her sobbing, Conner said, "Do you want me to say something to her?"

"No, please don't," I whispered back. "I don't want to embarrass or offend her. And honestly, she's giving me a way better story than if I just got to say 'I saw *Hamilton* in Chicago.' At least this is kinda funny."

"For $800 you shouldn't have a story like this," he fumed. "But that's fine, I won't say anything. I just hope you know how much I went through to get you these tickets and that you'll show me your appreciation later."

And there it was. Always strings attached. Of course he didn't do nice things for me because he loved me. He did them as leverage to ensure that he would get what he wanted from me, and now I knew I was going to be expected to give him sex that felt like it was as good as $800. I felt like I was his own personal sex worker. I snapped back to the sad reality that our relationship was transactional.

Our new friend Liv was having her 34th birthday party at a vineyard in the Tennessee countryside on a cool late April evening. I had only met Liv half a year prior, and she was vibrant, beautiful, and very, very single. She was obsessed with her singlehood and longed to have a husband. It's all she ever talked about. On the night of her birthday party, I sat with her as she talked about having met the love of her life, the one and only Tim Tebow.

She had met him at an event they both attended, and from the way she told it, sparks flew. She said God had given her a message that he was going to be her husband. She gushed as she spoke and her story made it sound like he had actually reciprocated her feelings. I left the party that night, confused at how she was so certain that God told her Tim Tebow was her guy after one meeting, and also a little impressed with her confidence and faith in believing something so wild. I mean, this is Tim fucking Tebow she was talking about. Was this even real?

On our drive home, I shared with Conner about my conversation with Liv, and he howled.

"There is no way that Liv is going to marry Tim Tebow. She's crazy," he said. "Why is she so obsessed with getting married, anyway?" he mused. "She's not a bad-looking girl ... but you know what her problem is? She's 34 and she already looks like a used and dried-up married mom of two. Like, she's a bit weathered or worn down or something. Like you can tell that she was stunning when she was younger, but now ... it's like life caught up with her. No one wants to marry that."

"Wow, that's super rude and superficial of you to say about her," I pointed out. I was shocked that he was able to so easily dismiss someone based on their looks, regardless of how boycrazy and Tebow delusional she may be.

"What? I'm saying she's beautiful ... but she's beautiful like YOU." He paused for a moment, and I let his words hang in the air because I was really curious about where he was going with this sudden comparison. He continued, "Like, you are beautiful, but you have two kids, and you've lived a life. You don't look like a fresh pick anymore. Liv has that vibe." I think he was trying to make me feel better about the fact that he just dogged my friend, but somehow he had also given me a backhanded compliment in the process.

"Oh my gosh, you should stop talking NOW," I said, completely offended on multiple levels.

"What? I'm saying you look as good as a 34-year-old who hasn't had kids, Ash. That's a compliment. You should be happy I see you this way."

"Are you kidding me? Clearly, you're not hearing the words that are coming out of your mouth. Please, just stop talking. This isn't helping," I replied.

"I don't get why you're upset. Sorry, I guess," he said insincerely. It was delivered more like a question than an actual apology.

I was trying to keep my motto of "Don't be easily offended," but this one felt like a real blow. How he really felt about me was obvious. He viewed me as used up and unworthy of love.

On a Saturday afternoon in late July, I found myself stuck in a house with three cranky children, ages 5, 7, and 38. It seemed that everyone needed something from me, and I wasn't serving anyone fast enough. Finally, after my efforts at lifting the mood in the house had failed, I waved my white flag of surrender and suggested that we all hop in the car for a Sonic happy-hour milkshake run. I was certain that a little sweet treat would help us all reset, and hopefully would be enough to let us have a nice evening together as a family.

I loaded up the kids and Conner got in the passenger seat. Once everyone was buckled up, I put on a movie for the kids because Conner wanted to talk to me. He was stressing about work and money, as usual, and wanted to process his thoughts with me. I used to enjoy talking with him about his problems. I loved that he seemed to value my opinion and would take my advice and suggestions. It used to make me feel like a part of his world. But I stopped loving it when the exchange was not equal, and he didn't make space for me to also share and process what I was going through.

At this stage in our relationship, I had so much going on with my whole family falling apart, and if he had just asked me how I was handling it all and made space for me to share, it would have gone such a long way. But that was not the case, and my heart was hardening and closing off to his need to process with me. I found it annoying and burdensome because he expected me to care deeply about everything he was going through while making it blatantly obvious that he couldn't care less about all the ways I was hurting.

Yet here I was, driving to a fast-food restaurant to get half-price milkshakes, held captive in a minivan I didn't want, listening to this man complain about the fact that he had lost out on a bid for a recent job that he was "clearly the best option for." The kids had their headphones on and were giggling and singing along to the movie, totally oblivious to the fact that their dad was in the passenger seat nearly on the verge of a self-righteous hissy-fit breakdown.

Conner, in mid-rant, suddenly snapped. "SHUT UP!!!! I can't even hear myself THINK," he growled, as he put his hands on his ears like a four-year-old boy when the music is too loud.

Startled and furious, I pulled the car over, looked at him, and said, "Get out of this car right now. We need to talk."

He folded his arms and turned his face away from me. "No, I won't get out of the car. Keep driving."

I got out and walked around to the passenger side, hoping that he would go with it and get out of the car so we could talk about what just happened without the kids hearing. He locked the door as I approached. I begged, "Please get out of the car so we can talk."

"No, I'm not doing that. You get back in here," he demanded.

I knew that insisting that he get out of the car was pointless. He was so stubborn, and now the kids were more aware of the fact that the car had been parked, and I was outside. I sucked it up and got back behind the steering wheel. "Never ... do that again," I whispered.

"Oh, they had their headphones on. They didn't know I was yelling at them," he excused.

"Yeah, well that means they probably think you were yelling at ME, which is also not ok," I calmly pointed out.

"I'm just so stressed out, Ash, and they were being too loud, and I couldn't even hear myself think. They need to be quieter," he said, still not getting the point I was making or even remotely willing to admit that his behavior was wrong.

I knew this conversation was going nowhere, so I decided to move on for now. I would try to bring this up again later after the kids went to bed. I parked the car and turned to the kids and asked, "What milkshakes would you guys like me to order for you today?"

They told me what they wanted, and I placed the order. Conner continued to lament his work situation while we waited for our order to be delivered, which felt like a lifetime as I listened to him drone on.

Finally, the milkshakes arrived and I handed all the straws to Conner while I passed out the milkshakes. The kids were ravenous and holding their milkshakes without yet having their straws must've felt like torture. Elianna could not contain her impatience any longer and blurted out in the whiniest sad voice, "I don't have a strawwwwwwww!"

Without hesitation, Conner turned toward her seat and chucked the entire handful of straws right into her face. "Here!" he snapped.

Shocked, Elianna gasped with hurt in her eyes and whispered, "I don't even know you."

Retelling this story, I have found the comedy in the dramatic reaction of a seven-year-old little girl who simply wanted a straw for her milkshake. But I can also still feel the pure heartbreak of my child in that moment. The father of my children was himself a fucking child who had zero self-control and could not resist having a physical outburst.

He didn't say anything in response to Elianna. He turned back to face the front and the drive home was completely silent.

I began to wonder how long it would be until throwing straws turned into other physical reactions. I could not allow my children to be in a position where they were not safe, and the trust I once had in Conner to be a loving and stable father was quickly evaporating.

Treat me badly, I can tolerate it. Treat my kids badly, you can fuck right off. They deserve better than that, and I was beginning to realize that I did, too.

chapter eleven

STRONG RIGHT HOOK

"Our destiny is not written for us, but by us."

— Barack Obama

It turns out that when you have so much intense drama and heaviness in your life, all the anger you've stuffed deep down in your heart begins to coagulate and morph into a huge beast that explodes out of the lockbox and pulses through your veins, in Hulk-like fashion. But I had no outlet for these feelings of rage, and it was eating me alive. I had never been so miserable, and I felt out of control and helpless.

"Some of the nicest, quietest people I've counseled end up being the angriest because we all believe the lie that nice people don't get mad," my therapist told me. "You've been through so much, and it's a miracle that you didn't give up and become an alcoholic or drug addict or something. But you're not giving your anger any outlet for safe expression, and you can't keep all that bottled up inside you. It's going to start seeping out in ways that you can't control and aren't safe. What can you do to help release your anger?" she asked me.

I thought for a second. "When I was in high school and college, my brother was taking boxing lessons from this guy ... He was the 1984 Olympic gold medalist, and he was training my brother to fight in actual matches. The workout looked fun, so my mom asked him if he would be willing to train us just for the workout and not for the fighting part. He agreed and we started training with him. We would hit the heavy bag or he would wear boxing mitts and make his hands moving targets for us to hit.

"It felt so good. I could channel all my feelings into the punches, and it was such a release. Every time he held mitts for me, he always said how strong my right hook was, and how no one could ever fuck with me. I miss boxing a ton, and I think that would be good for me now … but I don't know where to find someone like that here. I looked into this one place called Title Boxing, but it's too expensive and Conner would never agree to pay for it," I answered.

"Ok, well now we know something that you feel confident would help you, and we can start to look into it more." She gave me the assignment of just trying to find a place that I could go and hit a heavy bag for a few minutes a week, to help me channel all this anger in a positive way.

I prayed and asked God to help me find a place that I could afford and that Conner would be ok with me attending once a week. I was surprised when a couple weeks later, my daughter's Girl Scout troop announced that the next event was going to be at East Nashville MMA, where the girls were going to take part in a kid-friendly workout. When I arrived on the day of the event, I almost burst into tears.

This place was a little grimy and a lot smelly, but there were eight heavy bags hanging along one wall, and one of the trainers there was this badass woman, Vida Martinez, who had actually competed in MMA. I felt in my whole spirit that she was my person. It was like God was answering my prayer by sending me to Vida's gym. As soon as the kids' workout was done, I rushed to her to find out if she ever did one-on-one training or even some sort of group class, and she said yes.

A week later, I was back in the gym and spent an hour pounding out jabs, uppercuts, and right hooks. Vida echoed what my old trainer said, "Girl, you've got one of the strongest punches I've seen in a minute!" As I threw punches, I visualized that I was physically beating the shit out of every fucked up situation—or person—that I've ever encountered. I felt my anger subside with every punch. It was the exact release that I needed.

I was still holding out hope and trying to work things out with my mom, but whenever we would visit our hometown for the holidays, my visits with her grew increasingly more passive-aggressive. One time, she actually told me a story about two women she was training at her gym that she called "new Birdie and Ashley" because they were similar looking to us and were around the same age. What she was really saying was, "I've replaced you."

It was beginning to take a physical toll on my body as anxiety would build in anticipation of seeing her. While I tried to have deeper, real conversations with my mom when we were together, she would quickly change the subject to make sure we never talked about anything other than surface-level topics. I longed to connect with her and work out our problems, but she just couldn't (or wouldn't) go there.

For two years following our singular therapy session together, I tried to be the fun-loving, easy-going daughter she said she wanted. But I was physically breaking out in hives all over my lips from the anxiety I felt every time I knew I was going to see her. It was extremely painful. I would cry on the drive to Ohio, feeling overwhelmed with dread. And for a couple of weeks after our visits, my lips would swell up like I'd had some terrible lip filler injections from a plastic surgery Groupon.

I couldn't do it anymore. Even when she would FaceTime with my kids, she would barely look at me or acknowledge my presence. She'd look through me as I said hello and as soon as one of the kids was in sight, she would dive deep into silly Me-maw mode to get their attention and shut me up. I felt invisible and like such a phony trying to perform to meet her expectations of me as a daughter.

It was another sticky Nashville August, as I sat in Valerie's office and decided that maybe the classic (and super cliché) therapy exercise of writing a letter to my mom would help me to process my feelings and relieve some of the anxieties I was feeling. I wasn't sure if it would help, but I spent the next couple of weeks thoughtfully crafting what I wanted to say to her. After I finished writing it, I did feel better. I shared it with Valerie during my next session.

"This is so well written. You really have a way of expressing yourself with words, and everything you've said here is delivered with honesty and kindness. How do you feel about this letter? Do you think you want to send it?" she asked.

"I feel so much better having just gotten all these feelings and thoughts out of my body and into this letter. I know that it's getting close to the time when I will need to tell her how I'm feeling, but I haven't even heard from her in two whole months, so if I were to send this now, I think that it would actually create more drama than I want to deal with. Since the waters are calm at the moment, I don't want to rock the boat," I reasoned.

"I think that's wise. It's good that you feel better just having written it, and maybe that's all it has to be. Maybe you never send it, or maybe you hold onto it for a while until you feel like it is time to send it," she said. "Whatever you do, always make sure you are doing it from a place of love for yourself and for others. This way you're keeping your side of the street clean, and you'll know you did everything in your power to handle things with care."

I kept the note on my phone and didn't return to it for a couple of months. Then December arrived, and with it, the requests from Conner's parents about getting equal time with our kids on our upcoming holiday visit. Surprisingly, by the day before Christmas Eve, I still hadn't heard from my mother. I told myself I would just reach out to her when we arrived in town to work out what day she wanted to see her grandchildren.

On Christmas Eve, we decided to take our kids to the Opryland Hotel to see their over-the-top Christmas lights display. On our way there, my mom texted me:

"Hi, if you can fit me in when you are in Ohio for Christmas this year, I would like to be Target Memaw again."

The car suddenly started to shrink around me, and my stomach dropped as I read her message. Feelings of sadness and dread overwhelmed me. She didn't say, "Hi, I miss you and the kids and I'm dying to see you guys. Are you coming to Ohio? If so, I would love to spend time with you." Instead what I read was, "Hi, I want to buy your kids a bunch of plastic shit they don't need so I can tell all my friends how I filled an entire cart for you and then explain how you are so shitty to me and everyone will feel so sorry for me to have such an awful daughter."

I felt my breath go shallow with a rush of anxiety. I turned to Conner. "My mom just texted. She said she wants to be 'Target Memaw' again this Christmas. I think I need to tell her that I'm not open to seeing her this visit. I haven't even heard from her in months and all she says is 'I want to buy the kids some crap toys,' and that feels horrible."

He brushed me off. "Just keep the peace and see your mom.

Let the kids see her. It's like two hours of your life. You can do it."

I was willing to take his advice because I knew keeping the peace meant there would be no additional drama. But if I was going to stand up for myself, I knew I would need to pull up the letter I had written sooner rather than later.

I replied, "Hi Mom, we are only going to be in Ohio for a couple of days this trip. We can meet you on the 27th. Let me know what time is good for you that day."

"Oh, I can't see you on the 27th. I'm training a few people that day," she texted back.

I knew that she made her own schedule and could easily swap things around, especially since it was the week between Christmas and New Year's. Instead, she completely dismissed any possibility of changing her schedule. Was she really unable to take a little time out of her day to see *her grandkids*? Knowing how passive-aggressive she had been with me in other situations, I was convinced that she was intentionally being difficult as a means to punish me for the fact that I hadn't been her perfect little people-pleasing "yes girl" like I used to be.

I remembered this one time when I was in the sixth grade and we were driving to the mall. She was telling me about a falling out she had with an old friend, and she said, "I will be your most loyal and supportive friend until you cross me, and when that happens, you'll wish you never knew me."

Something about that memory irked me so hard now that I was on the receiving end of her wrath. I had never been on her bad side before, and now that I was, I remembered something my dad had said during their divorce. When he told us he was moving to Washington state, he said, "Ohio isn't big enough for both your mom and me, so I'm moving away."

I always thought it was preposterous that the entire state of Ohio was too small for him and my mom to live in, but now that

I was feeling the heat of her hatred, I finally understood what he meant. I wanted to be as far away from her as possible, and I was so grateful that we lived in Tennessee and that I didn't have to see her very often.

I looked toward Conner. "I really think I need to just send my mom the letter and not see her this visit. She's not even available the day that we are free."

"Do what you need to do, Ash," he said in a tone that let me know that he was disengaged.

I felt a strong knowing in my heart that it was time to send the letter. I could feel my lips begin to tingle with the onset of stress hives from the moment I first received her text, and I knew that the best thing I could do for myself would be to take a step back from my relationship with her and not see her during this trip.

I searched my Notes app on my phone and found my original letter. I knew that as much as I wanted to say this to her face, I needed to send it as a text because that was the only place she would even speak to me. I reread the letter and made a few slight changes that involved the current situation of visiting for Christmas, took three deep breaths, and hit send:

It hurts me to say this, but I don't want to see you on this visit. Your text about being "Target Memaw" seemed like just another sign to me that you are not interested in being a genuine and sincere part of our lives. You missed the opportunity to say "Hey, I care about you and would love to spend time with you when you are in town."

These past three years have been especially trying on my heart. It's so painful to know that you don't believe me or Birdie, and it hurts to feel only conditional love from you. Your passive-aggressive comments and cold demeanor take such a toll on my heart and body. I am constantly haunted by the fact that we are not close, and that we likely never will be because of all we have been through.

The thing is ... I think you are a good person. I'm proud of how you are helping so many people through your fitness training and living out your dream of owning your own gym. I know what a big deal that is for you, and I always make sure to ask you how it's going and to share my enthusiasm about it with you.

You, on the other hand, never ask me about my life, my projects, or how Conner is doing. You didn't call Milo on his third birthday or even send a card in the mail, and you never reach out to say hi to the kids without me setting it up first. I rarely hear from you.

When we do talk, I feel a sense of dread and anxiety every time. When we see each other in person, I find myself breaking out in hives and crying a lot before and after our time together. I long for a deep, genuine relationship with a mother who supports and believes in me. I've given it my best shot, but I'm sure it seems like a shitty attempt from your perspective.

In the past, I chose not to say anything for the sake of my kids and my sanity, but I cannot do that any longer. I tried to be who I think you want, but that is not who I am or who I want to be. I've been trying for two years to do what I can to mend our relationship, and all I've realized is that you cannot be the kind of mother I need and want, and I cannot be the daughter you need and want.

For my mental and physical health, I need to take a further step back from our relationship. I have made this choice after much prayer and counseling. As bad as it hurts, there is also a sense of peace that comes with knowing that I won't be living a life of obligation to you. I'm looking for authenticity in my relationships. I don't want to fake it. My relationship with my own mother isn't something that should be fake.

This letter is to let you know where I am and how I feel, and I hope it is received in a loving way, though I know it's probably coming off harsh. At holidays and birthdays, I won't be reaching out anymore. You won't hear from me for a visit when we are in Ohio. And I no longer expect you to reach out to me. Let's go our separate ways so we can both be a little freer from whatever pain and suffering we cannot seem to heal in our relationship.

I sat and stared at my phone screen for a moment after sending it, feeling numb and empty. I thought of the old man in the first *Home Alone* movie. The one who sits in the church with Kevin McCallister and confesses that his son no longer speaks to him and so if he wants to see his granddaughter, he has to go sit in the church during choir practice. I used to feel so sad for that man. How lonely he must be. How awful his son was to completely cut him out of his life. *I would never do that to my mom,* I remember thinking ... Yet here I was, a grown ass adult doing exactly that, and also wondering what toxic character trait Old Man Marley exhibited in his backstory that pushed his son away to begin with.

I was learning the very hard lesson that if you are forced to cut someone out of your life, it's because they are not safe for you, and sometimes there's no amount of Christmas magic that can redeem a relationship. But I was hopeful (or delusional?) that her response to my message could be one that looked like, "You are right. What I should have said was that I miss you and the kids instead of offering to buy you more shit. I'm sorry I didn't say how I was really feeling. I do miss you and want to see you. If there is any chance of that still happening, I will be there for you whenever you have time, but if you need to step back, I understand and I will be here when you are ready to talk."

Instead of that fantasy response, what I got was radio silence for two whole weeks. I assumed that she read it and got mad and decided I was dead to her. *Ok, that's fine,* I thought. I had played out a few different scenarios of what her response might be to this message. Being ghosted by her was one of the options and was the one I expected; the other was that she would become furious and open the floodgates of her wrath on me.

While I admit there was a small part of me hoping for the fantasy response, I knew there was less than a 1% chance of that happening, so I tried to adjust my expectations to match my reality. As the snow was stacking up outside my window on a rare Nashville snow day in mid-January that shut down the entire city, I received one of the most bizarre and upsetting text messages of my life from—of all people—Garth.

"Ashley. I wanted to let you know that I saw your message to your mother before she did, and I deleted it. It was extremely hateful and she doesn't deserve to hear that from you."

I was in complete shock reading his message, and I dropped my phone onto my bed and sat on the edge, looking out the window at the falling snowflakes. In every potential outcome of my sending this letter, I had never even considered the possibility of it being intercepted by her husband. I didn't know how to respond, if I should respond, if I should tell her he deleted it ... or if I should just go into full build-a-wall-between-us mode.

I looked down at my hands which no longer felt like my hands at all. They were shaking. My bedroom was suddenly closing in on me, and my furniture seemed to be getting larger. I was running out of space. I reached for my phone and texted my therapist, "Hey Valerie. I'm sorry to bother you, but I have kind of an emergency that I need to talk through with you ASAP."

She replied quickly since all sessions were canceled due to the few inches of snow covering the city, and a few minutes later I was on the phone explaining what had just happened. "I guess I just don't really know how to respond to this. I feel like he took my voice from me. She's my mom and even if she doesn't like what I have to say, I have every right to say it to her." My words came out in a rush.

"I want to resend it, but he'll probably delete it again. I guess I just don't want her to think that I ignored her for these two whole weeks. I wanted her to know why I was stepping back because going radio silent with her felt wrong to me. Now he has come in and manipulated the situation, and she probably thinks I've been ghosting her." I was so infuriated that he had interfered like this.

Valerie talked me through all my feelings and helped me come up with a strategy that would allow me to try to say what I needed to say to her. I decided that I would not reply to Garth's message at all, but I would send my mom the message again, this time via Facebook Messenger and email.

I decided to preface my original message with a short paragraph that explained to her that Garth had gone through her phone messages and deleted my note before she could have a chance to see it. I included screenshots of him confessing that to me, and then said, "If you choose not to read this message, that is totally fine, but I want you to be the one who makes that decision, not him."

Twenty minutes later, Garth texted me again. "I heard you went ahead and resent your message to your mother. Shame on you. We never asked for any of this; you brought it on yourself."

I haven't heard from my mother since resending the message. That was January 2018.

January of 2018 was not only the unraveling of my relationship with my mom but also my continued awakening to the fact that my marriage was completely out of balance. While I was never physically alone in my house—or anywhere I went—I had never felt more lonely. My entire life was beginning to feel like a never-ending ride on the F train from Astoria to Manhattan: sweaty, sticky hands constantly reaching for me, and the unavoidable bumping shoulders with a grouchy man who wouldn't make much eye contact with me, but would gladly press my body against a wall to feel me up just because he could.

I thought about life when we lived in New York. The red flags were all clearly marking my fate, but I couldn't recognize them yet, blinded by what I thought was love. Living in that apartment in Astoria, with no doors on any of the rooms except the bathroom, I remember how I would hurry out of the shower with my towel around my body toward the bedroom. Conner, sitting on the couch watching TV, would notice me and get up to follow me into the bedroom where I was preparing to put on my clothes.

I would feel a need to rush and get dressed before he made it into the room. If I wasn't fast enough and he caught me half-naked, he would grab my breast with his hand, squeeze, and make the same grunting sound he would make when he was eating a medium-rare steak at a fancy restaurant. I hated this and always felt dirtier than before my shower when he did it, but we were still newly engaged and I told myself he was just excited about being with me.

But even after 14 years with him, this was still part of my experience if he was around, and I was changing clothes. My body was not my own—it was his—and my opinion on how I wanted to be touched or not touched was not considered. As my husband, he believed he was entitled to my body whenever he wanted.

On his 37th birthday in late February, I knew what would be expected of me ... another expensive date night of food, drinks, and the requirement of sex. This year, he told me he wanted to use the "pull and pray" method instead of a condom. And because he was so good at pressuring me until he got his way, I agreed. But he didn't do his part of "pulling" and instead finished inside of me and then excused his actions as "I was just in the moment."

A couple of weeks later, when my period was late, all I could think was, *I'm about to have a third kid with this asshole who I don't even like.* Conner knew I had said I was done having kids, and so one day before I took a home pregnancy test, he came into the bedroom, looked me right in the eyes, and said, "If you're pregnant, are you going to give it up for adoption?"

"Excuse me, what?" I said, trying to make sure I heard him correctly.

"Will you want to give up this baby for adoption if you take this test and it's positive? I know you said you don't want to have any more kids, and honestly, I don't think we can even afford it."

"Are you fucking joking right now?" I said. "I would never give up my own child. Adoption? Really. You have no clue who I am." I got up and went into the bathroom to pee on a stick that three minutes later would give me the greatest feeling in the world: Not Pregnant with another spawn of Conner. Thank you, Jesus.

The 12 months Conner had been working in a trendy co-working space were some of the freest months I had during our marriage. He had recently bought a second car, and the kids were both in school. I finally had a few hours each day to focus on housework and grab the occasional coffee with a friend.

But when his contract at the co-working space ended, he decided not to renew it to save money. He was going back to working from home … which meant our dining room table. I braced myself for his expectations of me to be his servant-wife and captive audience again. We were together 24/7 unless he had a guys' poker night, a coffee meeting, a friend hang at the cigar shop (so gross), or the ultimate gift: an out-of-town video shoot. I prayed that God would give him all the out-of-town jobs, but his work was few and far between. We were struggling financially, relationally, spiritually—really every way imaginable —and it took all of my energy just to tread water in the relationship.

I spent my mornings rushing to get the kids off to school and my afternoons trying to avoid being asked for an "afternoon delight." If I passed him while he was working, a laundry basket full of dirty clothes in my arms, he would ask me to stop what I was doing to weigh in on which of two jackets I liked more so he could buy it for his next job. Whenever I passed him, I had to stop and look at something. He was sucking up all my time.

Not only would I make him lunch and bring it to him at his computer, but I would also clear his plate for him when he was finished. Then it was more of the same, me walking past him working at the dining room table, and him asking me to drop everything to sit down and give him my full attention on whatever he wanted to show me. If I objected, he would default to a lecture about how this is our family's livelihood and I needed to respect him and do whatever he asked because I didn't have a real job anyway. He had no respect for the work I did to manage our home and take care of our kids.

But choosing my battles was no longer something I did. He had worn me down and so my white flag of surrender was up and I bent to whatever he asked. I had resolved to fully betray myself in an effort to keep the peace in the house, but I was becoming more and more exhausted and overwhelmed, and it seemed like I had no escape. He dominated my time and body.

I was not my own, but I was growing and healing in other areas of life that began to shine a spotlight on how completely dysfunctional our marriage had become. I was standing at a fork in the road: Go to the left and continue to be miserable and insignificant in my marriage. Or, go to the right and set boundaries, start standing up for myself, and create a new destiny that could lead me to empowerment and joy.

I felt the first flicker of this awakening in 2017 at the beach with him on our first family vacation in seven years. He had taken photographs of me and the kids on the beach, and when I saw them, I didn't even recognize myself. I looked miserable and hollow, even though I was smiling. There was no spark there, just a shell of a person who was living on autopilot trying to survive each day.

As I made dinner that night, I promised myself that I would find a way back to me. I wasn't sure how to do that, but I had this staggering feeling that once I found her, I couldn't stay with Conner. Something told me that staying with him would require even deeper self-abandonment than I had already sacrificed, and if I turned back to my truth, I knew that without some sort of miracle, eventually our relationship would have to end.

chapter twelve

BOUNDARIES ARE FOR LOVERS

"You become mature when you become the authority in your own life."

— **Joseph Campbell**

In the months leading up to August of 2019, Conner was usually waking up complaining about how horribly he rested at night and blaming the mattress for how fucked up his neck was each morning. We had been snoozing on a bamboo mattress for two years after he had completed extensive research on what was the best-rated foam mattress to have. I never complained; I can sleep anywhere usually (unless there is loud snoring before I fall asleep, then all bets are off). But after a couple of years on this expensive piece of squishy foam, he was fed up with it and insisted that we go shopping for a new mattress.

"We can't really afford this right now, but I also can't afford to wake up in pain anymore," he reasoned.

"Do you just want to go try them out alone and then let me know what you decide on?" I asked, trying to get out of going to lay on beds while our kids jumped on every mattress in the store. I had stepped out of my state of denial about our marriage and had known since January that our relationship was truly falling into disrepair and now, eight months later, it felt foolish to me, buying a new mattress. But I was not ready to tell him that I was devising my exit plan from being his wife.

"No, we all need to go. I want you to be there for this. It's a big decision, Ash," he said.

We all piled into our Toyota Sienna and headed to the mall where Conner had planned to go to the Casper store to try out a few of the options he had studied during his online quest (again) for best-rated mattresses. I was armed with a couple of Ziplock baggies of Goldfish crackers and bribed the children to be on their best behavior by promising a cake pop from Starbucks afterward. (No, I am not being paid to endorse these brands.)

When we arrived at the store, Conner spoke to the sales rep about which models he was interested in, and I followed the kids from room to room as they bounced around and lay on each bed, letting me know whether they thought it was comfortable. The Casper store had each of their beds enclosed in smaller rooms that looked like cheerful little houses on the outside, so of course our kids thought they were in a fancy bounce house.

They were fascinated with everything there was to experience, from firm to pillowtop to quilts and pillows to cute little window cutouts on the display houses—they were having a blast. I was happy to let them enjoy it and tried to keep tabs on them as an excuse for not engaging in the search for Conner's perfect mattress. Soon though, he came to find us and was starting to get annoyed that I wasn't more interested in trying out the models with him.

"I need you to try these out with me. You'll be sleeping on this bed too, so you need to weigh in," he said impatiently.

"I mean, I already told you that I can sleep anywhere, so get whatever feels best to you," I replied, thinking what I really wanted to say was that he would be sleeping on the mattress alone very soon, so my opinion didn't matter. But it wasn't time to say that out loud yet. I had to prepare and save money before I could let him know that I wanted to separate.

It felt like we laid on each model at least four times, and we were there almost as long as it takes to purchase a used car, but he finally made an agonizing selection, and our overstimulated children were ready for their cake pops. I took them to the coffee shop while he finalized his purchase. I was relieved that this activity was over and wondered if I would ever get to sleep on that bed, or if I would be gone before the delivery in four to six weeks.

For the majority of our marriage, my cell phone was available to Conner anytime he needed it. I had nothing to hide, and it didn't bother me to show him the photos I had taken that day, or a funny Instagram post I had seen. But a few years into our marriage, he started a new practice that I never really understood. Whenever I would leave my phone unattended, like if I was cooking dinner or taking a shower, I would return to find him on it, scrolling through all my text messages. If he read a conversation where I even hinted at a complaint about him or shared with anyone how I was struggling in my marriage, he would confront me and tell me that I shouldn't be talking bad about him to my friends.

"It's a betrayal of our marriage," he lectured. "You shouldn't be badmouthing me to anyone. What happens between us needs to stay between *us*."

I learned quickly not to question or fight back, so I submitted like a good little Christian wife and stopped texting my friends about him, or deleted the messages once they were delivered, so he wouldn't see them. I was realizing, though, that it wasn't just a violation of my privacy, it was also a violation of my friend's privacy, too. What if they were telling me things they didn't want him to know?

In April 2019, after several years of this messed up pattern, I finally worked up the courage to ask him about it. "Conner, why are you always on my phone reading my conversations with my friends?" I asked one evening after getting out of the shower and once again not being able to find my phone where I left it.

"It's easier for me to read what happened in your day here than to ask you," he said coolly.

"Well, I'm letting you know that I don't want you to do that anymore," I replied.

"Why not?" he pushed back. "What are you worried that I might see?"

"Nothing. I'm just starting to feel like it's not fair to my friends that you read their business. They might not want you to know something they share with me in confidence," I explained.

"Who's saying stuff to you that is so private that your husband can't know?" he continued to push. Oh, the hypocrisy, from someone who once said I shouldn't be talking about our relationship to other people.

In an effort to work on our marriage, I had been reading this book called *Boundaries in Marriage*, and they had outlined several ways that I could begin to set healthy boundaries with Conner, and I was seeing that this phone situation was the perfect chance to implement a few of their techniques.

"When you are on my phone without my permission, I feel disrespected. I am asking you to stop, and if you don't, I will be putting a password on my phone that only I will know," I stated calmly.

"Are you SERIOUS right now?"

"Yes. If the only reason you are looking at my phone is that you'd like to know about what's going on in my life, I would prefer that you ask me directly instead."

"You are being ridiculous, Ash. This is asinine. You're crazy. Whatever, be like that," he huffed.

I added the password to my phone immediately and felt in that moment that I had taken one small stand for my little inner foster child to not be walked all over in every aspect of life. The feeling of victory was short-lived though, when the following evening while sitting next to him on the couch watching a show, I found a funny meme on Instagram and wanted to show him. I handed him my phone, and after he looked at it, he was back in my messages, reading. I asked for my phone back, and he got really upset.

"I don't know why you're being this way," he said. "You know, I read online that when a wife won't let her husband see her phone it's because she's having an affair."

"I can assure you, I am not having an affair. I am setting a boundary with you because I want you to talk to me about my day instead of reading my text messages."

"That's bullshit," he said as he got up and walked away, tossing my phone next to me on the couch.

This same scenario played out at least once a week in a variety of ways but always ended with him telling me how irrational *I* was being and accusing me of having an affair.

Several weeks later, after running errands, I had my phone in the dock so I could follow the directions to get us home. I've lived in Nashville for more than a decade, and I still get lost everywhere I go without the wisdom and guidance of my Waze app. The sky was filled with ominous-looking clouds.

"Do you think it's going to storm badly, or is this just a little rain?" I asked. I hate driving in Nashville when it rains. No one seems to know how to drive in wet conditions and an annoying number of people drive as if there was a sheet of ice covering the roads.

Conner reached to pull my phone off the dock.

"What are you doing?" I asked, realizing he was going to have my phone and free rein to go through all my messages. I was a little panicked, not because I was hiding any secret conversation with another man, but because since I had protected my phone with the password, it had become my safe space. My only safe space. And I had a select number of friends that I was starting to open up to about my struggles with Conner in our marriage, as well as a whole slew of secret journal entries on my phone's Notes app, where I was keeping track of all my feelings and the hateful things Conner had been saying.

I was desperate for support from my friends and needed a space to process all my feelings without the risk of him finding out. *If he has my phone right now, he will see all that I've been saying about him, and he will get mad like he did a few years ago,* I thought.

"I'm going to check the weather," he said.

"Can't you use your phone for that? I need mine up on the dock for directions," I asked.

"What's the big deal? I'm going to look up the weather," he snapped.

At that point, I had a mini freak-out moment, and I reached out and snatched my phone as quickly as I could, trying to be calm and not too dramatic. I didn't want him to see that I told my friend Raina that I had saved $1,000 toward funding my exit strategy. "I need this for directions. Please use your phone if you want to check the weather."

"I'm using my phone to try and get a video of this storm," he said. The winds were picking up and a couple of large tree branches were falling from tall oak trees on the corner ahead.

"Stop taking videos and just look up the weather," I said. "I'm nervous this storm is going to get worse, and I won't be able to drive."

"Then let me have your phone to look at the weather," he demanded.

"No," I said as I sat on my phone so he couldn't reach it.

"That's real mature, Ash."

The kids were in the back seat watching a movie, and Conner was starting to get really angry at me. He raised his voice and yelled, "I read that if a wife won't even let her husband use her phone to check the weather, she's definitely cheating."

"This is not what is happening," I said. "I am not cheating. I have set a clear boundary with you and told you why you're no longer allowed to have access to my phone."

I was not going to move my boundary. The *Boundaries* book I read said that there would be a lot of pushback and maybe even a toddler-style tantrum when setting boundaries with someone who wasn't used to having to respect them. I knew that my sitting on the phone so he couldn't grab it was not helping him to feel calm, but there was too much on the line for me, and I needed to stand firm.

I wasn't sorry that I held my ground with him, but I was sorry that our kids were in the car when all that went down. Even though they had headphones on, I knew that they were still picking up on the tension between us. And it was only getting thicker.

After my dog Roger died in September 2015, I felt like there could never be a dog as wonderful as him. He was truly special and was the best boy ever. About six months after he passed, I began to feel like our house was ready for another dog. The kids were continually asking for a puppy, and I was finally feeling my heart open up to the idea. I approached Conner about it one night after getting the kids to bed.

"We aren't ready for that yet," he said. He spouted off a list of stipulations that he wanted to happen first, including getting a second car, taking a family vacation, and a few other things that didn't seem relevant to getting a dog. I agreed to submit to his wishes and aligned myself with his preference that we wait.

As time passed, our kids kept asking. Elianna even pinned a string of yarn to Milo's shirt collar, and he would crawl behind her barking. "This game is called Puppy School," she would say. They were desperate for a dog.

I was, too, and everyone who loved me knew it. Even Conner's parents and grandma were telling him, "Your wife needs a dog." But *he* didn't want one, so we didn't get one. Three years after saying goodbye to Roger, I sat down with him and once more begged for us to get a family dog.

"It's been a whole three years, and you've accomplished so much of that list of stipulations you gave me when the kids and I first began asking for this. You have your own car now, we went on vacation, we got our taxes done … and I don't want to keep putting this off. When can we get a dog?" I asked softly.

"IF I agree to get a dog, here are my criteria: The dog has to be a puppy. It has to be a rescue. AND, it HAS to be a Golden-doodle," he said with a smug smile.

I think he thought that giving me this impossible combination would make it hard for me to find a dog that fit the criteria, and that I would eventually give up. But I had a resolve in me that I didn't even realize was possible at the time. I knew I needed a dog, I knew our kids needed a dog, and I was determined to find one.

I immediately messaged friends and family, told them what I was looking for, and within two weeks, a photo of the sweetest-faced Goldendoodle was sent to my phone. Lily, a five-month-old puppy, was being rehomed because of an illness in her original family that prevented her owners from being able to care for her properly. As soon as I saw her face, I knew she had to be ours.

She checked every single one of Conner's boxes, and just like that, I had manifested a puppy for our family. He tried to say no, but it was too late. I had already said yes. I made plans to go pick her up in Ohio and told him that he could come with us or he could stay behind, but we were going to get her over the weekend and he could not stop me. While he wasn't as thrilled as me and the kids, he decided to go with us to pick her up.

Meeting her was the happiest moment for me. I had not felt that kind of joy in the longest time, and I was so thrilled that she was officially coming home with us. We decided to stay with Alice and Matt as we always had when visiting Ohio, so once we picked Lily up from her foster friend, we headed back to their house. Lily was timid but seemed sweet and happy. Alice and Matt's dog, Goose, was not thrilled about her, and she had never met another dog before, so she had a lot of curiosity.

There was a lot of tension in the air (coming from Conner, mostly) regarding introducing Goose and Lily. When Matt let Goose out to meet her, Lily got very excited. She jumped up at Goose, and he didn't like that. He snapped at her, clipping her nose, and she yelped and was bleeding a little. Our kids and Matt and Alice's kids were all kind of stunned at what happened. Matt called Goose away from Lily and sent him to a different room.

At the sight of this, an angry flame ignited in Conner, and he began to yell, "Control your fucking dog! I swear, that better not leave a scar on this dog. We are not staying here. Ash, go pack everything up; we are leaving tonight."

No one said a word, all the kids scattered, and Conner went outside. I stood there holding Lily on her leash, and Alice handed me a towel for her nose, which looked like it had already stopped bleeding. "I'm sorry guys," was all I could think to say.

I had to follow Conner's orders. I took Lily outside so I could start packing the car. Conner wouldn't come back inside the house, so I said our goodbyes and then loaded the kids into the car. We began the drive back to Nashville as the sun was going down.

"Wait, why are we leaving tonight?" Elianna asked as I handed her and Milo headphones so that they could watch a movie on the drive (a distraction I clearly used often so they wouldn't hear their dad yelling).

"Well, Goose was kind of grouchy with Lily, like you saw ... and Dad thinks it's a better idea for us to get her home so she can get used to us in our own house." It was becoming harder for me to put a positive spin on his behaviors.

For the next hour while we were on the road, Conner lectured me about how terrible Matt and Alice were to not control their dog and kept repeating how if Lily had a scar he was "going to be pissed." He also ranted about how, "This dog is probably going to have tons of problems trusting other dogs now," and kept talking in circles about how traumatizing this was to have only had her for two hours before something bad happened.

I wanted to cry, but I had gone numb with embarrassment and sadness. I felt awful for poor Lily and knew that Conner's energy on the ride home probably didn't make her feel very welcome. I tried to shake it off and focus on getting her home and starting her new life with us. It had to get better once we were all in our own space, right?

After the first couple of days, Lily finally started feel more comfortable at our house, and that became a huge problem for Conner. She was a puppy and very high energy. She would steal entire bunches of bananas from the kitchen counter or Conner's hats that he always left laying out. She also had crazy puppy zoomies and would slam her entire body into furniture as she tore through our house.

The other thing about Lily was that she was terribly afraid of other adults coming to our house, especially if it was a man. Whenever a delivery truck would pull up, or our lawn guys would come to cut the grass, Lily would go and hide under our bed and wouldn't come out for 20 minutes. I wondered if she thought that someone was coming to take her away like she was taken from her last home. I had so much compassion for her nervous heart. Conner was the opposite and had no patience. If she got excited and jumped on him (as puppies do), he would get extremely nasty with her, shove her off him, and yell at her.

"She's out of control," Conner would say. "This is dangerous. You need to do something about this; she's going to hurt one of the kids." He wasn't wrong that her zoomies were a lot, so I hired a dog trainer and started walking her longer to help get some of her energy out.

Every morning I would wake up at 5:30 so that I could get out to walk with Lily by 6:00 and be back before anyone was awake or could even realize I had gone. After our walk, everyone would still be sleeping peacefully in their beds, so I would let Conner continue to snooze while I woke the kids, got them breakfast, packed their lunches, and took them to school.

After school drop-off at 8:00 a.m., I stopped at our local coffee shop and got an iced coffee for myself and a drip coffee for Conner. I would bring the coffee home and, while Conner was still asleep, I would quietly sit his hot coffee on his nightstand. I never expected him to say, "Hey, thanks for getting me a coffee," because that was never even something that he would acknowledge as special—more like something he felt he deserved and was entitled to.

Since he was working from home then, there was not a lot of opportunity for alone time or any autonomy at all, so his mood upon waking up would dictate how the rest of my day was going to go. I could just tell by the way he was breathing if he was waking up in a good mood or a bad mood. One morning, I heard him stirring in the bedroom, and he grabbed his coffee and made his way into the living room. He was breathing heavily through his nose, which usually meant he was annoyed and stressed.

Lily saw him and got excited and jumped up onto him a little. He shoved her and yelled "No!" and then came directly in front of me holding his arm and said, "That dog scratched me! Look at what she did to me." He shoved his forearm in my face, and I observed a scratch from her paw where she accidentally scraped him when jumping up to say hello. He wasn't bleeding, it was just a little red mark from her nails.

"This is fucked up. I have to endure all this for you, and you give me NOTHING in return," he fumed.

I looked at him blankly and thought to myself, *I literally let him sleep in this morning while I took our kids to school and brought him a coffee. I cannot spend the rest of my life with this boy. He can't even be kind to a dog, let alone his wife who does everything for him.*

I didn't know what to say, but I knew that this wasn't Lily's fault, and I was really noticing how he had become so reactive toward her. I felt sad and worried that he was going to continue to be unkind to her. I needed to protect her, so I started wearing a leash around my waist and kept Lily attached to it at all times, so that I could keep her from jumping on Conner and so that she could learn that I was her person.

I even took her to the playground every day after school so that she could get exposure to lots of different types of people and practice being greeted by other men who were more patient and kind than my husband. I did this for her first six months with our family so that I could protect her from Conner's angry outbursts, which were pretty much a weekly occurrence at this point. I was feeling increasingly more unsafe with him, emotionally and now physically as well.

A few mornings later, as I placed a hot to-go cup of coffee on his nightstand, Conner's first words of the day to me were, "I told a few of my friends at poker last night that you wake up every morning to go walk the dog for an hour, and they all think that's just as weird as I do." I had just returned from walking Lily, and he was still laying in bed, scrolling Instagram on his iPhone.

"Ok?" I replied.

"I'm just saying it's so strange that you wake up and go so early. I think you must be meeting someone on these walks," he accused.

I turned to head toward the door and said, "Well, I'm not. It's just me and Lily." As I slipped through the doorway, I grabbed my phone from my pocket to add this interaction to my Notes app, where I was documenting all the bonkers things he had been saying to me. I suddenly found myself being followed by him, to continue the conversation.

"I'm gonna be honest ... I never understood it when people would say that marriages suffer when the couple has a new baby. People say it's because the father is usually jealous of the attention that the wife gives to their baby, but I never had that with either of our kids." He paused. "But I do have that with this dog. Everything you do is for this dog. We have barely even had sex since we brought her home. I know that she is the reason ... You spend too much time with her," he said.

"You're telling me right now you are jealous of a dog and think that is why we aren't having sex as often? No, I told you weeks ago, and I will remind you now: I have set a new boundary regarding sex, and I am only giving you love in that way when you make me feel loved by respecting my boundaries and treating me with kindness. This has nothing to do with Lily."

"It has everything to do with her," he argued. "In fact, you should be giving it up to me even more because I let you adopt her."

The entitlement. The audacity. I repeated myself and tried to wrap up this insane conversation. "You will receive love from me in the ways you want it when you have shown me love in a way that I receive it. It could not be more obvious what my love language is—I run a business based on words of affirmation and encouragement. It's all spelled out for you, a very clear roadmap to my heart. I just wish you could be kinder to me."

He looked at me, emotionless. "You knew exactly who I was when you married me."

chapter thirteen

RICH WIFE'S HOBBY

*"A woman with a voice is, by definition, a strong woman.
But the search to find that voice can be
remarkably difficult."*

— **Melinda Gates**

I'm fairly certain that thanks to Conner getting a second car for our family, our marriage was given an extension of about three years. Having the minivan all to myself (and the kids) gave me more freedom and autonomy. I no longer needed to coordinate my grocery store trips or play dates or school schedules with Conner's work day. I was so grateful to have this freedom.

We brought his new Subaru Outback home on a Sunday afternoon in October. By Tuesday, I was preparing to go to a pop-up event at a local stationery boutique where I would set up a small table for Love Everywhere and have the opportunity to sell my designs. I did these pop-up shops from time to time, and Conner was usually annoyed that I was asking him to watch the kids so that I could go make a couple hundred bucks. But he agreed to it on this particular night. I needed to leave by 4:30 p.m. to get to the stationery store and set up by the time the event started.

At 4:15, my phone rang. "Hey, I haven't left my office yet. I'm letting you know that I am running a bit late," Conner said.

"Ok, how late do you think you will be? I am supposed to be all set up for this event by 5:30," I reminded him.

"Listen, your event isn't as important as this job I am working on, so you'll just have to get there when you get there. I'll leave soon though," he snapped at me.

Feeling all the pressure, I tried to take a few deep breaths. He finally pulled into the driveway with his two-day-old Subaru. Conner breathed heavily as he grunted at me about how annoyed he was that I was leaving. I kissed our kids goodbye, ran out the door, and quickly hopped into my car to head to the event. I was in an obvious hurry because Conner was so late.

I started the engine and admittedly wasn't paying much attention to my surroundings when I put it in reverse. I lightly hit the gas and looked in my rearview mirror. Everything looked clear, then suddenly it felt as though I had backed into a trash can.

What was that?, I thought as I looked in my mirror again. It was just barely getting dark outside, and I was still not sure what had happened. I got out of the car to see that I had backed into Conner's new car.

Oh shit, oh shit, oh shit, I thought. He had parked on an angle behind me that was perfectly situated in my blind spot. This, plus the fact that I was not used to having a car parked behind me for the past 11 years, contributed to my giant mistake. I panicked. The front driver's side bumper on his car was majorly dented. I had to go inside and tell him. I was petrified, worried sick about what his reaction would be. There was never any grace for me if I made a mistake. Why did he park right behind me when he knew I was leaving? I knew better than to ask him that question, so I went back inside with my tail between my legs, like the most frightened dog, to tell him the news.

He was already seated at his computer at the dining room

table, with his back to the door. The kids were in the next room watching TV. I said, "Conner, I just backed into your car. I am so sorry."

He turned, his eyes dark, and said, "You're joking."

"No. I'm so sorry ..." I said. My hands were shaking.

"You've got to be fucking kidding me," he huffed as he stormed outside to see for himself.

When he saw the dented bumper, he looked at me, angry, and yelled, "How could you do this? This car is only two days old, and you've already destroyed it. This is so fucking classic. You never pay attention to anything. You are so careless."

I began to cry. "I know. I am so sorry."

"You're not going to that event now; you need to cancel. This is a fucking nightmare," he said and chaotically stormed back into the house, leaving me standing alone in the driveway sobbing.

I looked up to see him through the kitchen window, rage-kicking a box from our recycling bin through the air. The box flew across the room, and all I could think at that moment was that our kids were inside, and he was throwing things. I went back inside, still crying, and tried to make sure that he got himself under control so that the kids wouldn't see him hulking out. He continued to reprimand me, and I tried to dry my tears as Elianna entered the kitchen.

"What's going on?" she asked.

"Your mom just wrecked both of our cars," he answered her. Then he went back outside.

"Are you ok, Mommy?" she asked me.

"Yeah, I am fine, sweet girl. I just feel really bad for messing up Daddy's new car." I was not successful in sucking up my tears.

"Well, it's just a car ..." she said. And she was right. It was just a car. How Conner reacted to me is what was really hurting my heart. What happened was an unfortunate mistake on my part, and there was so much anger toward me. The way he was yelling at me felt so awful. I felt like I had done something completely unforgivable. I felt worthless and hopeless.

I was pouring myself into Love Everywhere, my passion project, and had been asking God to bring me something to be excited about with this endeavor to help me feel like I had a purpose. I was desperate for validation, encouragement, and kindness. Conner was usually so self-absorbed that he didn't see how badly I was hurting, and I knew it was only a matter of time before my position as a stay-at-home mom was going to come under scrutiny again.

I thought that if I could do more with Love Everywhere, he would see my value, and I would be able to make money for our family without causing him the inconvenience of parenting our children. That's messed up, I know. Still, I would pray daily and ask God, "Please bring me something today that is good that I can be proud of."

One day in early spring of 2018, that prayer was answered when I got an email from a woman named Mia who followed Love Everywhere on Instagram. She worked in marketing for Reebok and wanted to pitch Love Everywhere as a new brand collaboration for a potential multi-season deal. I couldn't believe it, and I excitedly shared the news with Conner when he returned home from a coffee meeting.

"This seems cool, but make sure it's legit," he advised. "And see if we can get some free shoes," he added, always feeling entitled to more.

I planned a call with Mia to hear more about what she was thinking, and by the end of the call, I felt like I had made a new friend. She totally understood the mission of Love Everywhere, and Reebok wanted to put over 200,000 encouragement cards inside their sneaker boxes, as well as build out an entire collection of sneakers, apparel, and accessories to promote the collaboration. Reebok offered to fly me out to discuss the details of the first capsule launch at their headquarters in Boston.

As soon as Conner found out that they wanted me in Boston, he said, "You can't go there alone. You need me there with you. Ask Mia if Reebok will pay for me to fly out, too."

Of course, I was thinking that I could have enjoyed a little time alone, but he was my husband, so I did what he told me to, and in a few weeks we were flying into Boston Logan International Airport for a quick overnight trip. We arrived at the Reebok offices, got a tour of their building, and then stepped into meetings where designs were presented.

"After this first launch, you will get to have even more input on the designs of the next season, but for now what do you think of these?"

I was just happy to be in the room and would have said, "This looks great!" but Conner was there, and he spoke up before I could. "What was the intention of the design on the bomber jacket?" he asked.

Suddenly, I felt a shift in the room as the oxygen felt like it had been completely sucked out, and Conner went on to say that he would like to speak to the designer. As if he were Kanye putting out the first pair of Yeezys. I began to feel my cheeks turn hot with embarrassment, but what could I do? Either disrespect my husband in this conference room full of strangers and tell him to stuff it, or tell myself that he must be seeing something I wasn't and trust that he was looking out for what was best for my brand. I struggled to believe that, but he was my husband. I thought I had to yield to him in everything.

The rest of the meeting was so painful, and then finally we were able to go to the hotel and freshen up before an evening event at their flagship store. The entire time we were in the hotel room, Conner worked to plant seeds of distrust in my mind about this collaboration. We had already signed a contract, so we were locked into at least one season, but Conner was saying, "They showed you 18 SKUs of product, and they're set up to make so much more on this collaboration than you are. You need to go to them and ask for more money now that we have seen what they are planning. They need to be paying you more, or you can't do this collaboration."

Holy shit. How was I going to navigate this? Conner got on the phone with our attorney, told him to get involved, and then spent the next two weeks emailing back and forth with Mia, who was trying desperately to save this partnership. Conner would no longer allow me to email anyone at Reebok on my own from my business email. He wanted to be cc'd on everything and forbid me from sending any replies that he had not approved before. It all felt so awful. All I wanted to do was see this move forward and share love and kindness with strangers, but Conner was letting his greed get the best of him, and it was nearly killing my deal.

Somehow, miraculously, we were able to find a way forward, but he had severely damaged my relationship with the brand, and I knew that we would not get to extend our contract into future season collaborations. I was devastated at how things had turned out, but I put on my bravest face and tried to make the most of what I had accomplished, even with all the chaos Conner had created.

In preparation for the launch date of this collaboration, I lined up several podcast interviews and landed a guest spot with one of the biggest boss babe entrepreneur podcasts at that time. I had been a fan of the show for years and was extremely geeked out that they agreed to have me on their show. It was a total dream come true, and the interview process went so well.

The first 24 hours after my episode aired, my Instagram following shot up by more than 3,000 new followers, and I received countless messages about how people thought Love Everywhere was so inspiring. I was feeling validated and good about my work. People actually thought what I was doing was cool and wanted to be a part of it! My heart was so full and encouraged, for the first time maybe ever.

The next day, Conner woke up breathing heavily, and he was grouchy about our finances. He had a therapy appointment that afternoon, and when he returned home his mood had drastically changed. He was almost giddy.

"I just had one of the best sessions I've ever had with a therapist," he said.

I was unloading the dishwasher and looked up to see his smiling face. "That is so awesome!" I was legitimately happy he was in better spirits and had found a therapist that he seemed to like, after going through a series of people that he didn't "click" with.

"Yeah, John is great. He actually said something to me today that made me feel fully understood for the first time ever during therapy, but I'm not going to tell you what that was because I think it would hurt your feelings."

"Ok? Well, yeah, don't tell me because I am feeling pretty good about life right now. Did you see I have more than 3,000 new Instagram followers?" I said excitedly.

"Yeah, I shouldn't tell you this," he replied.

I thought it was so strange that he would tell me that his therapist said something that might hurt my feelings, but I was flying too high to let this get me down. Later, when I was cleaning up after dinner and the kids were playing in their rooms, he came up to me *again*, talking about how good his session was and how he couldn't tell me what his therapist said. Again I agreed, "Please don't tell me something if you think it will hurt my feelings."

When bath time and bedtime routines were complete, I hit the shower. I was longing for a relaxing night where I could just Netflix and chill (literally), but when I finally sat down on the couch at 10:30 p.m., Conner could no longer contain himself. He blurted out, "John said that Love Everywhere is nothing more than a rich wife's hobby, and we aren't rich, so it's time for you to start making more of a financial contribution around here."

I was completely crushed as he said this. I looked him in his eyes, which were sparkling like it was Christmas morning, and I said, "You are absolutely right. That did hurt my feelings, and I wish you hadn't said that to me."

I got up and went to bed where I lay awake, silently sobbing. He knew how hurtful it would be to tell me that, and yet he couldn't contain himself—he actually seemed to take pleasure in telling me. I was feeling so lost in my marriage, and I knew he did not value or respect me. I knew I deserved more.

Summer was winding down and the kids were heading back to school; Elianna was starting second grade, and Milo was headed to kindergarten. After school, I usually took the kids to the playground to get their wiggles out and see all their friends. I used this time to catch up with my other mom friends until one of our children inevitably interrupted our conversation because they needed to go home to pee.

On the afternoon of their second day of school, we went to the playground as usual. Conner said that he might swing by to see the kids at the playground on his way home from a meeting.

While standing in the shade of a tall walnut tree, I struck up a conversation with one of the dads.

"You don't have your dog with you today," the dad noted. He was one of the guys that would say hi to Lily when I brought her to the playground before school let out for the summer.

"Yeah, it's too hot today," I said. "I didn't want her to be miserable out here in this heat."

"Totally get that. How was your summer?" he asked.

"It was good," I answered. "We didn't do much other than hang out at the YMCA pool. How was yours?"

"Oh, it was fine. Our kids got to visit my parents for a week, and then we took a vacation to Gulf Shores," he said.

As he started describing their vacation, my attention shifted to Conner, who had just arrived and was walking up to where we were standing. He wore a blankly sour expression on his face, his thin lips dangling with every heavy step he took. Grouchy was an understatement.

When he reached where I was standing and chatting with the other dad, I introduced him.

"Hey, glad you made it," I said. "This is my husband, Conner. And …" I struggled to recall his name, and I was feeling sheepish. "I'm so sorry, I have forgotten your name …"

The dad stuck out his hand for a handshake. "It's Logan."

"Hey," Conner said dimly. He quickly shook Logan's hand, then immediately reached for his phone and stood there, disengaged.

"We were just talking about how our summers were," Logan said, trying to loop Conner in on the fact that he was not trying to be weird or creepy by talking to his wife on the school playground.

"Cool," Conner said without even looking up from his phone. After a moment, Elianna was calling his name, so he walked away toward the monkey bars to watch her do a trick.

"Your kids have great sneakers this year," Logan said.

"Conner actually picks out all their sneakers," I said, as I remembered how much Conner liked to receive credit for the small things he did to help our family, and was hoping that my nod to him here would somehow pay off as bonus points for me later.

"Well they're great," Logan said as Conner approached us once more. Conner didn't say a word, only got out his phone again and began scrolling his social media feed. "Conner, I was just remarking how your kids have great sneakers this year, and your wife told me that you pick out their sneakers. Great job, man!" Logan was really trying to appease the grouchy monster.

Without making eye contact with Logan, Conner replied, "Yeah, I have *impeccable* taste."

I was mortified. He was being so rude and unfriendly. He didn't even seem like he wanted to be there by the way he was so engulfed in his phone. I couldn't bear to stay there any longer. I stood up and announced to the children that it was time to go.

"Mom, we've literally only been here 10 minutes," Elianna protested.

"I know, sorry guys. It's just so hot today. Why don't we go get ice cream instead?" Obviously I am not against harnessing the power of bribery with my children. "Who wants to ride with Daddy?" I asked, assuming that Conner would want to get ice cream with us. But neither kid wanted to ride with their dad, so he said he would just go home.

When we got home, Conner was standing in the kitchen, smoldering. As the kids were walking by him with their backpacks and their ice cream, he approached me and loudly asked, "Who the fuck was that guy?"

"He's just a dad at the playground," I replied calmly, as I tried to quickly assess the severity of my transgression for having a friendly conversation with a man who had apparently threatened Conner.

"He's not just a dad," Conner said, mockingly. "That guy goes to the YMCA, and when you were on the elliptical machine once, he chose the machine right next to yours when there were six other machines open. That guy has an agenda." The vein in the middle of his forehead was pumping blood overtime and bulging.

"I have no idea what you are talking about, but I can assure you that there is nothing going on with me and that dad. I couldn't even remember his name today when I went to introduce you ..." I added, trying to appease him.

"Oh, yeah, how *convenient*. Something fishy is going on between you two," Conner retorted.

"This is ridiculous," I said. "I'm not having this conversation any longer."

"Well, mark my words, that guy will make a move on you at some point," he said, like a jealous Nostradamus.

"Whatever," I muttered under my breath as I left him standing alone in the kitchen and went to the bathroom to cry alone before making dinner. I shut and locked the door, and assumed my familiar position sitting on the side of the bathtub with a towel over my face to muffle the sound of my sobbing.

I could hear our kids in the hallway outside the bathroom. They were chasing each other and being rambunctious, laughing happily. I could hear Conner, annoyed, tell them to settle down and then loudly exclaim, "I don't know *where* your mother is." But he knew.

"I don't know how much longer I can do this," I prayed. "Please help. Please help. Please help." It seemed insane to me that he continued to accuse me of cheating, and my head was pounding and felt like my brain was going to explode trying to rationalize how he had just come at me like that. *I'm stupid to stick around for more of this,* I thought. *But I don't even know if I can survive on my own—especially as a single mom.*

I made a quick note in my phone marking what had happened between us so that when he tried to tell me he didn't say that or he didn't mean it the way I heard it, I would know what I heard, and that I wasn't crazy.

Eventually, I made my way out and back into the kitchen to cook a meal that he would complain about, before getting the kids to bed by myself, while he sat browsing the internet on his laptop. The next day at the playground after school, I told my friend Tess about what happened. She was shocked. "What are you going to do?" she asked.

"I'm going to start looking for a place to live, and I'm going to rent a house and get it furnished for me and the kids, and then I am going to tell him I am leaving," I said. "I can't do this anymore. He's only getting worse."

The next day, I found a place that looked doable, and called Tess and asked her to come see it with me so I wouldn't have to do it alone. She kindly agreed, and we met after dropping our kids off at school. The house was a duplex and only a couple blocks from the school. When we walked inside, it was tiny, but I kept thinking, *Anything is better than living with him.* We turned the corner to the kitchen. A dirty oven and stove top with missing burners sat next to a small refrigerator that was supposed to be white but was more of a grimy off-white. "Ok, so it needs a good cleaning," I said, trying to be optimistic.

Tess was trying to be supportive, so she just kept smiling. My positive vibes were really starting to drain out of my heart, and then we saw the bathroom. The bathtub looked hazardous to children, and it was filthy. Tess leaned into my ear and said, "This won't do."

She was right. There was no way I could bathe my kids in that bathtub. We left and went to get sandwiches. "I know I can't live there ... and that was the only place listed that I could even sort of afford," I said. We finished our food and went our separate ways. I thanked Tess for her kindness and willingness to go with me to that horrible duplex.

The rest of the day I felt like my whole body was underwater. I thought I was going to be sick. It was such a surreal feeling, taking that one action of looking at a place of my own. As much as I wished I didn't have to do this, I knew that if I stayed much longer, I was going to lose myself completely, and our kids would see my misery and think that all this tension and fighting is what love is supposed to look like. I wanted more for them. I wanted more for myself.

At my next therapy session, I told Valerie everything that happened. She looked at me with a most serious face and said, "He is holding you back, he's gaslighting you, and he's emotionally abusive. If you want to leave, I know that you can do it. But you both absolutely need a long-term separation for clarity so that you can get some space and see how that feels to you."

What she said felt so big to me, and I realized that I needed someone to tell me that I could do it. I didn't know if I believed I could, but if she thought that I was capable, maybe I was. I knew how difficult all of this was going to be, the separating of two codependent souls. I decided after telling her about my tour of the scariest duplex in East Nashville that it made more sense for our kids to get to keep their bedrooms and stay in their house. I needed to ask *him* to leave, but I wasn't sure how.

I knew I needed space to breathe and be myself without being overwhelmed by his presence, demands, and outlandish accusations every time I turned around. So I did more walking the dog and crying out to the heavens, begging for wisdom and courage, and the right words to say and to know exactly the right time to say them.

I knew I was unhappy in my marriage for several years before I finally understood why. I believed that the problem was me, and so I read all the self-help books and tried to work on myself. I found myself praying that God would change *me*. That I would become the wife that Conner needed, that I would become more supportive, that the gaps in our love could be repaired and filled. I truly believed I was the problem. And no matter what I did, it was never enough.

Eleven years into our marriage, and it turns out I wasn't doing as great of a job hiding the negative dynamics of our relationship from the outside world as I thought I was. This became abundantly clear in our financial planner's office one afternoon. Conner had been meeting with Miriam to get her help with his business finances and decided to tap her vast knowledge for our family finances as well.

He brought me to her office where we all sat with bottled waters and a manila folder of our expenses and debts. Miriam would ask me questions about our family situation and the bills, and every time, Conner would jump in and answer her, sometimes talking over me until I submitted to his answer (which did not take long). Eventually, I was just sitting in my chair quietly while he did all the talking.

Once he had guzzled two bottled waters, he needed a bathroom break. Miriam made a little small talk with me about our kids, and as soon as Conner was out of earshot, she looked right at me with the most serious face and said, "Are you safe? Are you ok?" and though I was taken aback at her directness, I was also relieved that someone else was seeing what was happening to me: the oppression, the silencing, the manipulation, the controlling.

I mumbled quietly, "Yeah, I'm safe," just as Conner's heavy footsteps were drawing nearer in the hallway.

"You let me know if that ever changes," Miriam said quickly before Conner reentered the room.

He returned to his chair, and it was back to business as usual with Miriam assigning action points for us to gather for her so that we could devise a plan to tackle our debts. As we left her office that day, I couldn't help but wonder how many other people saw what Miriam saw and just didn't have the guts to ask me the way that she did. If she could see it after being in a room with us for half an hour, it must have been worse than I thought.

A few years later, as I was preparing to ask Conner to leave, I immediately contacted Miriam. She met me for coffee and told me about this divorce workshop where I could learn about the financial ramifications of divorce and the reality of what life is like as a single mom. There would also be a divorce lawyer who would share their professional opinion on how the legal system works and hand out packets of resources to help us navigate the process.

"There's a meeting this Saturday. It's from 8:00 a.m. until noon. Can you get away?" she asked.

"I can probably make up a story about having to go help a friend or something and see if Conner will stay with the kids," I said.

"Do what you have to do, but I really think you need to be there. I'll pay for your seat so that he doesn't see any money leave your bank account." Miriam's generosity toward me was beyond gracious. I couldn't believe that someone who barely knew me was willing to go the distance to help me get out of a bad situation with my husband.

That Saturday, I arrived at the workshop to a room already filled with the most heartbroken and exhausted collection of women I have ever seen. The heaviness and sadness on their faces was undeniable. A scatterbrained little old woman, who sort of reminded me of my Bubby, handed us all folders stuffed with pertinent information. Her name was Annalise, and she was the organizer of this workshop. She was also a divorce financial planner.

She greeted us all and gave a presentation on how assets are divided in a divorce, as well as a few jaw-dropping statistics such as, "Baby boomer wives typically give their husbands control of their finances and 59% of these women have no idea what is going on in their bank accounts. More alarming than this is that 64% of millennial wives have zero involvement in their finances." I was part of that 64%, and I was shocked that so many of us had given so much power and the ability to control everything in the family to our husbands.

The other striking observation I made during this workshop was the fact that so many of the women in the room were well into their late 50s and 60s. Some of them asked questions and shared snippets of their stories, and all I could think was, *These women all stayed for their kids and are here now saying they wished they hadn't wasted those 25 years being unhappy. I do not want to get a divorce and start over at 65. I don't want to live a lie and waste my life being sad when I could take my power back now and finally be free.*

A few minutes into the presentation, I knew for sure that I was going to get a divorce and that Juliette, the attorney presenting that day, was going to be my attorney. She had more than 30 years of experience and had so much compassion for everyone that asked questions during the workshop. I booked an appointment with her one day in September and shared my situation. When I told her about how horrible he was to our dog, Lily, Juliette said, "The best thing you ever did was get that dog. She's showing you the truth and giving you unconditional love. You're going to need her in these coming months."

I knew she was right. This was going to be an excruciating process, and I was going to need all the emotional support I could get.

chapter fourteen

THE TRUTH LOOKS BEAUTIFUL ON YOU

"A person who deserves my loyalty receives it."
— Joyce Maynard

The pressure was building in my relationship with Conner. I knew that there was nothing else I could do to make it work; I had exhausted all my resources, and to stay in this relationship longer meant that I would have to become an actual zombie wife who only existed to make everyone else more comfortable in their lives. But would that actually be the best for my kids? Would they settle for less than they deserved because that's what they watched me do their whole lives? Would my daughter allow her spouse to treat her with disrespect? Would my son know how to truly love his partner?

I was still standing at the fork in the road, but now I could see that just because my current existence felt familiar didn't mean it was safe. My life was predictably miserable and would only continue to be that way with Conner's constant accusations that he thought I was cheating on him, along with the arguments and his increasingly controlling behaviors.

The bigger risk—the unknown of asking him to leave when I had no job and no family to fall back on for financial help—was less terrifying to me now than the thought of continuing to put myself through more relationship hell. Another early morning walk with the dog a few days after viewing that shitty duplex with my friend Tess brought more tears and more prayers. This time, when I spoke to God, I said, "I am ready to move on from this relationship. I trust that you will give me the right words to say and that you will let me know when exactly is the right time to say them."

Two days later, Conner had me cornered in our bedroom and was waving his fingers in my face about how asinine it was that I wouldn't bend my boundaries for him, clearly angry and ranting about how I must be hiding something since he wasn't even allowed to use my phone. As he talked in circles, I felt a pull on my spirit and got the message that it was safe for me to ask him to move out now. The time had come to finally speak my truth. I took a long, deep breath and began.

"I'm going to be brutally honest right now, and it should not come as a surprise to you. I have been setting all these bound-aries as a way to establish myself as a human being and to attempt to get our relationship in a healthier place. You have clearly not respected the boundaries I have been setting, and I have been miserable for a very, very long time. It has been so bad lately that last week I went to look at a rental house and was going to move into it with the kids. I took Tess with me to look at this place, and it was in awful condition, and that's when I realized that I can't move the kids out of their house. That wouldn't be fair to them.

"So I am telling you now; I need to be separated from you. I am feeling completely suffocated by you and what's worse is that your constant accusations and angry outbursts happen right in front of our kids. This is not the kind of environment I want them exposed to and definitely don't want them thinking that the way you treat me is ok. It's *not* ok. I am asking you for a separation for clarity. I need space to be myself without you for at least three months. This is not negotiable. You have to find somewhere else to go, and you need to do it within the next week."

I was so scared to say all of this, but as soon as I did, I felt a massive shift in my heart and within my body. I physically felt lighter as the weight of carrying these feelings lifted from my shoulders and shifted from me to Conner.

He immediately walked toward me. My back was up against the wall in our bedroom, and he got down on his knees directly in front of me, put his head down, lifted his prayer hands up toward me in perfect begging formation, and said, "Please don't do this to me. You have to understand that it has been *your* boundaries and *your* behavior that has made me act this way. Please. I am begging you. Don't do this. Don't throw away 14 years of our lives."

I could not believe that even in his apology and imploring me not to do this, he still could not accept responsibility for his actions and was blaming me. "Get up. That was not an apology. You need to get out of this house by Friday. I have nothing else to say to you right now."

"Where am I supposed to go? You can't just tell me to leave; I have nowhere to go."

"Go to Ohio, stay with your parents, call a friend in town ... I don't care. But if you're not gone by Friday, I will take the kids, and we will go somewhere until you're out of here." I wasn't angry with him. I was relieved, and I was fucking proud of myself for saying what I needed to say. For the first time ever in my life, I was saying what I wanted and it felt so good.

Speaking my truth was setting me free. I could hear the chains falling off and clanking onto the ground. I was stepping into my power—no, I was running toward it full force—and I was not ever going back to that dark and lonely place. My therapist had told me that once I asked him to leave, he would try to manipulate and weasel his way into not actually leaving. If I was serious about my request, I would need to be extremely firm and not budge even an inch. My ultimate objective was to protect myself and my best interest. Even though it was going to seriously suck seeing my truth hurt his feelings, it was time, and I needed to stand up for myself.

Conner requested we do an emergency marriage counseling session because he had no place to stay and wanted me to sit with his therapist (you remember—the one who said Love Everywhere was a rich wife's hobby) so that we could discuss our actual options and why we "couldn't afford" to get a divorce. Not because he valued me or our relationship, but literally because we didn't have the money. *I will find the money,* I thought. I went to the therapy session with only one agenda: I'm here because he needs to leave our house, and if he doesn't, I will. I maintained that I needed space and that I deserved to have this request honored.

His therapist agreed with me and told Conner that if he ever hoped to mend our relationship, how he behaved now was crucial. He told Conner to go to Ohio and stay with his parents for a bit to respect my request. Not without a lot of protest and excuses, eventually Conner agreed to leave. After the therapy session, he went to the house to pack a bag of his things, and I went to get the kids from school. When I got back, we told them that Conner had a job in Ohio and would be gone for a while, which was not unusual for them. When he left that day, I knew in my spirit that he would never be coming back, but I wasn't ready to say it out loud yet.

Conner's therapist (who mainly focused on therapy for creatives and entrepreneurs) suggested we meet with one of his colleagues, Fiona, whose primary focus was marriage and family therapy, so that we could have someone uniquely qualified to help us communicate and find a positive path forward.

I agreed to go to three of these appointments, and when I sat with her alone, I told her, "I am here because I want to help make sure that Conner is ok (the gray area of inner conflict at its finest) and able to hear that I want a divorce. I am not here to fix this. It cannot be fixed."

Fiona asked me a lot of questions about our relationship, and I answered them all with severe honesty. "Do you think that Conner is a narcissist?" she asked me.

"My experience with Conner has been one full of his controlling and manipulative behaviors. So I think he is manipulative and controlling."

"I would say those are textbook signs of narcissism," she replied.

"Well, then there you go," I said. I never wanted to go into any therapy session trying to diagnose my partner with any sort of disorder or mental health issue. That seemed in poor taste to me. I have always trusted that when I am honest about my personal experience, people can see what's happening without me having to put a psychology term on it. That was more powerful to me than me telling them. It also validated my experience so much more at a time when I needed every tiny nudge of encouragement I could get.

He went to Ohio for a week and then came back and rented a condo from Airbnb for another week which cost $500. We didn't have money for that and he knew it, but he said he had nowhere else to go.

"Why didn't you just stay in Ohio longer?" I asked.

"Ashley, my work is here. My life is here. I can't just stay in Ohio," he snapped back.

"Well you can't come back here, so you need to figure out what you're going to do when your time at this Airbnb is up," I said flatly. I had to stay emotionless to maintain my boundaries and keep him from finding a foothold to pull me back under his control. After his time ran out at the Airbnb, he moved into a friend's house who was out of the country for six months. It was furnished, and the house was in the neighborhood, so he was close by.

When he would stop by the house to pick something up or see the kids, it always ended with me being cornered and having to talk with him about why I was doing this to him, and how he couldn't figure out why I would throw away 14 years of our lives for no reason. "I don't think you understand what you're doing here," he would say.

Over the long Labor Day weekend, he was supposed to take the kids to Chattanooga. The day he was meant to take them, he still hadn't booked a hotel and kept pushing their pickup time back so that he could figure it out. By dinner time, he still hadn't been by to get them, and they had been packed and ready, sitting by the window watching for over two hours. I was heavily triggered by memories of being a little girl and waiting for my dad who was usually late to pick us up for his weekends.

I left a note on the door for him that said, "Conner, we have gone out to dinner after the kids waited over two hours for you, and you never showed. Don't bother taking them tonight. It's obviously too late at this point anyway."

I taped the note to the door and went in to get the kids. "Hey guys," I said. "Dad isn't going to be getting you tonight because something came up, but the good news is that we get to go have dinner and even go to Target after for a fun little toy to say thanks for your patience today."

The kids picked the restaurant and by the time we were

walking in the toy aisle of Target, Conner texted me. "I'm just going to get them tomorrow. I waited too long to book the hotel today and nothing was available."

"Fine," I said, disgusted with how he had left them hanging all day long. I wondered if this would be an indication of how life as co-parents would be after we were divorced, and my heart was heavy for this season of life and how our kids were going to have to navigate it all. But I moved through the guilt and found grace for myself.

About a month after Garth had overstepped his boundaries by telling me that he deleted my message to my mother, I still hadn't heard from her. It was mid-February when I got a call from my cousin, Birdie. "Arthur died. I just found out from my dad. I thought you should know," she said.

"Ok, thanks for telling me since I don't expect to hear anything from my mom," I replied.

"Yeah, that's what I was thinking, too." Birdie sighed. "I'm not going to his funeral. Alice and my mom aren't going either. Matt is going to go with my dad in solidarity so he doesn't have to go alone."

"Well, I'm not driving in from out of town for his funeral," I said.

"I wouldn't either if I were you, but I will let you know how it goes for my dad."

"Thanks." We got off the call not too long after that, and I hung up feeling nothing.

I always thought that when my grandfather died, I would be just as upset and shaken as I was when Nanny passed away. But having all the truth out in the light, and after not having any contact with him or my mom for so long, what I felt was the same feeling I had when I would watch the evening news and the reporter would announce that a celebrity had died—but like, a celebrity that I wasn't a fan of. *Ok, he is dead now,* is all I thought.

A few days later, I was notified of what happened at the wake and funeral by Birdie via text message:

"Your mom had a fake family at the funeral. She was introducing Jonah and Quinn and their three children as her 'kids and grandkids' to everyone there. They sat with her in the front row during the wake and the funeral service. People who know you were so confused."

As I read this text message, it felt like my entire life was exploding in my face. How could my own mother attempt to completely replace me and her actual grandchildren, and introduce these imposters to people who we've known our whole lives as if it were actual truth? Did she think that no one would notice that they weren't me and my family?

I know Jonah and Quinn. She replaced me with people I actually KNOW. Jonah's family and mine have been in each other's lives for more than 30 years. My mom and Uncle Rhett grew up with Jonah's parents in the same church youth group on Seventh Avenue.

To be replaced by Jonah and his wife and kids at my grandfather's funeral made so much sense to me and yet, at the same time, was completely unbelievable. After everything I'd been through with my mother over the past two years, I thought, *Even Shonda Rhimes couldn't make this shit up.*

I imagined the scene in my head and how truly fucked up my mom was. On her social media page, she had been referring to Jonah and Quinn as her "framily" and posted often about how sometimes this "framily" was better than actual family. *Good for her; they can have each other,* I thought. I wish I could say that being replaced at my grandfather's funeral by this fake family my mom had fabricated left me heartbroken, devastated, and angry. And maybe it did. But I was too numb to feel any of the grief that you might expect.

For a long while, I didn't even know how to tap into my feelings in regard to this bizarre plot twist. Over time, my suppressed grief found other ways to express itself. When I stuff my heartbreak deep within my soul, it eventually forces its way out in a scenario like this:

I am riding in the car with a friend who says something completely hilarious. We laugh and laugh until tears stream down our faces. Suddenly, my body recognizes that I am crying and decides, "Well, since the tears are already sort of flowing, let's really give her something to cry about." And before I can stop it, my laughter turns into unstoppable sobbing. My emotions run wild, and I am annihilated by all the grief, all at once. I feel out of control with intense loss and pain as every sad and terrible thing I haven't dealt with rises to the surface, and this aching inside my chest makes me fear that I might break in half.

This grief is devious. Stalking me until it finds an opening—a tiny weak spot in my usually fortified heart—and then it seizes my entire being, holding me down under the water while I thrash and gasp for air. It feels like violence because it is brutal. I am helplessly drowning in a sea of unacknowledged emotion and believing the lie that maybe I am entirely unlovable and completely expendable.

After my mom and dad told us that they were getting divorced, Dad moved out against his will. He didn't like it and took every opportunity to let my mom know this. She was fighting like hell to get free from him, but he could manipulate any situation and somehow always became the victim of every bad experience—as was the case with their tumultuous divorce.

Their fighting in marriage was nothing compared to their fighting in divorce. One day after school, I was home alone and making a snack in the kitchen. I was 12. On this day, my father decided it was a good idea to attempt to break into the house. He carried a baseball bat in his right hand as he approached the master bedroom window. Suddenly, I heard the pounding of his blows against the window. My dog was barking in full attack mode at the window, and in a terrified panic, I called my cousin who lived next door.

"Alice, my dad is here trying to beat down the window with a baseball bat, and I am afraid," I said.

"Oh my God, what should we do?" she asked.

"I don't know. I think we need to call the police. He's trying to break into the house," I said.

"I'll call the police, and you call Grandpa," Alice said.

My hands were shaking, and I called my grandfather. He only lived a couple minutes down the street, so he actually beat the police officers to my house. When he arrived, he confronted my dad. I could see them both through the sheers on the kitchen door as I sat at the table. They were yelling. I heard my dad threaten to hit my grandfather with the baseball bat, and his face was angrier than I had ever seen it before. I saw the squad car pull into my driveway, and two officers approached to get the story of what was happening.

I called my mom, who was thankfully already on her way home. "I might have to get a restraining order on your dad," she said. This was not the first domestic violence call to the police at our house, and it wouldn't be the last.

I didn't know what that meant exactly, but I knew that I didn't feel safe with my dad anymore. Even if he didn't know I was home, what he did that day frightened me, and I couldn't imagine ever trusting him again.

About a month after this failed break-in attempt, my mom and dad got into another terrible argument in the front yard of Fat Grandma's house. Mom was trying to leave, and Dad grabbed her car keys so he could keep her there longer. She reached to pull the keys from his hand, and he said that she scratched him. She left and returned home. We ate dinner, and around 9:00 p.m., when she was in the bathtub, there was a knock on the front door. I answered since she was still in the bath and opened the door to see two police officers who asked me where my mother was.

"She's in the bath right now," I answered.

"Please go get her," they said.

I left them standing on the porch and went to the bathroom. "Mom, there are two police officers outside, and they said they need to speak to you."

She looked a little confused as she stood up. I handed her a towel, and she grabbed her robe and headed toward the front door.

I stood out of sight in the hallway and heard them tell her that she was being arrested because my dad had filed a domestic abuse report against her for scratching his arm earlier that day. I heard my mom exclaim, "You've got to be kidding me," and ask if she could at least go grab her pants and call her parents so that someone could be here with my brother and me while they took her to jail.

I went and hid in my room and heard my mother and one of the police officers walking down the hallway toward her room so that she could get dressed. My grandparents arrived, and the police officers handcuffed my mom and drove off with her in the back of their squad car. I was confused and hurt that my dad was having my mom taken away like a criminal, and I was really scared for my mom. I didn't know what going to jail meant, or how long she would have to stay there.

The next day she was released, and she was pissed. When I got home from school, she was home and told me all about her jail experience.

"I'm ok," she assured me. "Actually, I cried a lot, and if I wasn't crying, I was doing push-ups or crunches. They brought me a gross breakfast, and I refused to eat it," she continued. "Here's something funny about when I was in the holding cell," she added. She was always looking for the silver lining or what made a terrible situation funny.

"When I arrived, they did my mugshot and fingerprints and then put me in a holding cell with several other women," she told me. "They were all sitting on these benches and one big Black girl stood up and started asking us all what we were in for. Some women said stealing, some said prostitution ... and then it was my turn.

"She came over and said, 'What are you in for, little white lady?' and I looked her right in the eyes and said, 'I beat up my husband,' and then everyone cheered, and a couple of the women high-fived me," she laughed as she did a strut around the living room. Then she got serious and added, "But I promise you that if he so much as breathes on me wrong, I will be putting him in jail. An eye for an eye."

For two weeks she waited, and then she finally had her revenge. They had another massive fight, and he tried to grab her arm as she was leaving. As soon as he touched her, she got kind of an "I got ya now!" look on her face, and she exclaimed, "Ha! You're getting what is coming to you now," as she got out her cell phone to call the police. She filed her report, and they took him away.

"You know what the best thing about all this is?" she asked

me as she retold the story. "It's Friday night ... So he is going to have to spend the whole weekend in jail because they don't process people on weekends," she said with a sly smile. "Payback is a bitch."

When I was a kid, one of my favorite shows was Jim Henson's *Fraggle Rock*. I loved the characters, the puppets were absolute perfection, and their songs were so catchy. One of the characters on the show that always stood out to me was Marjory, the trash heap. She was an actual pile of garbage that most people over-looked, but the Fraggles would always come to her seeking advice, and she would usually impart her golden nuggets of life wisdom to them via a fun song.

For much of my marriage, I felt exactly like I imagined Marjory did as a trash heap. Conner kept piling his shit, his expectations, and his problems onto me and always expected me to come through for him with all the things he wanted from me, and he wanted it served up with a cheerful smile and no needs of my own.

I was buried underneath all the trash, suffocating below the weight of his litter, and I believed I actually was garbage. I had lost myself so fully that I thought I was the trash. I didn't know that I could stand up and clean myself off, or that I could actually set a boundary and tell him not to put his trash on me. That thought hadn't even occurred to me because I was too busy with the song and dance of being the trash heap who made him feel better about his problems.

I didn't know that I was allowed to speak up and ask for what I needed. And of course, when I began to set healthy boundaries and refused to be the trash heap anymore, Conner did not handle the transition well. Once I asked for a divorce, he began to take every detail about my toxic family and hold it against me as a way to try and control me and get me to bend to his will.

One morning after dropping our kids off at school, he requested that I meet him for coffee so we could discuss our budget during this "married but separate" time. I had begun recording all of our conversations because he had a habit of saying things that later he would deny having said. Recording the conversations helped remind me that I wasn't crazy and that he was gaslighting me. On this particular day, he wanted to discuss the fact that our house needed new windows, and if I would not divorce him, he could take the money he was paying his attorney and put it toward fixing the house instead.

I was listening to him rattle off the details and all I could think was, *New windows might cost us $15,000, and I think my freedom is worth more than that. Getting new windows in my house is not a reason to stay miserable in this relationship. You cannot put a price on this freedom.*

I looked him right in the eyes and said, "There is nothing that will change my mind. We are not getting back together."

He paused for a quick second and then replied, "Well just so you know, this process doesn't have to be like it was with your parents. I am not your dad, Ashley. This divorce will only be crazy if YOU make it crazy."

I couldn't tell if that was a threat or an accusation. Like, "Ashley don't be crazy, let me still have control over you ..." or if it was more like, "I will be crazy if you don't give me what I want." I decided not to ask him what he meant by that because I was afraid of how he might answer. And more than anything, I wanted this meeting to be quick and then to get the fuck away from his manipulation.

When I wasn't with him, I felt like myself for the first time. When I was free of his presence, I felt like I was soaring. I was no longer the trash heap. I was a real person.

By November 2019, it was time for me to officially file for divorce. I sat nervously in my attorney Juliette's office. The paint on the walls felt ancient, and I wondered how many other anxious wives had sat in my seat and recounted the reasons why they were seeking to end their marriages.

"We need to create a document for the judge that will explain why you are asking for this divorce. You need to be able to paint a clear picture of why this marriage is no longer healthy for you. I know it is not going to be fun to think about these things, but you need to have as many examples as possible so that we can build your case," she instructed.

For three hours, we sat together as I recounted the various cruel and manipulative ways I had been treated or spoken to. After I got to the part about how Conner would throw a fit if I didn't want to have sex with him after an expensive date night out, she stopped typing and turned to look at me and said, "This is a lot of emotional abuse."

I paused. I had never told any of this to anyone else—not even my therapist knew *everything*. And here I was, sharing every detail of every awful experience with my attorney. For the first time, I felt fully seen. I began to cry. It felt so good to have my struggle finally acknowledged by someone else. I took a few deep breaths. I wasn't nearly finished, and I was emotionally drained. Since there was still so much more to add to the document, Juliette sent me home with the file so that I could address everything the judge would need to know on my own.

Doing this myself versus sitting with her or one of her assistants saved me a lot of money. A couple of days, several coffees, and 9,000 words later, I had a full report of our marriage and every fucked up thing I could remember him ever saying or doing. Seeing it all in a legal document was so surreal, but it helped me to solidify my resolve to fight for my freedom. I had combed through previous journal entries dating back as far as 2015 and audio recordings of the last couple months of our marriage and during our separation—all the tangible proof of the unraveling and the coming back to myself.

I returned to Juliette's office to sign the official papers for her to file.

"How are you feeling today?" Juliette asked.

"I'm ok … but I am nervous what Conner's reaction will be when he gets this document. I imagine that it's going to make him really angry," I admitted.

"The best advice I can give you in regard to your nervousness on how he might respond to your truth is that someone who treats you nasty during your marriage does not get nicer in divorce," she said. "You can't expect kindness from him. If you could, then you wouldn't be sitting in my office at all."

That hit me right in the gut when she put it that way. What I was doing was bracing for the fallout, knowing that I had the proper armor and tools to protect me. It was going to be scary, but I would survive this hell—just like I had survived all the other hells of my life.

The best part of going through hell one more time was that on the other side of it, I would finally be free to be myself and make my own life choices. I would be fully me, once and for all.

With the 9,000-word document and a notarized signature from me, my divorce papers were ready to be filed. That meant that Conner would need to be officially served. He had recently moved to a new rental house, and so I requested him to provide me with an address. For two weeks I asked for his address, and he never responded. He knew that I was going to be serving him the divorce papers, and I think he assumed that if I didn't know where he was, he wouldn't be served and could possibly delay the impending destruction of our marriage, legally speaking. Even my sweet friend Kylie's husband, who was friends with Conner, was telling him to give me his new address. But Conner refused. My lawyer was getting frustrated.

"Legally, once these papers are signed, we only have a short window of time to serve him," she noted. "Is there anywhere you know he will be other than his house that we could send someone to serve him since we don't have an address?" she asked.

"Well, our daughter's eighth birthday party will be at my house this weekend. I know he will be here then, but I don't want to do that to him during her birthday," I said, still trying to think of how to be respectful of his feelings, even though he had been so awful to me.

"Can you have them arrive after the party? Maybe ask one or two friends to hang back in case he gets angry that he was served," Juliette suggested. "We have to have this done by Monday, otherwise the papers are no longer valid, and we have to start over."

I made arrangements to have someone deliver the paperwork to Conner during our party cleanup, and asked Kylie and her husband to stick around afterward for a few moments while the delivery happened.

Once the paperwork was in his hands and he realized what was happening, he approached me with the mustard yellow envelope, waved it in my face, and angrily exclaimed, "THAT WAS A LOW BLOW," as he breezed past me and out the door.

The feeling was bittersweet. I hated that he had to be served at Elianna's birthday party, but I also felt a massive sense of relief knowing that it was done and that I was finally on my way to not being his wife anymore. My freedom was drawing closer every day, his grip on me was slipping, and I was stepping into my truest potential and power.

I knew the journey would be long and painful, but I was happy and so proud of my courage to leave a relationship that was not safe in pursuit of myself. I wasn't leaving for anyone else, and I wasn't staying for anyone else. I was doing this for me, and I was taking back my broken heart, mending each shard with every new boundary and small act of self-care I could. I was healing. I was beginning to bloom.

A few months later, in early January 2020, our first court date was scheduled. It was the first week the courthouse was open after the holidays, and the courtroom was overcrowded. The judge assigned to us decided that mediation would be a better way for us to solve our issues, and that day, our two attorneys were invited into a room with a mediator to discuss our case. I thought it was very unfair that both Conner and I were not even allowed to be in the room. I began to question if I had explained my situation enough to Juliette, or if she would be able to relay why I wanted—*needed*—this divorce.

After 30 excruciating minutes, our attorneys emerged. Conner's attorney met in a corner with him, while Juliette came and sat next to me on a bench. She pulled out a slip of paper from her notebook with several bullet points scratched out on it. She leaned into my ear and whispered, "He is saying that he can no longer afford to live in his rental house and is demanding that you either start paying some of his bills, or he will need to move back into the house with you."

My whole body began to shake with anger and adrenaline.

"So he can just send his attorney into a room to say, 'My client has no money to support himself or his family and so he needs to move back into the home where he emotionally abused his wife?' This is absurd. Juliette, I cannot live in the same house as him. It would be so toxic for our kids—especially at this point. Things are so volatile between us. The kids would be exposed to so much negativity, tension, and hate. I don't want that for them, that's why I am getting a divorce."

"I know. Don't freak out," she said. "I think this is their way to strongarm you into taking on some of these bills, so we are going to have to give them something."

She asked my monthly budget, and we sat with her legal notepad doing basic math and trying to figure out what payments I could agree to make in order to keep him out of the house. My freelance writing job at that time was barely covering our groceries and gas. Conner never once during our separation asked me if we had groceries for the kids, and never offered to help pay for their needs during that time. And here he was now, with his hand out toward me, saying he is the victim of my grounds for divorce.

"I cannot go back to having him in my house. That is the one thing I will not allow," I said.

"Ok then we need to take three of these bills," Juliette encouraged. We picked three that I thought I could handle paying, and Juliette went back into the mediation room to present our offer. I had never been more grateful that I stuck to my guns during this first court date as it was just two months later when the entire country went into lockdown due to COVID-19.

"Could you imagine if I was quarantined and stuck in my house with Conner every day during this pandemic?" I often said in disbelief when I was FaceTime-ing my friends. "What a complete nightmare. There would be no escape, and I would be so miserable."

I truly believed that it was a gift from God that I was able to be in the house with our kids and NO FUCKING CONNER.

chapter fifteen

NOTHING CAN WEAR DOWN A DIAMOND

"Character is revealed when pressure is applied."

— Rahul Kumar

A couple weeks before I asked Conner to move out, I decided to book an appointment with Daisy, an amazing intuitive coach, for a psychic forecasting reading. I had been so distraught and heartbroken the past few months and was searching for any point of wisdom or direction I could find. I had hoped to ask Daisy what she saw for my marriage and how I might be able to fix it, or if I should leave him.

The appointment was scheduled for two weeks out and the waiting felt like agony. I longed for answers, for a pep talk from someone who might be more tuned in than me. I was still looking outside myself for that "hero" figure to swoop in and rescue me. A couple of days before my appointment, I had already decided that it was time to ask Conner to leave. He officially moved out the day before my first meeting with Daisy. I hadn't shared this news with anyone yet, and I arrived at the appointment anxious to hear from Daisy about the energy she might be picking up on.

I sat in the waiting room, nervously paging through a magazine and trying to act natural. Daisy opened the door, and she stepped out with the brightest smile and kindest eyes, totally putting my anxious heart at ease. The warmth of her spirit felt like a giant hug as she welcomed me into her office and invited me to have a seat. After a quick centering meditation, she began the reading, which to my surprise felt almost exactly like my days receiving prophetic prayer in church.

"The first thing that came up for you when I was meditating on you this morning was a separation," she said, holding her hands together in front of her heart, then pulling them apart with as much distance as her reach would allow.

I'm certain that my jaw fell right out onto the floor at that point. The rest of the session was life-giving to my exhausted spirit. Daisy had so many words of encouragement for me that helped me to find belief in my own power to change my situation. I was already taking steps toward my freedom and a more peaceful life, and while I was terrified, I found confirmation that God was seeing me.

The timing of the appointment and asking Conner for a separation was so serendipitous and pivotal for my soul to recalibrate to my truth. The message was clear: the journey wouldn't be easy, but I could trust that I would be supported every step of the way.

When I started telling my friends that I was getting a divorce, they were not surprised, and they were incredibly supportive. The overall sentiment was, "FINALLY!" Clearly I hadn't been hiding the murkiness of my marriage as well as I had convinced myself. Not a single one of my friends said, "Oh no, I thought you guys were so perfect together," or, "Really? You guys seemed so happy!"

Most of the reactions were, "I've never been more excited for someone to get divorced!" or, "Ugh, he is the actual worst.

We only tolerated Conner because we wanted to be around YOU."

My friends and I now call him Gollum—you know, the fictional monster from *The Lord of the Rings*? I first gave him this moniker because my therapist told me that changing his name to something silly would take away the power dynamic, so that he didn't have the power over me that he did before. There are other reasons I chose to call him Gollum, as you have now seen.

While there was so much to celebrate, there was also so much grief. I wasn't even sure how to begin to process such bittersweet emotion. Because my usual way to cope was to stuff my own feelings deep into my heart, I mostly went through life feeling numb to the things that hurt me the most. I knew that I was going to have to deal with these feelings, but no matter how much I tried, I couldn't access them. My body had developed too many protective mechanisms to keep me from feeling all that pain. The idea of scheduling time to grieve the loss of my marriage sounded good until I actually tried to execute my calendar entry of "Cry at 2:00 p.m."

I remember thinking, *I'll cry about this for 25 minutes on Tuesday at 2:00 when I don't have any work calls and my kids are still at school.* When the time came to cry, I would sit in a chair and journal to try and tap into my emotions, but nothing I was doing could unlock the feelings box.

I was starting to wonder if my survival mode instincts needed more time to realize that it was safe for my feelings to come out. Just because it was finally safe for me to express myself fully for the first time in 36 years didn't mean my body would immediately believe that it was actually safe.

The feelings dam broke late one morning at the end of October 2019 when my friend Teagan sent me a song to listen to by Selena Gomez (thank you, Selena!). The Spotify link in our text message thread said, "Lose You To Love Me," and I assumed it was just a typical pop song. I was driving home from therapy when I heard the song for the first time.

Every word of this song resonated and pierced my heart. I felt like the lyrics were pulled directly from my experience of being Conner's wife. Something about it caught me completely off guard and cracked me wide open at the most inconvenient time—but when has grief ever been convenient? I sobbed the whole way home, and by the time I pulled into my driveway, I was fully inconsolable. I could not stop crying; I couldn't even move my body out of the car to get back into my house. I just sat there wailing in my car for an hour.

My limbs were heavy, my face was puffy and wet with tears, and my chest was tight with overwhelming sadness. I was feeling it all, and even though it hurt like hell, a true release was happening. As I cried, I felt layers of darkness being peeled off my body like the skin of an onion. Layers of hurt and heartbreak, shame, fear, and self-doubt were lifting. I was learning that in order to heal, I needed to feel.

After the divorce was finalized, Conner became relentless in his attempts to control me, and it required me to hold very firm boundaries. I had enough friends who were aware of the situation to help me navigate the toxicity Conner was throwing at me. I had to continually and consciously choose to come back to myself. After 14 years of marriage, certain enabling habits were extremely hard to break, so I was grateful to have friends help me stay accountable.

My friend Raina would regularly remind me of who I was by telling me, "Nothing can wear down a diamond" every time Conner would get nasty and say horrible things to me.

On my darkest days, I would feel so worn down and hopeless

that I would lie on the cold tile in my bathroom and sob. I needed to physically be positioned as low as I felt, and strangely, laying on the ground was the closest feeling I could imagine to being held and comforted. On those days it took all of my strength to peel myself up from the floor just to be a functional person. Raina's reminder really helped me, so I wrote it on the giant mirror in my bedroom in bright red lipstick. That way, I could see it first thing every morning and last thing every night before I closed my eyes.

nothing can wear down a diamond.

Navigating divorce forced me to learn to really listen to my body and care for myself in ways that made me feel empowered. One of the practices that I began just as Conner was initially moving out was to give myself mirror pep talks. I would look myself in the eyes and say out loud how proud I was of the progress I was making. I would point out how my growth was beautiful and how grateful I was to myself for taking all these hard steps toward my freedom.

It's funny how hearing my own voice speaking these kind words out loud was providing my heart with healing and a true sense of support and love. I learned how to step up to protect and guide myself on the path toward healing. The greatest gift was to give myself space to feel safe to express my feelings. Talking to my reflection in a mirror felt silly, but these pep talks were so pivotal in helping me navigate hard days when Conner was unrelenting.

My worldview was shifting and suddenly my heart was opening up and everything felt more vibrant. I was beginning to view myself as all the wonderful things I was saying each day, believing that I was worthy of love and kindness and healthy relationships.

There were so many things I never thought I would be able to do without a husband that I have found a sense of confidence and hope in now. Since leaving Conner, my therapist's words, "He's holding you back," echo in my heart every single time I do something for me. Like when I bought the skincare I wanted without having to justify why I spent $30 on myself at Target. Or when I landed a full-time job that I loved. Or when I booked a trip to California so that I could start writing this book.

One of my biggest accomplishments was refinancing my house and getting Conner's name off the mortgage. During the mediation process, Conner agreed that the kids and I could remain in the house. We would own it together for up to 24 additional months, at which time I would have to either refinance to get it solely in my name, or we would sell, and I would have to move out.

After the divorce was finalized, Conner reminded me more than a handful of times how kind it was of him to allow the kids and me to stay in the house. "I don't think you recognize how generous it was of me to allow you guys to stay in the house instead of just selling it now," he said.

The two-year timeline on my option to refinance the house was a giant question mark for me. I wasn't sure if I would be able to swing it. I worked my ass off—at one point holding two full-time jobs—to pay off my debts and start making progress toward this lofty goal. When I asked Conner to move out, I didn't have a steady job or family to fall back on.

But I believed that I deserved to be free. So I stepped out armed with a little bit of faith, a lot of hard work, and a stellar community of friends who cheered me on through the entire process. I never could have accomplished any of what I did without the encouragement and support of so many sweet friends who went above and beyond—as a shoulder to cry on, helping hands when things needed repairs, recommending me for jobs and helping me to find meaningful ways to support my family, volunteering to keep my kids so that I could work or have a little bit of sanity, holding me up in prayer, and giving me pep talks every step of the way. That saying, "It takes a village," is so very true, and the one I have has made it possible for me to thrive.

Throughout the process, Conner kicked and screamed and asked me condescending questions like, "Are you even sure that you'll be able to get approved for a loan on your own?"

The house was the final tie (other than our kids) to our life as a married couple. It was the one place where he still had a tiny bit of power, and he regularly reminded me of that by saying, "I still own that house, Ashley."

But now he can no longer say that. He can no longer claim to have any power or control over me whatsoever. I take responsibility for how I feel and how I live and who I love. I am finally free. I am finally, fully myself.

I often think back to the days when I would sneak out for an early morning walk with the dog at the airpark. Begging God, with every step I took, to send someone to help me get out of the mess of my life. Back then, I had no confidence in my own ability to dig out of the darkness. I wanted someone, *anyone*, to tell me what to do—how to fix it, how to not feel rejected, alone, and abandoned in my marriage. To show me how to leave, or at the very least, to give me permission to leave.

I didn't yet realize that I had to do that for myself.

I don't have all the answers. There's still so much mystery about what lies ahead and so much that I have to hope for in my future. But now I know that it's all possible because I have been under the heat of pressure and I have emerged with confidence, gleaming like the kind of diamonds Rihanna sings about.

Being a human is complicated and hard and wonderful and magical, and I wonder if maybe we're all diamonds—refined by the trials and pressures of life. If we love ourselves enough to keep our hearts open, we can step into the power of being exactly who we were created to be.

AFTERWORD

dearest reader,

There was a time when I believed I only mattered if I was able to live a "perfect" life and please everyone around me. I now recognize that imperfection is what has molded me into who I am. When it comes to diamonds, every blemish, discoloration, scratch, and pit is how professional jewelers can recognize a true diamond from a phony. The imperfections developed over the course of a diamond's journey are literally what gives every gem its own character and unique, one-of-a-kind value.

That's how I feel—finally—after a lifetime of being everything to everyone else. Thinking of all the challenges of divorcing such a controlling personality helped me to view myself as the diamond. I knew that on the other side, I would come out stronger and more sparkly than ever before.

In returning to myself, I decided to take a big risk on ME and write this book. I hired a writing coach to help me organize my story. I wasn't even sure if I had something worthwhile at the time, but I knew that I needed to write for my own healing process. I didn't have to ask anyone's permission; Conner could no longer tell me what to do, and that felt incredibly freeing.

I booked a flight to Los Angeles in early February 2020 to spend a day with my writing coach. I sorted through key moments in my story like a single strand of yarn knitting a sweater together, my hands positioned intentionally on the knitting needles. Knit, purl, knit, purl, knit.

At the end of the day, my entire life lay before me, organized on index cards on her living room floor. "That's your book!" she said.

"How surreal," was all I could think to say to mark the moment. "Do you think this is actually something, or am I crazy to be writing this?" I asked, suddenly feeling like this whole thing was a totally bonkers idea.

"No, this is something," she encouraged.

For a long time while working on this book, I wondered if this was my Alexander Hamilton moment. I was "writing my way out" of my brokenness and stepping into living life my way. I thought maybe this story was the only offering I would have to give to the world. What actually happened was that this story has unlocked all of my potential for a future that I am writing as I go. I'm not just the author of this book, I'm the author of my life now. And knowing what it has cost me to get here, that really feels like something to celebrate.

I thought that my value and my worth were two inter-changeable words that meant the same thing, but there is a strik-ing difference. A quick Google search will tell you that something with value is defined as an item that holds both monetary and emotional costs. Whereas an item's worth only refers to the financial expense attached to it.

People always say that it's good to have self-worth, but I think what might actually serve us better is to develop an understanding of our own *self-value*. While these two terms are also used interchangeably, I've got this hunch that they are significantly different. We've been missing the point and ex-hausting ourselves trying to perform perfectly to meet the impossible expectations of a person or culture that idolizes per-fection and has us convinced that our flaws must be hidden, no matter the cost.

Your time here in this world on your individual diamond

journey will come with deep and profound value if you're willing to dig deep and invest in the emotional cost of the adventure, chase after your dreams with ferocious fervor, and do the dirty work of getting vulnerable and setting firm boundaries with the people in your life who may try to force you into a surfacer role when who you really are is a miner.

What's ironic about writing the closing statements of this book is that I know that this is so far from the end of the story for me. I certainly have heaps more to learn, and I'm already stretching and growing in ways I never dreamed possible for myself. That's something I'm both extremely proud of and also continually frustrated by. I thought that eventually there would be this grand moment where it felt like I had "arrived."

What I have actually experienced is yet another level of growth, opportunities to cultivate healthy relationships, and tests from the Universe to see if my boundaries are really as firm as I think they are. I am still arriving. What they say is true; healing really is a lifelong journey.

All the energy I used to put into hiding the crazy and imperfect elements of my life, I now put into opening my heart to connect with others and to remind myself that we are all so very remarkable and resilient.

Maybe we're all diamonds? YES. We are all absolutely the most dazzling diamonds. A diamond without imperfections is boring, and perfect is you being exactly who you are.

Grateful for you,

Ashley

ACKNOWLEDGMENTS

The idea of putting the simple words "thank you" down onto the page feels completely insufficient to the amount of gratitude that floods my heart for each and every soul who has been a part of this book process (not to mention my life process). I'd much rather pull an Oprah, put you all in the same room, get you in slightly uncomfortable folding chairs and then announce, "Please reach under your seats to find *pause for dramatic effect* THE KEYS TO YOUR BRAND NEW CAR!" Since I can't do that yet, I hope this will suffice.

Thank you to Charlotte and Wyatt, my greatest teachers for knowing what unconditional love really feels like, and my motivation for every single good thing I do in this life.

Brandi, you are the reason I ever believed I could write this. You have been instrumental in my life. I love you heaps, dear heart.

Christyn, Emily, and Gennean, for inspiring me beyond belief with the way you each chase after your dreams so fiercely and love others so well. I am a better person because of your friendship.

Katherine and Beth, for the constant solidarity and coffee commiseration.

Holly D. and Olivia, for your endless inspiration, love, fun, and memes.

Towne, for your kindness and infectious joy. You are totally my soul sister!

Holly L., Jenna, and Kaleigh, for being the greatest Mother Fuegers I know.

Chris B., for your sweet friendship, real estate guidance, and our neighborhood walks. I really love you!

Candis and Cassie, for being my on-call text warriors so many nights. You both helped me stick to my boundaries and fight for myself when I did not have the strength to stand on my own two feet.

Carie, Jefferson, Harper, and Lige. I have no words for the love and appreciation I feel for your wonderful family. I could not have survived without your friendship.

Cara and Maria, you both kept me afloat and equipped me to support myself in ways I never dreamed possible.

Amanda T., your family means the world to me. I am beyond grateful for our FaceTime coffees and your friendship that feels like pure sunshine.

Morgan, had you not moved into that house next door to me, I might have lost my mind! Your family is precious to me and I love you endlessly.

Kaci, your friendship is truly a gift. Thanks for pulling me out of the field and helping me to get unstuck.

Carla and Felichia, there is no doubt in my mind that God wanted us to know each other. I am so thankful for the many ways you both have taught me to be more of a badass. Love you both to the moon!

Mel and Sarah P., for your thoughtful encouragement and prayers.

Laura and Matt H., for the hope I see in your love for each other, and especially to Laura for always bringing hugs when I needed them most.

To my family, who I will not name individually for your privacy, thank you for your forever love, encouragement, and prayers. I love you.

To my parents. While I hate having lived it, I love my life now, and I love who I have grown up to be. I have gratitude and love for you for your part in that, and my boundaries remain firm.

Misty and Lindsay, you both changed my life when you saw my pain and helped me find the confidence to get free.

Caroline, I could not have survived the dark times without your trust in me for sweet Lily. Thank you.

Kim D. from the lovely Lawrence & Clarke Cacti Co., I am forever grateful for your radical generosity towards me.

Mike and Kayla, for your constant encouragement and kindness. I love your family massively. Kayla, thank you for always wading through the coconuts of life with me.

G, if you've made it this far into the book, I want you to know that I'll always cherish our trip on "April 31st." Te amo mucho!

To the lovely Joanna Dee, thank you for the most perfect cover design and especially for your beautiful heart.

Allison and the team over at Find Your Voice, many thanks for your guidance and for kickstarting this writing train.

Christie, thank you for your friendship and for suggesting Clare as my editor.

Clare, you are a beautiful angel heart that is straight from heaven. The many conversations about this book and the love and care you have invested in my story have been vital. I am a better writer because of all that you have taught me, and *Maybe We're All Diamonds* would not be possible without you.

Mary, for polishing the little details of this book to a shine. Thank you for your proofreader's eye.

Shanda and the team at Transcendent Publishing, your guidance and endless knowledge have been a godsend. Thank you for this opportunity to share my story.

To anyone I might've failed to mention here, thank you for your grace. Know that you are loved so very deeply.

And last but not least, my deepest thanks to you, dearest

reader. Thank you for being here. I am humbled and honored that you chose to spend time with me. I have so much love for you.

ABOUT THE AUTHOR

Ashley Robyn is an expert on dysfunctional family dynamics because she lived through them. She is an artist, a stand-up comedy lover, a living room dancer, and a connector of people. She deeply loves boba tea and spaghetti, but never together.

While this is her first book, it's not her first circus. She spends her time as the ringleader of her family circus, living in a small house in Nashville, Tennessee, that she shares with two large fluffy dogs and two wonderfully human children.

Ashley enjoys cultivating a community of kind hearts and good vibes through the simple act of sharing words the same way friends share coffee. Graciously, sincerely, and with love.

Connect with Ashley at ShareLoveEverywhere.com.

TOOLS FOR YOUR
DIAMOND JOURNEY

Thank you for reading *Maybe We're All Diamonds*. I've created a few fun and reflective resources to support you on your diamond journey. Whether it's digging deep to unearth your sparkle or sharing love everywhere with others, I hope that these resources bring you closer to who you are meant to be.

Scan the QR code below to access your FREE resources:

Printed in Great Britain
by Amazon

39593058R00175